Dave Maynard's
Tried and True
All-Night Radio
Secret Family Recipe
Cookbook

Dave Mayna

Tried and True All-night Radi

Addison-Wesley Publishing Company   Reading, Massachuse

Edited by Dave Maynard

rd's
Secret Family Recipe Cookbook

Menlo Park, California   London   Amsterdam   Don Mills, Ontario   Sydney

**Library of Congress Cataloging
in Publication Data**

Maynard, Dave, 1929—
    Dave Maynard's Tried and true all-night radio
secret family recipe cookbook.

    1. Cookery. I. Title. II. Title: Tried
and true all-night secret family recipe cookbook.
TX715.M473   641.5   80-20824
ISBN 0-201-05008-0 (pbk.)
ISBN 0-201-05009-9

Illustrations courtesy of Dover Publications,
*Food And Drink: A Pictorial Archive From
Nineteenth-Century Sources.*
Selected by Jim Harter.

ISBN 0-201-05008-0
ISBN 0-201-05009-9

ABCDEFGHIJ-DO-8987654321

Second printing, February 1981

Cover photograph by Marshall Henrichs.

This book really began in 1939, when a skinny ten-year-old boy started to realize that cube steaks, corn niblets, and hot rice with milk and sugar were not the only answer to a poor but picky kid's prayer. It was then that I, the aforementioned skinny kid, learned to make Italian meat sauce from the matriarch of the Italian family downstairs. She spoke but a few words of English and couldn't understand why a *perocchi*—as I was nicknamed—would want to know about cooking. But then she must have realized that two small boys, living with only their father, were not eating high off the hog.

Looking and cooking over the last forty years, I can truly say that the *therapeutic* value alone of dicing, mincing, stirring, squeezing, rolling, kneading, mixing, folding, beating, tasting, and serving has easily made the effort worthwhile. Nothing is as steadying on the nerves as kneading six loaves of rye or turning out two hundred raviolis on a Saturday afternoon. And look at all the dishes I've never had to wash! When I do the cooking, I *don't* do the washing. Remember, a good cook is a somebody. Souffles give stature; pates, prestige; and casseroles, charisma.

These realizations were driven home to me when I started a television cooking show on Boston's channel 4 in 1977. Over the past years, I've come to know good cooks, closet chefs, try-harders, know-it-alls, pan-fry pontiffs, and all those in between. I'm convinced that at least 90 percent of our total population know the way to gastronomical heaven, while the other 10 percent are waiting to break out.

Whenever I'm at the home of friends or in a restaurant and my taste buds react to something new or something better, I immediately begin making plans for the acquisition of the recipe. But it was Robert Burns who said, "The best laid plans of mice and man aft go astray" (he obtained that quote from his mother who was being bilked out of her haggis recipe). Often the replies to my inquiries about certain specifics of preparation are shrouded in mystery. It's very curious as to why some people guard their trade secrets as though they belonged in Fort Knox, while others offer them readily and lovingly, wishing only to share. Those latter people are my kind of folks.

It's been a great source of pleasure for me over the past year to read, evaluate, compile, and test these jewels of recipes that have been living with families all over the United States for generations. My love of cooking and my desire to improve upon ordinary meals that become the dreary routine twenty-one times a week have resulted in this easy-to-read, novel collection of recipes that I hope will bring many enjoyable hours in the kitchen, good eating at your table, and much great comment thereafter.

Although many generous viewers of my television antics have submitted culinary ideas, I dedicate this book to the 7,434 people who responded to my pleas over the radio (WBZ 1030, Boston) as part of my all-night telephone talk show. God and the Federal Communications Commission blessed us with a strong thirty-eight-state signal (and six provinces in Canada). To say

Preface

the response was heartwarming would truly be an understatement. Many women *and* men sent those recipes that are the very essence of their home life and that have been handed down from generation to generation, some coming from the native homelands of parents and grandparents. It is this type of cooking that we've chosen to share with you in this book. Something as basic as a white sauce or a pie crust will be welcomed by your family and make a staple for everyday meals.

The spirit of this book is neatly and warmly stated in a letter from Marion Abbott of Detroit, Michigan:

Many of us who have cooked without recipes much of the time have produced delicious meals. That's why interest in these lasting old dishes has stayed with us. For me, these old recipes are real treasures. My German forebears loved good food but pinched pennies as well, as you will see this in the recipes. Honest, thrifty, hard working, yet educated, these people were leader-type citizens (not politicians!). No wonder I keep their recipes from the "good old days!"

Along with their recipes, many listeners have sent in stories, tales, and explanations about the origins of the various dishes. Some accompanying notes of my own are included to suggest further tryouts and experimentation.

For the response, cooperation, time, and effort of those who sent in recipes, whether or not they have been included in this book, my wholehearted appreciation. If your recipe was not included, please, as they say in the auld sod, don't go away with a sad face. It may be that your family favorite will be in another book. After all, over 7,500 recipes were sent in. We were expecting only about 1,500, and I do have to squeeze in a few of my own.

Again, thank you, my far-flung friends, for opening up your hearts and sharing your cooking ideas and general all-around kitchen sense. It is *your* book. Treasure it!

Apology

For some reason, several contributors neglected to provide us with addresses. Rather than omit the recipe, I used the contributions of those good folk who forgot or, in some cases, had their address misplaced. I can't believe it was my fault inasmuch as I've never made a mistake in my life.

If *your* name appears in the book, please correspond a.s.a.p. so I might keep my end of the bargain.

Dedication

This book is dedicated to over 9,000 people, including the burnt finger people —Denise, Grace, and Vicki—and the burned souls, Harriet and Brian.

Contents

This, perhaps, is my favorite part of this book. I'm the type who unfortunately (for my stomach) loves to pick at good cooking and loves tasting morsels, both hot and cold. What follows is good news and bad news. The good news is that all of these hors d'oeuvre, or canapes, or whatever, are simply delicious and in some cases very inexpensive. The bad news is that a lot of main meals are going to be ruined. When you serve these appetizers, be prepared to see food left on plates further on in the meal. As a matter of fact, shouldn't you plan to serve fewer hors d'oeuvre? I'm sure the money you save will be far more gratifying than walking around feeling paranoid about food that has not been eaten. And woe to the hostess or host who sets out a couple of dips with crackers and chips and expects raves. Oh, by the way, these delights are especially good when you have to invite dull people to dinner. It'll give them something to talk about. —Dave

Appetizers

Hot Cheese Dip

More people have requested this recipe than any other I have. It is for raw vegetables, cauliflower, carrots, celery, broccoli, or crackers.

½ cup dry white wine
1 can mushroom soup
4 ounces cheddar cheese, grated
1 pound processed cheese spread

Put all ingredients in a fondue pot and stir over low heat. Keep warm and dip cauliflower, celery, carrots, zucchini, or melba rounds. Makes about 3 cups.

Dave's note: Raw turnip fingers are great and inner broccoli stalks also.

JANE SMITH
HAMILTON, OHIO

Butter Dips

⅓ cup butter
2¼ cups flour
1 tablespoon sugar
3½ teaspoons baking powder
1½ teaspoon salt
1 cup milk

Heat oven to 450°. Melt butter in the oven in a 13 x 9½ x 2-inch pan. Remove the pan once butter is melted. Sift dry ingredients into a bowl and add milk. Stir with fork until dough just clings together (about 30 strokes), then turn out on a floured board. Knead lightly about 10 times. Roll out dough ½ inch thick into rectangles 8½ x 12 inches. Cut in half lengthwise, then crosswise into 16 strips. Dip each strip on both sides into melted butter. Place close together in two rows in pan. Bake 15 to 20 minutes until golden brown. Serve piping hot. Makes 32 dips.

ANONYMOUS
INDIANAPOLIS, INDIANA

Hot Crabmeat Dip

2 8-ounce packages cream cheese
½ cup mayonnaise
3 tablespoons sauterne
4 teaspoons sugar
¼ teaspoon salt
½ teaspoon onion juice
1½ teaspoons prepared mustard
2 cans crabmeat or 2 boxes fresh Maine crabmeat

Combine all ingredients except crabmeat in top of a double boiler. Heat in top of a double boiler over water, stirring constantly until mixture becomes a smooth paste. Blend in crabmeat. Serve in a chafing dish with dipping crackers and watch it disappear!!
Makes 4 cups.

Dave's note: This recipe could be cut in half for smaller parties, although it would do as a first course for four. Place on buttered shells, dust with bread crumbs, and put under broiler for a few minutes. Serve with lemon wedge.

JUNE KINNE
CUSHING, MAINE

Steak Tartare

Good as a first course or as an hors d'oeuvre.

1 pound extra-lean hamburger or ground sirloin
½ teaspoon prepared mustard
½ teaspoon soy sauce
½ teaspoon Worcestershire sauce
2 tablespoons brandy
 salt and pepper to taste
1 onion, grated
 parsley, chopped
1 egg yolk, whole

Mix meat and seasonings well. On the serving dish, shape into a patty. Make dent in the center, sprinkle all over with parsley, and drop egg yolk into dent, being careful not to break yolk. Cover and refrigerate until needed. Serve alongside toast points or crackers. Before eating, break egg yolk and push into meat with cracker. Serves 4.

MRS. JOYCE SILVA
PROVINCETOWN, MASSACHUSETTS

Marinated Mushrooms — Continental

This is an original recipe which I started thirty-five years ago with artichoke hearts and developed into the final recipe. The marinade can be used for both vegetables and is also very good for mussels and squid. It is a combination of Italian, Greek, and French styles; hence the name.

1 pound small mushrooms
2 cloves garlic, crushed
½ red onion, sliced
½ teaspoon celery salt
¼ teaspoon basil
¼ teaspoon oregano
1 teaspoon parsley, minced
½ teaspoon msg (optional)
 salt and pepper to taste
1 cup salad oil
¼ cup vinegar

Boil mushrooms in salted water for 10 minutes. Drain well. Put into a large bowl. Add garlic, red onion, and spices. Stir in salad oil and vinegar. Mix well. Store in a glass jar in refrigerator. Makes about 3 dozen.

ROBERT STRESCINO
GLOUCESTER, MASSACHUSETTS

Hot Spinach Hors d'Oeuvre

These are delicious! Even diners who do not usually enjoy spinach will enjoy eating these hors d'oeuvre! They are very simple to prepare and can be made ahead of time (flash freeze on a cookie sheet, slip into a plastic bag to keep in freezer until ready to use, and simply place as many as wanted on a cookie sheet and bake). These can be kept on hand for emergency use or for unexpected guests. One recipe makes quite a large batch.

2 10-ounce packages frozen chopped spinach
2 cups seasoned herb stuffing mix
4 eggs
1 cup Parmesan cheese
¾ cup butter, melted
½ teaspoon thyme
1 garlic clove, minced
    pepper to taste

Cook and drain spinach (squeeze to drain well). Mix all ingredients together thoroughly. Chill for 2 hours or longer. Roll into 1-inch balls. Place on cookie sheets, uncovered, to freeze. When frozen, remove from cookie sheets and place in a plastic bag or a container to store in freezer until ready to use. To bake, place on a cookie sheet (as many as you need) and bake for 30 minutes at 300° until golden brown. Makes about 6 dozen.

MRS. VICKIE E. SHARP
JOHNSTOWN, PENNSYLVANIA

Hot Cheese and Bacon Hors d'Oeuvre

3 large onions, chopped
2 large green peppers, chopped
1 pound bacon, chopped
8 ounces or more cheddar cheese, grated
1 loaf party rye

Cook bacon until just crisp and drain. Sauté onions until golden. Add green peppers and sauté for 1 or 2 minutes. Drain. Add crisp, drained bacon and cheese. Stir together off stove. Cool. Heap onto party rye slices. Freeze if you wish and then store in plastic bags. Before serving, bake frozen at 350° for about 20 to 25 minutes. Makes about 50 servings. For variation, heap on pumpernickel rye with onions, mushrooms, Swiss cheese and sherry.

MRS. WALTER E. GOODRICH
KENNEBUNK, MAINE

Armenian Stuffed Grapevine Leaves

This recipe has been in our family for as long as I can remember, which would be over fifty years. I am of Armenian parentage: my father was born in Turkey and my mother in Armenia.

Serve this as a main dish with a salad or as an appetizer.

1 large green pepper, chopped
3 large onions, chopped
1¼ tablespoon oil
    a few sprigs of fresh parsley, chopped
    dash salt and pepper
    sweet basil and mint
1 8-ounce jar grapevine leaves, drained

3 cups rice
6 cups water
juice of 1 lemon

Sauté green peppers and onions in oil and simmer until tender. Add parsley, sweet basil, mint, salt, and pepper, and let simmer for 15 more minutes. Add 3 cups water and rice. Continue to simmer until water evaporates and rice is half-cooked. Let stand for 20 minutes, then take a teaspoonful of rice mixture and wrap each in a grapevine leaf. Place wrapped leaves back into pot and add 3 more cups of water and lemon juice. Cook until rice and leaves are tender. Makes about 2 dozen.

MRS. PEARL AXTMAN
CAMBRIDGE, MASSACHUSETTS

Ham Puffs

The ham puff recipe was clipped from a newspaper some time ago. These have remained popular through the years with family and guests.

1 8-ounce package cream cheese, softened
1 egg yolk
1 teaspoon baking powder
dash salt
4½ ounces canned deviled ham
10 to 15 slices thin bread
mayonnaise
paprika

Combine cream cheese, egg yolk, baking powder, salt, and deviled ham. Mix until blended and smooth. Cut each slice of bread into 4 triangles. Spread lightly with mayonnaise and then with generous amount of mixture. Sprinkle with paprika. This much can be done ahead of time and appetizers can be frozen. Bake at 350° for 12 to 15 min-utes, or until puffed and brown. Serve hot. Makes from 40 to 60 puffs.

Dave's note: I cut the crusts off the bread. I entertain fancy people.

MRS. KEMP SHOAF
GREENSBORO, PENNSYLVANIA

Italian-Style Clam Appetizers

24 littleneck clams opened on half shell
1 tablespoon butter
¼ cup olive oil
¼ cup light vegetable oil
1 clove garlic, halved
1½ cups fresh bread crumbs
¼ cup fresh parsley, finely chopped
¼ teaspoon black pepper, freshly ground
1 teaspoon salt
2 tablespoons Parmesan cheese, grated
1 teaspoon oregano

Chop clams, then distribute back into lightly buttered shells, reserving the clam juice. In a heavy skillet, heat oils, then add garlic and sauté until just about golden; discard garlic. Add bread crumbs to oil and sauté on low heat until crumbs absorb oil and are beginning to brown. Place crumbs and oil in a mixing bowl and add parsley, pepper, salt, cheese, and oregano. Mix well. Add clam juice if too dry. Place a generous teaspoon or more on each shell, which should be placed on a broiler pan. Brown lightly under broiler. This should take only about a minute. Serve hot. Makes 24 appetizers.

Dave's note: This is very rich, but good. Double the amount of cheese for less of a "brandy" flavor.

ANONYMOUS

Corned Beef Party Loaf

2 cups celery, diced
1 12-ounce can corned beef, chopped
1 onion, chopped
2 hard-boiled eggs, chopped
1 3-ounce package lemon-flavored gelatin
1 cup boiling water
½ teaspoon vinegar
1 cup mayonnaise
1½ teaspoon horseradish

Combine celery, beef, onion, and eggs. Dissolve gelatin in boiling water to which vinegar has been added, and pour over mixture. Mix in mayonnaise and horseradish and mix again. Put in a greased 7 x 9-inch glass dish. Refrigerate; to be used as needed. Use a spatula to remove from dish. Serves six as an entree and lots more as an appetizer.

Dave's note: It seemed a little sweet when I tested it, so I substituted unflavored gelatin for the lemon-flavored gelatin. This could be served as a light summer luncheon, garnished with lettuce, tomatoes, and black olives.

ELLEN F. TOOKS
DORCHESTER, MASSACHUSETTS

Miniature Cream Puffs

This recipe was originated by my great-grandmother, improved upon by my grandmother, perfected by my mother, and enjoyed by me!

½ cup water
¼ cup margarine
½ cup flour
  dash salt
2 eggs

Heat oven to 400°. Bring water and margarine to a boil. Add flour and salt; stir vigorously over low heat until mixture forms a ball. Remove from heat; add eggs, one at a time, beating until smooth after each addition. Drop by teaspoonful onto an ungreased baking sheet. Bake for 30 to 35 minutes. Remove from the baking sheet immediately. Nice to know: These appetizers can be made ahead and frozen. Reheat at 375° for 30 minutes. Makes 2 dozen cream puffs.

Dave's note: These can be filled with so many delectable combinations. Check "Fish and Shellfish" for one terrific filling, Cheryl's "Ambrosia from the Sea."

CHERYL M. HOFFMAN
ITHACA, NEW YORK

Orange Balls

The following recipe can be made ahead of time and frozen. Remove orange balls from freezer approximately thirty minutes before serving time. They make an attractive platter, especially during holiday times when unexpected guests seem to drop in frequently.

1 box vanilla wafers, crushed
1 box confectioner's sugar
1 stick margarine, melted
1 small can frozen orange juice concentrate, thawed
½ cup pecans, chopped
2 cups shredded coconut

Mix all ingredients except coconut well and form into 1-inch balls. Roll balls in coconut. Note: Coconut may be tinted for use at different times of the year. Example: red and green at Christmas, orange for Halloween. Makes about 3 dozen.

LARRY J. LAY
CANTON, NORTH CAROLINA

Cheese Balls

I am not sure about the origin of this recipe; however, it was used in my family (in Atlanta) more than thirty-five years ago.

2 cups flour
2 sticks margarine
13 ounces sharp cheddar cheese, grated
   dash Worcestershire sauce
   small pimiento stuffed olives
   paprika

Mix flour, margarine, cheese, and Worcestershire sauce. Form into small balls or biscuits, wrapping the dough around each stuffed olive. (Pinching up a small peak at the top makes them more attractive.) Sprinkle with paprika and bake at 425° on an ungreased cookie sheet about 10 to 12 minutes. Can be frozen but thaw partially before baking. Cheese balls may be baked ahead of time and reheated to serve. Makes about 3 dozen balls.

MRS. HENRY FICKBOHM
NAHANT, MASSACHUSETTS

Eggplant Balls

This is a Sicilian recipe that was given to my mother during the Depression era. It is used as a substitute for meat. I would name this "Sicilian Eggplant Balls," but I'm not Sicilian; I'm of German descent.

1 eggplant
1 cup bread crumbs
1 large clove garlic
¼ cup grated Romano cheese
1 egg, beaten
   salt and pepper to taste
   oil

Peel and cube eggplant. Steam it until tender. When cool, mash and mix in all other ingredients. Form into balls. Fry in a heavy pan in about ¼ inch of olive oil or any other cooking oil. The balls may be served plain or covered with tomato sauce. Makes about 2 dozen.

MRS. T. R. SLIFER
BUFFALO, NEW YORK

Stuffed Mushrooms

This recipe was given to me a few years ago by a friend of the family. I have made them many times when we have friends in for a Christmas or New Year's Eve party. Everyone seems to love them.

24 medium-size mushrooms
½ stick margarine, melted
1 teaspoon oregano
   dash of salt
1 teaspoon Italian seasoning
½ teaspoon fennel seed
½ teaspoon black pepper
½ cup bread crumbs
4 tablespoons onion, minced
8 tablespoons Romano cheese
3 tablespoons vegetable oil

Stem and peel mushrooms. Blanch for 30 seconds in boiling water and then dip in cold water. Drain and pat dry. Chop stems finely, add seasonings, bread crumbs, onion, and cheese. Add 1 tablespoon vegetable oil and grease a cookie sheet with the remainder. Blend mixture and stuff mushroom caps. Bake 10 minutes at 375°. Makes 24.

Dave's note: Try soybean flakes instead of bread crumbs. There's really no need to peel the mushrooms.

MARJORIE CLARK
ROCKLAND, MASSACHUSETTS

Zucchini Appetizers

3 cups zucchini, thinly sliced and unpared
1 cup biscuit mix
½ cup onions, finely chopped
½ cup Parmesan cheese, grated
2 tablespoons parsley, chopped
½ teaspoon salt
½ teaspoon seasoned salt
½ teaspoon marjoram or oregano
   dash pepper
1 clove garlic, chopped
½ cup vegetable oil
4 eggs, slightly beaten

Heat oven to 350°. Grease pan, 13 x 9 x 2 inches. Mix all ingredients and then spread in the pan. Bake until golden brown, for about 12 to 15 minutes. Cut into pieces, about 2 x 1 inches. Makes about 4 dozen.

MRS. VERA B. NAVICKAS
HAVERHILL, MASSACHUSETTS

Olive Cheese Snacks

I have made and served the Olive Cheese Snacks for ages as an hors d'oeuvre, and it has always proved to be very popular. These may be made weeks ahead and chilled, then put in plastic bags and frozen. They will keep in the freezer for quite a long time.

1 5-ounce jar bacon-cheese spread
4 tablespoons butter or margarine
   dash hot pepper sauce
½ teaspoon Worcestershire sauce
¾ cup flour, sifted
1 small jar medium-size stuffed green olives (about 30)

Blend cheese spread and butter or margarine until light and fluffy. Add hot pepper sauce and Worcestershire sauce. Mix well. Stir in flour, mixing to form a dough. Roll into balls, using about 1 teaspoon dough for each. Push olive into center. Place on an ungreased baking sheet. Bake at 400° for 12 to 15 minutes, or until brown. Makes about 40 snacks.

Dave's note: You know these will be delicious. They sure do look great.

MRS. LEONARD C. TAYLOR
ASHLAND, MASSACHUSETTS

Mock Pâté de Foie Gras

½ pound cooked liver (chicken livers cooked in 1 tablespoon butter, keeping centers pink)
¼ cup mayonnaise or salad dressing
1 tablespoon prepared horseradish
½ teaspoon paprika
½ teaspoon salt
¼ cup onion, chopped
   parsley

Process liver in the container of a food processor with steel blade or put through food chopper, using fine knife. Combine with mayonnaise or salad dressing, horseradish, paprika, and salt. Place in a serving bowl. Chill. Garnish with onion and parsley. Serve with crackers or crudités. Serves 6.

Dave's note: A good flavor. For variation, add 1 clove minced garlic. This can sit for a couple of days.

MRS. SYLVIA F. COFFIN
PLYMOUTH, MASSACHUSETTS

Crabmeat Cocktail Dip

Crabmeat cocktail dip is good served on Triscuits. This elegant cocktail party food may be made in advance and frozen. Makes a great gift for special friends and family at holiday time, birthdays, and other gatherings.

8 ounces cream cheese
1 tablespoon milk
6½ to 7½ ounces crabmeat, flaked
2 tablespoons green onion, finely chopped
1 teaspoon horseradish
¼ teaspoon salt
   dash pepper
¼ cup sliced almonds, toasted

Combine cream cheese and milk to soften. Add all other ingredients except almonds and put in an ovenproof dish. Sprinkle with almonds. Bake at 375° for 15 minutes. Serve with crackers or rye thins. Makes about 2 cups.

Dave's note: Freeze first, then mix well after heating. With 1 full teaspoon of horseradish for added flavor, a delicious combination.

MARY L. AND BOB AMBRIOLE
FORT WAYNE, INDIANA

Krispy Nibblers

These crunchy goodies developed one day when I was making large shells stuffed with ricotta cheese and spread with tomato sauce and baked. I found I had more shells than filling and, not wanting to waste them, I deep fried them after frying the "Swedish Rosettes." We found the shells to be crispy and tasty. They were even better with left-over lobster salad in them.

1 pound large shell macaroni
   salt
   assorted fillings

Cook shells in 2 quarts boiling water to which some salt has been added; 10 to 15 minutes should be sufficient, but check for tenderness. Drain and rinse with cold water, then drain again. Spread out on several layers of absorbent paper and let dry thoroughly. In a deep frying pan, fry about 8 shells at a time in deep fat for 5 to 8 minutes, or until they have turned a nice golden brown. Drain on absorbent paper and sprinkle with salt to taste. When cool, fill with egg salad, shrimp salad, or cream cheese mixed with chopped olives and mayonnaise, or any other favorite you may have. Makes about 5 dozen.

ELEANOR R. WILSON
BOOTHBAY, MAINE

Shrimp Wheels

1 4½-ounce can shrimp, drained and mashed
¼ cup mayonnaise or salad dressing
2 tablespoons pimiento-stuffed green olives, chopped
2 tablespoons chili sauce
1 tablespoon celery, finely chopped
1 package refrigerated crescent roll dough

Combine all ingredients except rolls. Unroll and separate crescents into four rectangles. Do not separate to form triangles. Spread ¼ of shrimp mixture on each rectangle. Roll up jelly-roll fashion. Cut each roll into 10 slices. Place cut side down on a greased baking sheet. Bake at 375° for 10 to 12 minutes, or until golden brown. Serve hot. Yields 40.

RITA PELISSIER
BARRINGTON, RHODE ISLAND

Crabmeat Canapes

I was given the recipe by my sister, Mrs. Pauline Redway, a gourmet cook, who has been making these for many years — at least forty! It's very popular with my friends, to whom I've served it countless times over the years.

2 8-ounce cream cheese
1 can shrimp
½ onion, minced
   salt and pepper
1 7-ounce can king crab
2 tablespoons cream
1 teaspoon horseradish
   slivered almonds, toasted

Mix all ingredients except almonds together and put in a casserole. Bake for 15 minutes at 350°. Sprinkle almonds on top. Serve warm. (Put on hot tray.) Yields about 40.

VIRGINIA EGAN
BELMONT, MASSACHUSETTS

Herbed Cheese Spread

16 tablespoons cream cheese
1   small carton whipped cream cheese
8   tablespoons whipped butter
2   cloves garlic, chopped
¼   teaspoon ground cloves
1   teaspoon dill weed
½   teaspoon marjoram
½   teaspoon basil
½   teaspoon chives

Let cheeses and whipped butter soften. Mix well and add spices and herbs. Place in plastic cartons and refrigerate. Can be frozen if desired.

Dave's note: Cheese spreads are so darned expensive these days that I'm glad Mrs. C. sent this one in. It tastes great and its refrigerator life is, I bet, trés admirable!

MIRIAM CARSON
QUINCY, MASSACHUSETTS

Old Country Antipasto

This is a very old recipe, brought from Italy by a friend's parents way back in the early 1900s. I have made it and find it truly delicious. Can be made at any time of the year.

5 large carrots
1 bunch celery
1 large cauliflower   } diced
1 pound small onions
4 large green peppers
1 quart vinegar
1 cup olive oil, salted to taste
2 cans mushrooms
1 pint sweet mixed pickles
3 cans ripe olives
1 can tuna fish
1 bottle catsup
1 bottle chili sauce
1 pint green cooked beans

Start with carrots and boil in vinegar for 10 minutes. Then add cauliflower and cook for 10 minutes. Repeat, adding another vegetable every 10 minutes until all vegetables are added, using more vinegar if needed. Add mushrooms, olives, green beans, and tuna. Mix well. Add catsup and chili sauce, boil 5 minutes, and stir. Seal while hot in sterilized jars. Makes 9 to 10 pints.

FRANCES CANFIELD
MEDFORD, MASSACHUSETTS

Chinese Meatballs

1½ pounds ground beef
1   garlic clove, crushed
½   cup soy sauce
1   tablespoon powdered ginger

Combine all ingredients well, and form meatballs 1 inch thick. Put in a roasting pan. Bake uncovered 1 hour at 275°. Shake occasionally. Also can be cooked on top of the stove over low heat in a little butter. Makes about 50.

ESTHER H. THOMPSON
WEST NEWTON, MASSACHUSETTS

Sweet and Sour Sausage Balls

My mother, who came from Sicily, was a fantastic cook. After she died, I carried on her tradition of having the family holiday dinners and family gatherings. I had to experiment and look for recipes that were easy and could be made up quickly. These Sweet and Sour Sausage Balls were passed on to me when a dear cousin heard I wanted a new recipe for the christening of my first grandson. Everyone who was there wanted the recipe, and the sausage balls disappeared very quickly.

4   pounds bulk sausage (fine ground Italian with seasoning)
1½ cups soft bread crumbs
4   eggs
½   teaspoon salt
¼   teaspoon pepper, freshly ground

Mix all ingredients well. Shape into small cocktail-size balls. Sauté or broil (cooks in sausage fat), turning several times. Drain and place in a large, flat pan. Prepare sauce.

Sauce

3   cups catsup
½   cup white vinegar
¾   cup brown sugar
½   cup soy sauce

Combine ingredients and pour over sausage balls. Simmer 30 minutes uncovered. Sausage balls may be frozen without sauce and when ready to use, mix sauce and simmer in sauce. Makes about 6 dozen.

Dave's note: Thicken sauce by adding 1 tablespoon cornstarch with a little water after 20 minutes.

MRS. NINA PILLA
WALTHAM, MASSACHUSETTS

Kay Bixler's Sauerkraut Balls

The only problem with these goodies is that once you make them, your family and guests will expect you to make them again and again! They have a mysterious and delicious taste, and one would never guess they contain garlic, as it is seldom used with sauerkraut. And the smoked ham and sauerkraut make for an excellent blend of flavors. These are traditionally served at our Christmas Eve buffet, and are most popular with everyone.

4   tablespoons butter
1   onion, minced
1½ cups smoked ham, chopped
½   cup sauerkraut juice
3   cups raw sauerkraut, chopped
1   tablespoon parsley finely chopped
2   cloves garlic, crushed
4   tablespoons flour
1   egg
1   cup bread crumbs
    oil for frying

Cook all ingredients except flour in a large skillet. Sprinkle flour over the top, and mix and stir well. Cool the mixture for several hours in order to roll more easily. Roll into small balls about the size of a walnut, dip into flour, then in beaten whole egg, then in freshly ground bread crumbs. Brown in deep hot fat or oil. Serve hot. Serves 8 to 10.

Dave's note: I made these balls for the first time on the ship, the Queen Elizabeth II. *Even with all the luscious food that was served, every last bit of sauerkraut was devoured—and at 11:00 in the morning!*

MRS. DENNY BIXLER
JOHNSTOWN, PENNSYLVANIA

Stuffed Grape Leaves
(Greek)

This recipe has been in our family for four generations. It's a hit every time. It's delicious, a perfect delight served warm or cold. Gather fresh grape leaves in June or early July. Cut off stems, wash, pour boiling water over them, drain, and pack in rolls in freezer bags. When ready to use, unroll. One can freeze grape leaves by omitting the boiling water and packing them wet and green.

1½ pounds ground beef
½   cup long-grain rice, washed
2   large onions, finely chopped
2   cloves garlic, minced
    salt and pepper
2   cups tomato juice
1   jar grape leaves or fresh leaves
    (with stems removed)
2   tablespoons olive oil
2½ cups water

Mix ground beef, rice, onion, garlic, salt, and pepper in a large bowl. Moisten with tomato juice until mixture is soft, of a firm consistency. Boil fresh grape leaves until half done (5 minutes). Cool in cold water. If frozen or canned leaves are used, rinse under cold water and drain. To roll, spread grape leaves dull side up on a large plate. Add a little beef mixture at base of leaves; fold sides of leaf in and roll like a cigarette. Place in a heavy kettle; pour olive oil over top; add remaining tomato juice and water until you can just see the leaves. Cook slowly 1½ hours. You may place in the oven uncovered 20 minutes at 375° to dry out. (optional). Makes about 40.

Dave's note: I found these delicious, especially with garlic.

MRS. JAMES THEODOROS
LITTLETON, MASSACHUSETTS

Coconut Sweet and Sour Meatballs

½ cup soft bread crumbs
½ cup milk
1 pound ground beef
1 small onion, minced
2 teaspoons salt
dash pepper
½ cup packaged coconut
¼ cup flour
1 egg, slightly beaten
2 tablespoons butter
¼ cup sugar
1 tablespoon cornstarch
1¼ cups water
¼ cup vinegar
1 tablespoon soy sauce
⅓ cup green pepper, thinly sliced

Mix crumbs and milk. Let stand 5 minutes. Add beef, onion, salt, and pepper. Mix gently; form 16 medium or 25 small balls. Mix coconut and flour. Dip meatballs in egg and roll in coconut mixture. Melt butter in a skillet; add meatballs and brown. Mix remaining salt, sugar, cornstarch, water, vinegar, and soy sauce. Add to meatballs. Add peppers. Cover and simmer 10 minutes. Add peppers when adding liquid; otherwise too much boils away, and meatballs get overcooked. Also might have to add a bit more water. Yields about 2 dozen meatballs.

DEE CONLEY
ROCKLAND, MASSACHUSETTS

Turkey Stuffed Mushrooms

I hate hot turkey sandwiches the day after, and then tetrazzini and hash for days after that. Instead I freeze leftover turkey and use it this way.

½ pound large mushrooms
2 tablespoons onion, finely chopped
2 tablespoons celery, finely chopped
1 tablespoon butter
½ cup turkey, finely chopped
2 tablespoons mayonnaise or salad dressing
1 teaspoon lemon juice
½ teaspoon salt
dash pepper
2 tablespoons butter, melted
pimiento

Remove stems from mushrooms, chop and sauté with vegetables in 1 tablespoon butter for 2 to 3 minutes. Add turkey, mayonnaise or salad dressing, lemon juice, and seasonings. Dip mushrooms into melted butter and place in a buttered baking dish. Fill caps with stuffing. Garnish with strips of pimiento. Bake for 20 minutes at 350°. Serve hot. Makes about 12.

DAVE

I'm a soup person. Perhaps it's the robust New England weather, or maybe it's the remembrance of the deep-flavored, hearty soups my mother used to make during the Depression. As I look back on those steaming hot bowls with great fondness, I remember that no matter how many times a week soups were served, no matter how small the amounts of meat in them, the taste and smell were so satisfying that I never realized we were poor.

Since those days, I've had cream of barley soup in North Carolina, conch chowder in Florida, a fish broth in Hangchow, China, cabbage soup in Jerusalem, potato soup in Ireland (Sligo, it was, I think), and many more soups nearly everywhere in between. I can therefore truthfully say that these recipes will burn a lot of tongues for those who venture into the kitchen and are overpowered by the aroma. At the end I've tossed in my recipe for a good, tangy soup using a leftover. If you're prone to heartburn, forget it. — Dave

Soups, Stews, and Chowders

Oxtail Soup

This recipe has been in our family for quite some time and always enjoyed by everyone. It has never had a special name other than the above.

2 pounds oxtail
    dash of vinegar
1 medium onion, chopped
4 tablespoons salt
1 small can stewed tomatoes
    salt, pepper, garlic powder, oregano, seasoned salt, and sage to taste
6 carrots, cut into ½-inch pieces
3 ears corn, broken into 3 pieces each
1 can garbanzo beans
1 can green beans or ½ pound fresh green beans, chopped
4 medium potatoes, quartered
2 medium zucchini, sliced 1 inch thick

Soak oxtails in enough water, to cover. Add a dash of vinegar, and quite a bit of salt and let sit for several hours or overnight in the refrigerator to remove the unpleasant taste. Boil oxtails and discard liquid. Then start again with enough water to cover and add onion, and tomatoes seasoned to taste with spices. Cover and simmer about 2½ hours. Add carrots, beans, and green beans. Cook 15 minutes. Add potatoes, zucchini, and corn, and cook until almost tender. Cook until just done, about 20 minutes.

Serve soup from a tureen at the table. Pass lemon wedges separately for individuals to add to soup. Serves 8.

Dave's note: Hearty and delicious.

MRS. MILDRED FERGUSON
FINDLAY, OHIO

Souse's Soup
(Korhelyleves — Hungarian)

This soup is usually served in the wee-wee hours of the morning to revive and "bring to" guests in a private home or restaurant after an all-night party or when a two- or three-day Hungarian wedding celebration is coming to a close. This traditional Hungarian soup, which is guaranteed to perk up all the tired, dizzy, and confused senses, can be made in several different ways, but two things must be common to the variations: the soup must be slightly fatty and must have a very sharp taste.

With good bread and wine, this is a good meal.

1 pound sauerkraut
2 tablespoons bacon fat from smoked bacon
2 tablespoons flour
1 small onion, minced
1 tablespoon paprika
½ pound smoked sausage (kielbasa), thinly sliced
3 tablespoons sour cream
    salt

Squeeze sauerkraut and save the juice. Cook sauerkraut in 2 quarts water until it softens. Meanwhile heat bacon fat in a frying pan, add flour, and stir and fry until the mixture is light beige. Then add onion and cook for another 5 minutes. Take off the heat, stir in paprika, and *immediately* add 1 cup very cold water. Whip until smooth.

Pour sauerkraut juice (saved earlier) into a soup pot; add flour and onion mixture, sliced sausage, and cooked sauerkraut. Cook for 10 to 15 minutes.

In a soup tureen, mix the sour cream and a cup of the hot sauerkraut broth. Add salt if needed. Adjust the taste of the soup to make sure that it is quite sour, and pour into the tureen. Mix with sour cream and serve. Serves 8.

Dave's note: Very tasty and if you desire a milder flavor, add more sour cream.

SHIRLEY AND JOHN SOVAK
STROUDSBURG, PENNSYLVANIA

Syrian Lentil Soup

1   cup lentils
1½ quarts water
2   teaspoons salt
2   onions, chopped
3   tablespoons olive oil
2   cups spinach, chopped, cooked
    and strained

Wash and cook lentils in water to which salt has been added. When cooked, sauté onions in oil until tender and add with spinach to lentils. Season to taste. May be served with a slice of lemon. Serves 4 to 6.

Dave's note: A little freshly ground pepper when serving would be nice. This one is for a cold winter's day.

JO MAURIN
LIVONIA, MICHIGAN

Stew Ukraine

This is quite different from regular beef stew, and very flavorful. One may add cut potatoes and carrots to it for variation.

1   cup onions, sliced
2   teaspoons salt
1   #2 can tomatoes
1½ pounds beef, cubed
1   bay leaf
1   teaspoon paprika
    caraway seeds
1   large can sauerkraut, drained
1   cup sour cream

Cook onion in a little oil until soft; then add tomatoes, meat, and seasonings. Cover and simmer until meat is tender (about 1 hour). Add sauerkraut, cover, and simmer for 30 minutes longer. Remove from heat, add sour cream, and serve. Serves 6.

Dave's note: If you add some potatoes 10 minutes after adding sauerkraut, you have a more complete meal. A very tasty combination of ingredients.

GRAMIE RODENHISER

Kielbasa with Schav Soup

My mom used this recipe for over fifty-five years. She used to grow a big batch of schav in her garden every summer. She'd chop it and salt it and put it in jars for the cold months. When she ran out of schav, she improvised by using canned spinach and vinegar.

1 ring kielbasa
1 jar schav or 1 pound sour grass
1 to 2 quarts water
4 or 5 potatoes
3 tablespoons flour
½ pint sour cream
  salt and pepper to taste

Cut up kielbasa and put in a pot with 1 quart water (if jar of "Schav" is used; if fresh sour grass is used, use 2 quarts water). Peel and quarter potatoes and add to the pot along with seasonings. Cook for 40 minutes. In small bowl, mix flour with sour cream and a little stock until smooth. Add to soup slowly and cook 5 minutes more. Serves 8.

ANN MERENSKI
STAMFORD, CONNECTICUT

Georgia Brunswick Stew

This recipe has been in my family since 1915.

1 2- to 3-pound frying chicken
½ pound salt pork or other shortening
1 onion, chopped
2 quarts water
1 pint tomatoes, chopped
¼ pound hot peppers
1 pound lima beans
3 cups corn (fresh or canned)
½ tablespoon Worcestershire sauce
  (optional)
  salt and pepper to taste

Start with a large soup kettle. Cut the chicken as for frying. Dice pork and brown slightly. Add chicken and brown slightly. Add onions; cook slightly. Add water, tomatoes, and peppers. Continue cooking until meat separates from bones. Discard bones, cut the meat in small pieces, and return to liquid. Add beans, corn, and seasonings and cook until vegetables are done. Serves 4 to 6. Rabbit or squirrel can be used in place of chicken.

Dave's note: I'd advise thickening with a little flour and water just before adding the vegetables. Good flavor.

MRS. MERLE BACKUS
PRINCETON, MASSACHUSETTS

Italian Wedding Soup

1 whole chicken
1 large head endive
6 eggs
½ cup Romano cheese, grated

Meatballs:

½ pound ground beef
½ cup bread crumbs
½ tablespoon salt
1 egg
2 tablespoons milk
2 tablespoons Romano cheese, grated

Combine all ingredients and make tiny meatballs the size of large peas and set aside. Simmer whole chicken in 3 quart salted water until tender. Remove meat and cut into small pieces. Discard skin and bones. Cook meatballs in chicken broth for 30 minutes, then add cut-up chicken.

While meatballs are cooking, chop endive and cook in salted water for 10 minutes. Drain well and add to chicken broth. Cook 2 minutes. In a small bowl, beat eggs. Add Romano cheese and stir slowly into chicken broth. Cook a few minutes until broth clears. Serves 6.

Dave's note: Looks good—tastes even better.

MARIE CERESA
CRESSON, PENNSYLVANIA

Tamari Soup

This takes only about fifteen minutes to make, but is so delicious your guests will think you slaved over a hot stove all day to make it! Serve as an appetizer, buy a couple of takeout orders of Chinese food, and PRESTO! You have a sumptuous banquet!

1 clove garlic, crushed
1 tablespoon parsley, chopped
¼ cup olive oil
¾ cup cauliflower florets, broken into singles
½ cup mushrooms, sliced (or 1 large jar sliced mushrooms)
½ cup tomatoes, diced
½ cup string beans, asparagus, or other seasonal green vegetables, chopped
¼ cup celery, diced
¼ cup onions, diced
6 cups water
⅓ to ⅔ cup soy sauce (tamari sauce, if possible)
¼ cup sesame seeds
   salt and pepper

Sauté garlic and parsley in olive oil. Add vegetables and water to cover; steam for 5 minutes. Add the rest of water—about 4 cups. Then add ½ cup soy sauce or more until flavor suits you. Add sesame seeds, salt, and pepper. Makes approximately 6 ½-cup servings. Serves 6.

Dave's note: Use the full ⅔ cup soy sauce. A very colorful soup. And the sesame seeds are a nice touch.

CARLEE L. HOWE
BURLINGTON, MASSACHUSETTS

Misov Spannak
(Spinach Stew)

I'm not really sure where I got the recipe. It is easy to make, but unfortunately lamb is inexpensive only in the spring. If you are like Popeye, who loved his spinach, you will like this dish, for the blend of tomato juice, onion soup, spinach, and lamb makes for a unique flavor. It will make anyone forget any prejudice against spinach.

2 pounds shoulder of lamb*
¼ cup butter
1 package (½ ounce) dry onion soup
3 cups tomato juice
2 pounds spinach, trimmed, washed, and torn into large pieces
   salt and pepper

Cut meat into 1-inch cubes. Brown meat on all sides in butter. Add onion soup, water, tomato juice, and spinach. Cover and cook for about 1 hour or more (depending on cut of meat), until lamb is tender. If you use a pressure cooker, set on "cook" for 15 minutes, then let pressure go down by itself. Serve with chunks of hard, crusted bread for dunking. Serves 4.

*You can substitute lamb bones with meat or pieces of lamb neck, back, or shoulder. To prepare, cook in a little water, drain, degrease, remove bones, cut meat into pieces, and reduce cooking time after adding rest of ingredients. Helps cut costs!

Dave's note: Nice combination of flavors. This tastes great reheated.

MRS. RICHARD W. HOWE
STONEHAM, MASSACHUSETTS

Linsen Suppe
(Lentil Soup)

1 pound lentils
¼ pound bacon, diced
2 medium onions, sliced
2 medium carrots, diced
2 quarts water
1 cup celery, sliced
2½ teaspoons salt
½ teaspoon pepper
½ teaspoon dried thyme
2 bay leaves
1 large potato, peeled
1 meaty ham bone
2 tablespoons lemon juice

Wash lentils and soak overnight, covered, in cold water. Early the next day, drain lentils. In a dutch oven sauté bacon until limp. Add onions and carrots and sauté until onions are golden. Add lentils, water, celery, salt, pepper, thyme, and bay leaves. Grate potato into lentil mixture. Add ham bone. Simmer, covered, for 3 hours until lentils are tender. Remove bay leaves and ham bone. Cut all bits of meat from bone and return meat to soup. Add lemon juice when ready to serve. Serves 6 to 8.

Dave's note: A meal in itself. Smoked ham hocks are even better than the ham bone.

J. MALLE
NORWOOD, OHIO

Cuban Black Bean Soup

Puerto Rico is famous for its Black Bean Soup. The city of La Zaragozana (old San Juan) is noted for this soup, which originally came from Cuba.

1   pound black beans
2   quarts water
2   tablespoons salt
5   cloves garlic
½   tablespoon cumin
½   tablespoon oregano
¼   cup and 2 tablespoons white vinegar
½   cup and 2 tablespoons olive oil
½   pound onions, minced
½   pound green peppers, minced
½   cup rice

Soak beans overnight in water. Add salt, and boil beans until soft. Crush garlic, cumin, and oregano into vinegar; set aside. Heat oil in a pan and add onions (reserving 6-8 teaspoons for marinade) and peppers. Fry until onions are brown. Then add crushed ingredients, frying slowly. Drain some of the water off beans before adding onion-pepper mixture to them. Cook slowly until beans are tender.

Boil a small portion of rice and marinate it and very finely chopped raw onions in oil and vinegar. Add one teaspoon of this to each serving of soup. Serves 6 to 8.

VERONICA McKINNON
KIRKLAND LAKE, ONTARIO, CANADA

Portuguese Kale Soup

This recipe was brought over from the Azores in the 1950s but has been in the family for centuries. It is an inex-pensive soup to make and feeds a large family. Freezes well, so a small family can eat some and save some for later.

3   tablespoons oil
1   clove garlic
2   large onions, sliced
1   large stalk celery, sliced thinly
2½ to 3 pounds cheapest cut of beef around
1½ pounds linguica (Portuguese sausage), cut into 1-inch chunks
2   pounds potatoes, peeled and cubed
1   pound carrots, chopped
1½ to 2 pounds kale (remove heavy stems, wash well, and chop into 1½-inch pieces)

In a *large* pan, heat oil and sauté garlic until golden brown. Discard garlic. Sauté onions until clear and add celery and beef and 15 cups water. Simmer, covered, for 2 hours and add linguica. Simmer 1½ hours. Remove beef (it should fall apart). Break it up into pieces, discarding all bone and fat, and return to the pot. Skim any fat from the pot. Add potatoes and carrots and simmer ½ hour. Add kale, simmer ¼ hour, and let sit 10 minutes. Serves 8 to 10.

Before serving you may add ¼ to ½ pound precooked (in a separate pan) elbow macaroni. (I do.)

Served with sweet bread, a complete meal.

Dave's note: Cooked just right, everything comes out beautifully. If you'd like a little variation, use chourico instead of the linguica.

MICHAEL SILVIA
HALIFAX, MASSACHUSETTS

Watercress Soup with Meatballs

Meatballs:

½ pound ground beef
½ teaspoon salt
½ teaspoon sugar
1 teaspoon light soy sauce
½ teaspoon blended whiskey
¼ teaspoon sesame oil
2 teaspoons cornstarch
1 egg white, beaten

In a large bowl, stir all ingredients (with chopsticks, if available) until mixture becomes soft and thoroughly blended. If too soft, add one more teaspoon cornstarch. Form into small balls and set aside.

Broth:

2¼ cups chicken broth or chicken
    soup
2¼ cups water
1 slice ginger (or ½ teaspoon ground
    ginger)
2 to 3 large bunches watercress,
    washed thoroughly, stems cut to
    about 1½ to 2 inches.

Bring chicken broth and water to a boil with ginger. Add meatballs, bringing liquid to another boil. Meatballs are cooked when they float to the top (8 to 10 minutes). Then add watercress and bring to a boil once again. Serve immediately. To give watercress a bright green color, add ½ teaspoon baking soda; not necessary if served immediately and not overcooked. Serves 4 to 6.

Dave's note: Nice texture and taste. The meatballs and watercress make it delightful.

MRS. NICHOLAS W. BILTCLIFFE
FALL RIVER, MASSACHUSETTS

King's Soup

All I know about this recipe is the notation that came with it from a friend that it was first published in *The Lady's Companion* in 1753 in the Virginia Colony.

2 large Bermuda onions, thinly sliced
1 cup butter or margarine
2 teaspoons salt
¼ teaspoon mace
¼ teaspoon pepper
4 cups milk
2 cups light cream
2 egg yolks
    parsley, chopped

In a soup kettle, sauté onion in butter until very soft but not brown. Add salt, mace, and pepper, and cook for 1 minute. Then add milk and cook just below simmer for 30 minutes. *Always heat slowly but do not allow to boil or soup will curdle.* Beat yolks and cream in a small bowl; blend in 1 cup hot soup, then stir into kettle. Cook, stirring constantly, for 5 minutes. Ladle into soup tureen and garnish with chopped parsley.

This soup is more flavorful if made the day before and chilled 30 minutes until serving time. Then reheat. Serves 6 to 8.

PAULA TOWNSEND
WEST ROXBURY, MASSACHUSETTS

Rantasipe Cauliflower Soup

1 tablespoon butter
1 heaping tablespoon flour
1 pint veal stock (or chicken stock)
1 pint light cream
  buds from 1 cauliflower, cooked
  salt
  ground white pepper

For stock:

1 carrot
¼ onion
¼ leek
1 parsnip
  stalks of 1 cauliflower
  black and white pepper
2 ounces butter

Cut stock ingredients into small pieces and cook in 2-ounce portion of butter over low heat for about 15 minutes. Then melt tablespoon of butter, add flour, and cook for 10 minutes over low heat. Add veal stock and cream, both gently warmed, to stock, and mix vigorously until blended. Add stock vegetables and cook all together for 20 minutes. Strain into another saucepan. Discard stock vegetables, then add cauliflower buds and flavor with salt and ground white pepper. If soup is too thick, add cauliflower stock. Take care to avoid lumps. Serves 4 to 6.

Dave's note: Garnish with chopped parsley or chopped scallion tops.

K. CREPPIN
OTTAWA, ONTARIO, CANADA

Mediterranean Bean Soup

This recipe originated in northern Greece and Albania, which is very mountainous country inhabited by poor peasants who do a little farming and sheep raising. The bean soup is very hardy and nutritious. It's also very popular and inexpensive to make. My grandmother migrated from Greece in 1916 and brought the recipe with her. But it's hardly a secret recipe because many Slavic, Greek and Turkish people are familiar with it and enjoy it immensely.

I'm sure whoever makes this soup will enjoy it. It goes well with braised lamb or chicken, good rye bread, dill pickles, and cauliflower.

½ cup green peppers, chopped into ¼-inch pieces
½ cup celery, chopped into ½-inch pieces
½ cup onion, finely chopped
½ cup carrots, diced
½ teaspoon dried parsley
1 large potato, diced
½ teaspoon dried mint
½ small can stewed tomatoes (#303) or equivalent amount of tomato paste
⅓ cup vegetable oil
½ teaspoon oregano
1 large can northern beans or red kidney beans

Combine all ingredients except beans, cover with water, and cook slowly until vegetables are soft. Add the northern beans or kidney beans (uncooked) and enough water to yield soup of the consistency you like. Simmer for 30 to 45 minutes. Add garlic and more mint and oregano if needed. This makes a good Lenten soup. Serve hot or ice cold. Serves 6.

.Dave's note: A substantial soup that was even better the next day when reheated.

CARL EVANOFF
LANSING, MICHIGAN

Rivel Soup

I am sorry but I have no story regarding this recipe other than it is old and really called Rivel Soup. (I suppose this is the Pennsylvania Dutch word for "lump.") I remember my mother making it when I was a young tot. I am now a seventy-six-year-old widow. I was raised with Pennsylvania Dutch foods, pork and sauerkraut, Schnitz and Knepp, rich pastries, etc.

2 cups flour
½ teaspoon salt
1 egg, beaten
8 cups chicken broth
2 cups corn, cooked

Place flour, salt, and egg in a bowl. Blend with your fingers until crumbly. Bring broth to boiling point. Add the crumbly "rivels" and corn. Simmer for 12 minutes. Serves 8.

Dave's note: A little too salty for my taste. Also, I'd cut the flour down to 1 cup. It's very filling.

MRS. PAULINE MILLER
DALLASTOWN, PENNSYLVANIA

Kentucky Potato Soup

4 cups potatoes, diced
1 small sprig parsley
2 small onions
  salt and pepper to taste

Dumplings:

1 cup flour
1 to 2 eggs
  water

Boil onions, parsley, and potatoes until well cooked, making sure the water level remains ¼ inch above potatoes.

Then prepare dumplings as follows:
Combine flour and egg(s) with enough water to form a stiff dough. Roll the dough until it is about ½ inch thick. Pinch off small piece (about ½ inch square) to drop into cooking potatoes. Allow dumplings to cook only until they feel firm. Serves 4 to 6.
Now try to stop eating this—if you can.

HAROLD L. EKAS
WHITE OAK, KENTUCKY

Cockle Soup

From Dublin, Ireland.

2 dozen cockles or clams, mussels, scallops, or combination
1 heaping tablespoon butter
1 heaping tablespoon flour
2 cups cockle or fish stock
½ pint milk
2 tablespoons parsley, chopped
¼ cup celery, chopped
¼ cup light cream
  salt and pepper to taste

Scrub shells well. Put in a saucepan, cover with water, and bring to boil. When shells are opened, remove cockles and dispose of shells. Strain juice and reserve. Melt butter in a separate saucepan and stir in flour and juice. Add 2 cups of stock; then add milk, stirring constantly until smoothly blended. Add parsley, celery, and seasoning and simmer gently 5 minutes. Finally, add cockles and simmer another 5 minutes. DO NOT BOIL. Serve with a little cream for each portion. Serves 4.

Dave's note: A tablespoonful of minced onion would be good when serving.

MARY W. SULLIVAN

Oyster Bisque

I first tried this bisque when I was a bride at the home of another bride. This was the first course she served, and I was so impressed with it that I asked her for the recipe. I think it is over seventy-five years old, at least. I have had it for fifty years.

½ pint oysters
1 cup water
2 cups milk
1 small onion, chopped
1 stalk celery, diced
3 sprigs parsley
1 small bay leaf
⅛ teaspoon mace
2 tablespoons butter
2 tablespoons flour
1 teaspoon salt
⅛ teaspoon pepper
  paprika

Chop oysters; add water and simmer 10 minutes. Scald milk with vegetables; add oysters and strain, rubbing oysters and vegetables through a sieve. Melt butter; add flour and stir to blend; add oyster-milk mixture; add seasonings and simmer until smooth and thickened to desired consistency. Sprinkle with paprika when serving. Serves 4.

Dave's note: A very subtle flavor. Something special.

MRS. RUSSELL S. HAYDEN
WHITE STONE, VIRGINIA

Pemaquid Point Fish Chowder

2 pounds fish fillets (preferably haddock)
4 medium potatoes, diced
  few celery leaves, chopped
1 bay leaf
1 clove garlic, put through garlic press
2½ teaspoons salt
4 whole cloves
3 medium onions, sliced
½ cup butter
¼ teaspoon dill seed or dill weed
¼ teaspoon white pepper
½ cup dry vermouth
2 cups boiling water
2 cups light cream

Place everything except cream in a large casserole and bake at 375° for 1 hour. Heat cream to scalding and add to chowder just before serving. Serves 6 to 8.

MADELINE COWING
CONCORD, MASSACHUSETTS

Scallop Chowder

This recipe came from Ireland. It is very popular at Shannon Airport Restaurant.

3 slices bacon, diced
2 onions, chopped
4 large potatoes, diced
6 cups bottled clam juice
3 tomatoes, seeded, chopped, and peeled
1 teaspoon salt
  dash freshly ground pepper
½ pound sea scallops, diced
1 cup heavy cream
  parsley, finely chopped
4 crackers, crushed

Cook diced bacon over low heat until almost crisp. Remove and cook onions in bacon fat until soft. Add potatoes and clam juice and cook mixture 15 minutes. Stir in tomatoes, salt, and pepper, and simmer 10 minutes longer. Add scallops, crushed crackers, and cream. Simmer a few minutes. Stir in a generous amount of parsley before serving in preheated bowls. Serves 6 to 8.

Dave's note: It tastes better if you double the amount of scallops. So sell one child. And instead of cooking onions in bacon fat, remove all but one tablespoon of fat. Add 2 tablespoons of butter and then sauté.

ROSETTA REILLY
CONCORD, MASSACHUSETTS

Galway Stew

2 pounds stew beef
2 tablespoons oil
1 large soup bone
2 large onions, diced
1 green pepper, diced
1 teaspoon prepared mustard
1 teaspoon instant coffee
1 can tomato soup
4 carrots, sliced in 1-inch pieces
6 potatoes, quartered

Brown beef in oil. Add onions, peppers, soup bone, and water. Cook until meat is tender (60 to 90 minutes). Add water if necessary. Then add mustard, coffee, tomato soup, carrots, and potatoes. Cook until vegetables are done (20 to 30 minutes). Serves 4.

MRS. HAROLD G. BOYDEN
LEOMINSTER, MASSACHUSETTS

Redwood Sorrel

Redwood sorrel, one of several allied species sometimes cultivated for use as a green vegetable or in salads and sauces, is a perennial herb found in shaded woods. The following recipe makes a delicious soup. Chopped violet leaves — which come from the wilds, not from a house plant — may be substituted for the redwood sorrel.

1 tablespoon butter
1 cup fresh sorrel leaves
1 cooked potato, mashed or pureed
2 cups milk
  salt and pepper to taste

Melt butter in a saucepan. Add well-washed sorrel leaves, without stalks, and brown lightly. Add potato and seasoning. Mix in milk slowly and heat, being careful not to boil. Serves 4 to 6.

M. GAMBLIN
KINGSTON, NEW HAMPSHIRE

Polynesian Beef Stew

I used to cook this stew prior to my husband's death, but I haven't cooked for over eight years now as I live alone. I do very little cooking now, as I eat out most of the time. The Polynesian Stew is very good, though.

1   green pepper, chopped
1   small onion, chopped
1   tablespoon butter
1   tablespoon cornstarch
1   tablespoon water
1½ pounds beef stew, canned
1   13½-ounce can pineapple chunks, drained
¼   teaspoon ginger
1   tablespoon sugar
1   tablespoon vinegar
1   teaspoon soy sauce
¼   teaspoon salt
1   3-ounce can chow mein noodles

Sauté green pepper and onion in butter until tender, not soft. Mix cornstarch with water and add with remaining ingredients, except noodles. Simmer and stir gently until thickened. Serve with noodles. Serves 4.

Dave's note: Rather standard fare with sweet and sour taste and canned stew, but the ingredients all work well.

RUTH W. FODREY
ELIZABETH CITY, NORTH CAROLINA

Cabbage Patch Stew

A hearty dish for the male folks.

1   pound ground beef
2   medium onions, chopped
4   cups cabbage, coarsely chopped
½   cup celery, diced
1   quart canned tomatoes
1   can kidney beans
2   cups water
2   teapoons salt
2   teaspoons pepper
1   to 2 tablespoons chili powder

Cook ground beef in a dutch oven, stirring occasionally, until the color changes. Add onions, cabbage, and celery. Continue to cook, stirring, until vegetables are wilted. Stir in tomatoes, kidney beans with liquid, water, and seasonings. Heat to boiling; reduce heat and simmer until vegetables are completely cooked.

If desired, dumplings may be added when the vegetables are almost done. Drop by spoonfuls into simmering stew. Serves 4 to 6.

Dumplings

1   cup flour
2   teaspoons baking powder
½   cup milk
¼   teaspoon salt

Put all ingredients in a bowl and mix. Drop by spoonful into stew. Cook 10 minutes uncovered, then covered for 10 minutes.

Dave's note: Very hefty combination. Very tasty dumplings.

ESTHER STEVENSON
OAKLAND MILLS, PENNSYLVANIA

Pink Soup

My maternal grandmother brought this recipe from Poland. It always was and still is the highlight of the summer season. All we ever had to do was call and tell each other we were making Pink Soup, and you can believe in the next day or two we had visitors.

No matter who made it or how many times you had the soup the previous year, come summer you couldn't wait to make it or go where it was. It's especially great when the vegetables are fresh out of the garden.

This has a Polish name, but it was years since I heard it, so I can't give it to you.

2 or 3 bunches red beet tops (all green removed)
2 medium cucumbers
2 medium onions
5 stalks celery
2 or 3 sprigs fresh dill
1 pint sour cream
2 quarts boiled water
¼ cup vinegar (start with this amount, but after it sits overnight, you may find you'd like a little more, so add to your own taste)
salt and pepper

On the first day, wash and dice beet tops; then cook them until tender and drain. Peel and dice cucumbers and onions; cut up celery. Put all these ingredients in a bowl, sprinkle with salt, then cover and refrigerate overnight.

On the second day, add sour cream to water and vegetables and stir until very well blended. Place some of this mixture in a bowl and gradually stir in ¼ cup vinegar. (It's okay if it looks as though it's curdling.) Stir well and add salt and pepper to taste. Cover and let sit overnight refrigerated. Add this to remaining mixture . This soup will turn a nice shade of pink and will keep for better than a week if properly refrigerated. It doesn't usually last that long around here, but I have set some aside to give to others in a jar, and it is sometimes a week before they get around to getting over here for it!. Serves 8.

Dave's note: The name in Polish is Chodnik. For a stronger flavor, use beet roots as well, julienned and boiled along with diced tops.

MRS. JOAN HUGHES
NILES, OHIO

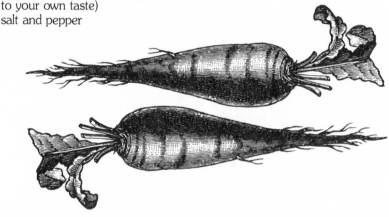

Swedish Fruit Soup

This recipe has been in our family since I was a child. For us it was a treat and it still is. This should be called Elna's Swedish Fruit Soup, as that is my mother's name. She came to America when she was eighteen, married, raised a family, and never went back to Sweden.

The Scandinavian people love to gather together with their relatives and friends for a festive meal. Needless to say, even while in America they still serve many of the traditional dishes they learned to prepare in their homes in Sweden.

1   package dried mixed fruit, chopped coarsely
½   cup raisins
½   cup sugar
1   slice lemon
1   stick cinnamon
5   cups water
1   pint grape juice
1   large jar white cherries
1½ teaspoons cornstarch

Combine fruit, raisins, sugar, lemon, cinnamon, water, and grape juice and simmer for 20 to 25 minutes until fruit is tender. Mix cornstarch with a little cold water and, while stirring, add to soup. Add cherries and simmer for 10 more minutes. Chill for 3 to 4 hours and serve cold. Serves 6.

Dave's note: Very, very sweet. Add 4 tablespoons lemon juice, and it's still sweet. I suggest using ¼ cup sugar, then adding additional sugar once fruit is cooked, if necessary. Good served with a dollop of sour cream.

EBBA WITTKONSKI
GRAND RAPIDS, MICHIGAN

New England Cider Soup

3   pints apple cider
⅓   cup brown sugar or granulated sugar
2   cups dried bread cubes
3   tablespoons butter
    salt
3   eggs
2   tablespoons granulated sugar
1½ cups cream
2   tablespoons flour
    allspice
3   tablespoons dark rum

As slowly as possible bring cider to a boil, and carefully skim off the beads that will appear on the surface. Stir in ⅓ cup of sugar (brown sugar is preferable). Set this mixture aside, keeping it warm. Brown bread cubes in butter and add salt to taste. Set aside, also keeping warm. Beat eggs as for making an omelet, and add to them, while beating, the extra 2 tablespoons of sugar and cream, to which have been added flour, dash of allspice, and rum. When mixture is well blended, pour it slowly and steadily into hot cider. When ready to serve, sprinkle fried bread cubes over soup and serve immediately.
Serves 6 to 8.

Dave's note: Very pleasant soup for a crisp fall day.

JAMES W. PAPPAS
IPSWICH, MASSACHUSETTS

Potage con Carne

(Leftover Chili con Carne)

My wife made a double batch of really good chili one time, and we had no show for dinner. Instead of freezing it, I pureed it, thinning with the juice, bouillon, and wine until I liked the taste. Experiment with wine by changing the amounts.

1 large can tomato juice
  couple sprigs fresh parsley
1½ cups red wine or 1 can of beer
1 can beef bouillon
6 frankfurters

Cut frankfurters into rounds and fry until brown, then drain. Simmer this concoction for about 30 minutes. Serve with franks floating on top. If no hot dogs are available, herbed croutons will do.

DAVE

Is there a more glorious way to add roughage to your diet? Cold crisp greens, thinly sliced vegetables, fresh fruits, sprouts, nuts — but not all at the same time! Salads are so foolproof, so good-looking. Easy — nutritious — and successful (can you tell I eat one every day?) if certain rules are followed:

1. Use the freshest, cleanest ingredients.

2. Serve cold (warm lettuce has very little charm).

3. Don't flood with dressing: It's supposed to enhance but not smother the salad.

4. A little garnish (freshly grated cheese, coconut, artfully carved radishes and carrots) is great.

5. Serve salads just before the main meal and don't give me any arguments about after or during.

6. There are so many combinations — why not use some of them?

7. Don't cover brown lettuce with paprika. You won't fool anybody.

—Dave

Salads and Salad Dressing

Dutch Salad Dressing

This recipe has been handed down from my grandmother to my mother and then to me. My grandmother lived in Kutztown, Pennsylvania, a small Pennsylvania Dutch town near Reading. The dressing can be used cold on lettuce or hot on dandelion or endive. It even makes a good dressing on potato salad and can also be stored in the refrigerator.

2 slices bacon, chopped
1 or 2 eggs
¾ cup cider or white vinegar, diluted with ¼ cup water
1 cup sugar
dash salt
1 cup milk
1 tablespoon butter, melted
1 small onion, thinly sliced
flour thickening (about ¼ cup flour mixed with water)

Fry bacon until crisp. Set aside. Beat eggs well in a bowl and add vinegar, sugar, salt, and butter. Add to bacon. Then mix milk and flour thickening together. Add to first mixture and cook, stirring constantly, until mixture thickens. Remove from heat. Add onion to mixture. Let cool, stirring occasionally to prevent skin from forming on top.

MRS. ADELE FISHER
HAZLETON, PENNSYLVANIA

Irene's Salad Dressing

A delicious Russian-style dressing that can be made for a fraction of the cost of commercial preparations. The recipe was developed by my stepmother, who was tired of paying high prices for salad dressings. For dieters, substitute packets of artificial sweetener and it's just as good.

1   can condensed tomato soup
12 tablespoons white vinegar
1½ cups salad oil
1   small garlic clove
1   small onion
¾   cup sugar (more if you like a sweeter dressing)
2   teaspoons dry mustard
2   teaspoons salt
2   tablespoons Worcestershire sauce
1   teaspoon paprika

Put all ingredients into a blender and mix thoroughly. Makes 2 large bottles of dressing. For best results, age dressing 2 to 3 days.

SUSAN NASON
NEWTON CENTER, MASSACHUSETTS

Million-Dollar Dressing

This recipe won a million dollars.

1   can tomato soup
4   bay leaves
6   garlic buds or ½ teaspoon garlic salt
4   teaspoons mustard seed
2   teaspoons salt
½   cup sugar
10 whole cloves
¾   cup vinegar
1   cup vegetable oil

Mix all ingredients in a jar and shake well. Put in the refrigerator for three or four days and strain before using.

Dave's note: Someday soon, Violet, you'll have to tell us when and where this dressing won a million. Did you spill some on a lottery ticket?

VIOLET MITCHELL
EAST WEYMOUTH, MASSACHUSETTS

French Dressing

During my childhood in Long Beach, California, we ate occasionally at Knotts Berry Farm where they served a delightful French dressing at their chicken and steak house restaurant.

Years later, I'm still trying to duplicate their dressing and this is as close as I've come. I don't think I can take credit for this recipe. Each time I serve this dressing to my family, I say, "Just like at Knotts Berry Farm." My family has heard this so often that they now tease me by saying in unison, "Just like at Knotts Berry Farm."

¼ cup dried onions
2 cups sugar
2 cans tomato soup
1 cup salad oil
1 cup vinegar
1 tablespoon prepared mustard
2 teaspoons salt
1 teaspoon pepper
  touch garlic salt or powder

Combine everything in a bowl and stir until well mixed. Store in the refrigerator. Will last a month or two. Makes one quart.

JUNE HOLST
MEDWAY, OHIO

Salad Dressing

Delicious.

3 eggs, beaten
2 tablespoons sugar
½ teaspoon dry mustard
1 tablespoon flour
  pinch cayenne
½ cup vinegar
½ cup water
½ teaspoon salt
½ pint medium cream

Combine eggs and water with sugar, mustard, flour, and cayenne. Heat vinegar and add a little to this mixture. Stir well and add rest of vinegar. Cook until thickened. Remove from the stove. When cool, add salt and cream.

EDITH L. SARGENT
DEER ISLE, MAINE

Endive Salad

1 large head endive
2 hard-cooked eggs, sliced
2 medium potatoes, boiled in skins and diced
6 slices bacon, fried crisp and cut up

Dressing

½ cup sugar
2 heaping teaspoons flour
1 teaspoon salt
½ cup vinegar
½ cup milk
½ teaspoon dry mustard

Mix dressing ingredients and stir into bacon fat left over from frying bacon slices. Cook, stirring, until thickened. Toss with endive, eggs, potatoes, and bacon bits.

MARIE CERESA
CRESSON, PENNSYLVANIA

Bouquet of Flowers Salad

This salad will give the effect of a bouquet of flowers. A pretty sight if done correctly.

1 medium cauliflower
   salt and pepper to taste
2 tablespoons oil
2 tablespoons lemon juice
2 medium potatoes, boiled
2 tablespoons mayonnaise
   heart of lettuce or sprig of parsley
4 hard-boiled eggs, quartered
2 medium tomatoes
1 green pepper
⅓ cup milk
   green olives

Cut stems off cauliflower and discard. Wash remaining cauliflower and cook whole in a small amount of salted water, covered, until tender (overcooking will make cauliflower unappealing). Drain well. Place in a salad bowl in the shape of a mound. Sprinkle with salt, pepper, oil, and lemon juice.

Mash potatoes, Add salt, mayonnaise, and milk. Mix and spread evenly with a spatula all over cauliflower, applying most of the mixture around the base of the mound.

Dip a small, pointed knife in cold water and make lengthwise slits in cauliflower. Garnish top of the salad with hard-boiled eggs. Place pointed ends of eggs up with yolks on the outside to give the appearance of a flower. Place small heart of lettuce or sprig of parsley in the center.

Slice tomatoes. Garnish bottom part of salad bowl. Cut green pepper in strips and place on tomatoes. Cut a few green olives in half and place around eggs.

Dave's note: If you want to make this salad look fancier, use a biscuit cutter on your tomatoes. The more artistry, the bigger the raves.

ANONYMOUS

Strawberry Salad

Very colorful and a bit of a mystery, this salad has been my hallmark at church suppers and potluck dinners and has proved popular at both.

1 package strawberry-flavored gelatin
⅔ cup boiling water
1 10-ounce package frozen strawberries
1 8-ounce can crushed pineapple, undrained
1 cup sour cream

Dissolve gelatin in boiling water. Add and break up frozen strawberries, then add pineapple and stir. Turn half of this mixture into a mold and chill in the freezer for about 10 minutes. Spread sour cream over set mixture, then spread remaining mixture over sour cream and chill again.

Dave's note: I'm a big layered man myself. The presentation is wonderful.

ELIZABETH ASHLEY GARDNER
CONCORD, MASSACHUSETTS

Radio Salad

This is a recipe a lady gave me quite some time ago. Believe it or not, it is the true name of the recipe.

1   10-ounce can tomato soup
1   3-ounce package lemon-flavored gelatin
½   envelope unflavored gelatin
½   cup cold water
½   pound cream cheese
1½ cups celery
1   green pepper   finely chopped
1   small onion
½   cup almonds, slivered
1   cup salad dressing

Overnight, allow cream cheese to soften out of the refrigerator. To prepare salad, heat tomato soup in a saucepan until hot. Dissolve lemon-flavored gelatin in soup. Mix unflavored gelatin with cold water and add to soup. Then add cream cheese and stir until tiny lumps appear. Add remaining ingredients and mix thoroughly, but do not cook. Set in a loaf pan and chill. Cut in squares and serve in lettuce leaf. Excellent with hot rolls and cold cuts.

BEA BENN
SIMCOE, ONTARIO, CANADA

Mary's Spring Salad

1   3¼-ounce package lime-flavored gelatin
1   3¼-ounce package lemon-flavored gelatin
2   cups water
1   cup evaporated milk
1   #2 can crushed pineapple
1   pound cottage cheese
1   cup mayonnaise
1   tablespoon horseradish sauce
1   cup nuts, chopped

Dissolve both gelatins in nearly boiling water, then cool slightly and add milk. Add pineapple, juice and all. Let jell partially in a mold. Add cottage cheese, mayonnaise, horseradish, and nuts. Let set until firm.

MS. MARY MAURIN
APO NEW YORK, NEW YORK

Yum Yum Salad

1   can fruit cocktail, drained
1   can pineapple, drained
1   package instant vanilla pudding
1   package miniature marshmallows
1   package dream whip, prepared as directed

Mix all of the above together, except dream whip. When all are blended well, fold in dream whip. Put mixture in refrigerator to set and chill. Serve as a dessert or salad.

MRS. MARJORY A. RETTIG
BUTLER, PENNSYLVANIA

Spinach Souffle Salad

This is an old recipe that my mother used when we were children. I do not know whether she got it from someone else or whether it was one she made up. My mother was an excellent plain and fancy cook and made up most of her recipes with a pinch of this and a few drops of that.

I'm afraid I have nothing too exciting to say about this except that we all loved it. And this was before Popeye made it popular to like spinach.

1   10-ounce package frozen chopped
      spinach
1   envelope unflavored gelatin
½   cup sugar
¾   teaspoon salt
      dash pepper
1   cup cold water
¼   cup lemon juice
⅓   cup mayonnaise or salad dressing
1   cup cream-style cottage cheese,
      drained
¼   cup celery, finely chopped

Cook spinach according to package directions. Press against sides of a sieve to drain very thoroughly; cool. In a small saucepan, soften gelatin in ½ cup cold water; heat and stir until gelatin dissolves. Add sugar, salt, dash pepper, remaining water, and lemon juice. Mix well. Place mayonnaise in a small bowl; gradually stir in gelatin mixture. Chill until mixture begins to set. Beat gelatin mixture until light and fluffy. Fold in spinach, cottage cheese, and celery. Turn into a 5-cup mold; chill 4 to 5 hours or overnight.

Dave's note: Very pretty and, much as I like a tossed green salad, this is a welcome change.

MRS. MYRTLE WOODWARD
EXETER, NEW HAMPSHIRE

Walloon Potato Salad

This recipe is something no gourmet cooks would want to lose track of, once they try it. Concocted first by a lady resident of the Walloon Lake community of Michigan's North Woods (where Ernest Hemingway's family summered in his youth), this potato salad is often served as an entire meal on warm summer evenings.

1   pound small new potatoes, scrubbed
1   pound new green beans, sliced
3   scallions
1   tablespoon capers, drained
      salt and pepper
¼   cup olive oil
2   tomatoes, quartered
¼   cup vinegar

Place potatoes in a saucepan of water to which a dash of salt has been added. Cook for 20 minutes, or until tender. Drain, quarter any potatoes larger than 1 inch, and place in a bowl. Cook green beans in salted water for 12 minutes or until tender. Drain beans, refresh under cold tap water, and combine them with potatoes. Add scallions, chopped with the tops, and capers. Add salt and pepper to taste. Pour on olive oil while vegetables are still warm. Toss to incorporate oil. Let cool to room temperature, add tomatoes, and toss with vinegar.

JOHN WESLEY COOK
DRAYTON PLAINS, MICHIGAN

Yummy Potato Salad

A handed-down recipe. My lifelong girlfriend gave it to me forty years ago (I'm now sixty-nine). It is a most convenient recipe for potato salad, for picnics and cookouts, as it is used at room temperature and does not require refrigeration.

1 tablespoon flour
2 slices bacon, chopped and fried
¾ cup sweet vinegar or ½ cup vinegar, ¼ cup water, and 1 tablespoon sugar
½ teaspoon celery seed
½ mango pepper, chopped
6 medium-sized boiled potatoes, sliced
4 hard-boiled eggs
½ pimiento, chopped
1 medium onion, chopped
½ teaspoon parsley, chopped

Make a paste of flour and bacon drippings. Add vinegar and celery seed. Cook, stirring, until thick. Mix with all other ingredients in a bowl and let sit about 1 hour. Serve warm.

Dave's note: This has to be a great picnic potato salad. Ever had mayonnaise turn rancid on a hot summer's day?

MRS. GEORGE W. FRYE
CINCINNATI, OHIO

Pickled Cole Slaw

This is an old German recipe given to me by a friend's mother. It keeps in the refrigerator for ages. Of course when we were kids it was kept in an icebox and was, we thought, the best thing a mother could keep in it. She always wondered, though, with such a quizzical look on her face, how the salad was disappearing! Maybe a mouse got in the hole in the bottom of the icebox. We would titter like little idiots because we knew where it went! Mother is no longer with us, but the memory and the recipe linger on.

1 large head cabbage, finely shredded
2 large onions, sliced
¾ cup sugar
1 teaspoon salt

Sauce:

1 cup white vinegar
2 teaspoons prepared mustard
2 teaspoons celery seed
¼ cup sugar
¾ cup salad oil

Toss together cabbage, onions, sugar, and salt. Let stand while making sauce.

To make sauce, boil vinegar with mustard, celery seed, and sugar. Then add salad oil and let bubble. Pour over cabbage, mix, and chill. This will keep in the refrigerator for several weeks.

MRS. HILDA DEAK
LONDON, ONTARIO, CANADA

Molded Crabmeat Salad

1 can tomato soup
6 ounces cream cheese
2 envelopes unflavored gelatin
½ cup water
½ cup green pepper
½ cup celery, chopped
  a little onion (optional)
1 cup mayonnaise
2 7-ounce cans crabmeat, lobster, or
  salmon

Heat tomato soup. Stir cream cheese
until smooth. Dissolve gelatin in water
and add to soup and cheese mixture.
Cool. Stir in rest of ingredients and
place in a mold. Chill in the refrigerator until it solidifies. To serve,
run a knife around the salad, then
let it sit in lukewarm water very
briefly. It should slip out easily.

ANONYMOUS

Tempura Side Salad

This is so simple yet so delicious. It's
very light and is the ideal accompani-
ment to a tempura meal.

½ red cabbage
½ white cabbage
1 good sized onion (sweet Bermuda
  or pink)
2 green peppers
1 cucumber, seeded
3 or 4 large celery stalks
12 mushrooms
4 tomatoes, seeded
½ head cauliflower

Chop everything fairly small. Serve on
a bed of lettuce with only Japanese
rice vinegar. No oil or anything else.
You can add broccoli stalks, leeks,
turnip. Eat two dishes of this and you
can race out of the house and help a
Boy Scout across the street.

DAVE

One cold, snowy Saturday, I turned out sixteen loaves of bread. Egad! It was an expensive afternoon. The bread didn't cost that much really, but proud bread makers give their breads away. Freely, gladly, with a modest shrug that denotes "it's really nothing" when actually the baker realizes it's the best-tasting bread you've ever had in your life. Fresh bread, rising in the warm oven, gives any kitchen a nice-place-to-be atmosphere. Bread baking builds character too. Many's the time, frustrated beyond belief, I've been on the verge of beating up my children, kicking the dog, and putting the house up for sale. But instead, I kneaded four loaves of rye and was so tired afterward that I wouldn't have been able to arm wrestle my wife's hair-dresser.

I served every one of the breads in this section in one week on successive mornings in the radio station cafeteria. By Thursday, I had a sellout. Later on, I was chosen employee of the month. Why not? I waited twenty-two years.

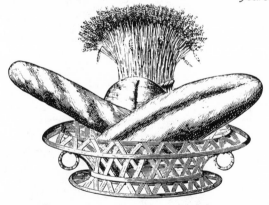

Breads

Murph the Surf's Zucchini Bread

This zucchini bread is freezable!

3 eggs
2 cups granulated sugar
1 cup vegetable oil
3 teaspoons vanilla
2 cups zucchini, peeled and grated
3 cups flour
1 teaspoon salt
1 teaspoon baking soda
¼ teaspoon baking powder
1½ teaspoons cinnamon
1½ teaspoons nutmeg
1 cup nuts, chopped

Beat eggs until light and foamy. Add sugar, oil, vanilla, and zucchini, mixing lightly but well, and set aside. Combine flour, salt, baking soda, baking powder, cinnamon, and nutmeg, and add this to egg and zucchini mix. Stir well to blend. Stir in nuts. Pour into two 9 x 5 x 3-inch loaf pans, greased and floured. Bake at 350° in a preheated oven for 1 hour. Cool on racks.

Dave's note: Great! Just spicy enough—plain or toasted. A real diet wrecker.

BRIAN M. KNEPP
FRAMINGHAM, MASSACHUSETTS

Apricot Oatmeal Bread

This delightfully different oatmeal bread freezes well, toasts well, and tastes superlatively well, but doesn't last well. It disappears all too quickly!

2 cups biscuit mix
1 cup quick-cooking oatmeal
¼ teaspoon salt
1 teaspoon baking powder
⅓ cup dried apricots, chopped
¼ cup walnuts, coarsely chopped
4½ teaspoons artificial sweetener
1 egg, beaten
1¼ cups milk

Combine biscuit mix, oatmeal, salt, baking powder, apricots, and nuts. Blend sweetener, egg, and milk, and add to dry ingredients, stirring just enough to blend. Pour into a greased loaf pan and bake at 350° for 1 hour or until the bread tests as done. Makes 12 to 15 servings. For peak flavor, serve bread warm or oven hot.

Dave's note: Two pieces with sweet butter and a cup of tea—ah, yes!

INGRID M. PARIDON
CLIFTONDALE, MASSACHUSETTS

Rhubarb Nut Bread

In my yard I have quite a few varieties of rhubarb, some of which came from as far away as Canada. The more I give it away, the more it grows! Since it has a long growing season, I like to use it in many ways so my family does not tire of it. We like breads, and the rhubarb nut bread is different and a good conversation piece. It also makes a good gift.

Here are some fascinating rhubarb facts:

The red coloring is in the outer covering, so don't peel strings.

Movie extras often say the word "rhubarb" over and over to sound like an angry mob.

Rhubarb is low in fat, fairly high in protein, and contains calcium, iron, phosphorus, potassium, folic acid, niacin, thiamin, and vitamin C! In other words, it's good for you.

Although rhubarb stalks are good for you, the leaves contain a poison, oxalic acid.

This bread is delicious served plain but is also good with strawberry jam or preserves spread on top of each slice.

1½ cups brown sugar
⅔ cup salad oil
1 egg
1 teaspoon baking soda
1 teaspoon salt
1 teaspoon vanilla
1 cup sour milk
2½ cups flour
1½ to 2 cups fresh rhubarb, diced
½ cup chopped nuts

Topping:

½ cup sugar
1 tablespoon butter

Beat sugar, oil, and egg. Mix baking soda, salt, vanilla, and milk and add to the first mixture. Fold in rhubarb. Grease two loaf pans into which mixture should be poured. For the topping, combine sugar and butter and sprinkle on top of loaves. Bake at 325° for one hour or until cake tester inserted in center of loaf comes out clean.

Dave's note: I really hate rhubarb, but not in this bread.

MRS. ELIZABETH S. MILLER
WHITINSVILLE, MASSACHUSETTS

Orange Honey Bread

2½ cups flour, sifted
1 tablespoon baking powder
½ teaspoon salt
½ teaspoon baking soda
2 tablespoons butter or margarine
1 cup honey
1 egg
1 tablespoon orange rind, grated
¾ cup orange juice, freshly squeezed
¾ cup walnuts, chopped

Sift together flour, baking powder, salt, and baking soda. In a separate bowl, cream butter, then beat in honey until light and creamy. Beat in egg and orange juice and rind. Stir in walnuts. Pour into a 9 x 5 x 3-inch loaf pan. Bake at 350° for 70 minutes, or until a toothpick inserted into the bread comes out clean. Let cool in pan for 10 minutes. Serve in thin slices with whipped cream cheese or softened butter.

Dave's note: I gained two pounds eating this bread. Thanks a lot, Mary.

MARY ROBILARD
PROVIDENCE, RHODE ISLAND

Bonanza Bread

I am one of those who doesn't take time to eat breakfast. I find this very quick and nutritious for breakfast. Hope you like it as much as I do.

1 cup flour, sifted
1 cup whole wheat flour
½ teaspoon salt
½ teaspoon baking soda
2 teaspoons baking powder
⅔ cup nonfat dry milk powder
⅓ cup toasted wheat germ
¼ cup walnuts, chopped
½ cup brown sugar, firmly packed
½ cup unsalted dry roasted peanuts, chopped
½ cup raisins
3 eggs
½ cup vegetable oil
½ cup molasses
¾ cup orange juice
2 bananas, sliced
⅓ cup dried apricots, chopped

Combine flour, salt, baking soda, baking powder, wheat germ, walnuts, brown sugar, peanuts, and raisins in a large bowl and blend thoroughly. Then in the container of an electric blender, whirl first the eggs until foamy. To the whipped eggs, add oil, molasses, orange juice, and bananas, whirling the contents of the blender after each addition. Add apricots, and whirl just to chop coarsely. Then pour mixture into a bowl with dry ingredients. Stir only until all flour is moistened. Pour into two 7⅜ x 3⅝ x 2¼-inch greased loaf pans.

Bake in a slow oven at 325° for 1 hour until center is firm when pressed lightly with finger. Cool the bread slightly in the pan on wire rack, then remove from pan and cool completely.

When cool, wrap tightly and store overnight to mellow flavors.

Or, baked in greased muffin tins at 350° for 20 minutes. Half the recipe makes 3 cups batter and 1½ dozen muffins.

Variations: For a tangy orange flavor, add ½ small orange, including peel, to liquid ingredients in the blender. Use other nuts instead of walnuts, but don't substitute anything for peanuts in order to keep the nutritional balance. Substitute raw chopped apples, grated carrots, applesauce, fresh ground apricots, peaches, pears, or even grated zucchini for the bananas.

Dave's note: I've seen this recipe in a dozen different places and always passed it by. Dumb me.

JEAN SWINEHART
FREMONT, OHIO

Pumpkin Bread

1 cup pumpkin
⅔ cup sugar
1 teaspoon salt
½ cup shortening
1 cup milk
½ yeast cake dissolved in ½ cup lukewarm water
5 cups flour

Use fresh pumpkin that has been stewed and strained, or canned pumpkin. Combine pumpkin with sugar, salt, shortening, and milk. When mixture is lukewarm, add dissolved yeast and flour. Cover and let rise over night in a warm place. Then shape into loaf on a buttered cookie sheet and bake at 375° for 20 minutes. Reduce heat to 350° and bake for 40 minutes longer.

STANLEY DROST
BOSTON, MASSACHUSETTS

Date Nut Bread

1 cup dates, coarsely chopped
1 teaspoon baking soda
1 tablespoon butter
¾ cup boiled water, cooled
¾ cup sugar
½ teaspoon salt
1 teaspoon vanilla
1 cup flour
½ cup nuts
1 egg, separated

Combine all ingredients in the order that they are listed. Fold in egg white last, after beating until stiff. Bake at 325° for one hour in a loaf pan.

Dave's note: Someday, Norma, I'll get even for all the luscious things you've made for me.

NORMA H. DAY
PROVIDENCE, RHODE ISLAND

Apple Bread

An apple a day has 70 calories per day.
An apple a day is a source of vitamin A.
An apple a day could save on food bill dismay.

½ stick butter or margarine
⅔ cup sugar
2 eggs
2 cups flour
1 teaspoon baking powder
1 teaspoon baking soda
1 teaspoon salt
2 cups apples, coarsely grated (for best results, use more than one variety of apples)
1 teaspoon lemon peel, grated
⅔ cup nuts, chopped

Cream butter or margarine with sugar until fluffy, then beat in eggs. Sift together flour, baking powder, soda, and salt. Add alternately with apples, lemon peel and nuts to form a stiff batter. Bake in buttered and floured loaf pan at 350° for 50 to 60 minutes. Bread will be moist and good — wait until cold to slice.

MAREA THEODOROS
LITTLETON, MASSACHUSETTS

Post Grape-nuts Bread

I liked the sound of this recipe. I received it from a friend

1 cup Post Grape-nuts
2 cups sour milk
4 cups flour
1 cup sugar
1 teaspoon baking soda
4 teaspoons baking powder
pinch salt
2 eggs, well beaten

Soak Post Grape-nuts for 10 or 15 minutes in sour milk. Sift together flour, sugar, baking soda, baking powder, and salt. Alternately mix in with dry ingredients the Post Grape-nuts mixture and eggs. Place in a greased and floured loaf pan and let stand for 30 minutes. Bake at 375° for 35 to 40 minutes, or until done.

Dave's note: I ate an entire loaf. What a great way to make friends.

KAY SHERMAN
FALL RIVER, MASSACHUSETTS

Short'nin' Bread

¼ pound butter, softened
¼ cup light brown sugar
1½ cups flour

Cream butter with brown sugar, then add flour. Roll mixture out quickly on a floured board. Cut dough with a small biscuit cutter. Place cookies on a lightly floured cookie sheet. Bake approximately 20 minutes in a preheated oven at 350°.

Dave's note: Very simple, easy, and good.

MRS. MARION R. WILLIAMS
FRAMINGHAM CENTER, MASSACHUSETTS

Portuguese Sweetbread

2 packages dry yeast
½ cup lukewarm water
¾ cup milk
¾ stick butter
1 cup sugar
¾ tablespoon salt
4 jumbo eggs, beaten
6 cups flour

In a small bowl, soften yeast in warm water. Heat milk until almost boiling and add butter, stirring until it melts. Place sugar and salt in a large bowl. Add milk mixture, beaten eggs, and yeast mixture. Add flour little by little to form a soft dough. Knead for 8 to 10 minutes. Place in a greased bowl, cover dough, and turn once. Let rise in a warm place for about 2 hours, then punch down. Divide in half and place in 2 greased bread pans. Let rise again for 1 hour. Bake at 325° for 40 minutes. Makes 2 loaves.

Dave's note: I used to buy this all the time in Provincetown and usually finished half a loaf before I got home —a brown bag bread junkie.

LOIS DAVIDSON
GLOUCESTER, MASSACHUSETTS

Cowboy Graham Bread

An old recipe — over one hundred years old.

½ cup sugar
1 egg
4 tablespoons shortening, melted
1 teaspoon baking soda
½ teaspoon salt
1 cup white flour
1 cup graham flour
1 cup sour milk

Mix together sugar, egg, and shortening. In a separate bowl, mix together dry ingredients. Combine the two alternately with sour milk. Mix well. Bake in a greased loaf pan for 50 minutes at 350°. Or make muffins instead: bake at 425°.

Dave's note: Nice and subtle—great for sandwiches.

MRS. A. DEAN HOLMER, JR.
EXETER, NEW HAMPSHIRE

Easter Bread

This recipe has been in the family for years. My parents came here from Italy in 1903, and my mother brought it with her. When our daughter was learning how to bake, all the ingredients were assembled and, excited, she put the batter in the oven. Being in a hurry to see the results, she raised the temperature. After a little while, she checked it and everything was perfect —color, smell—it made your mouth water. But after it cooled off and she snuck a piece, she found it was raw inside!

2   yeast cakes
1   pint milk
12 eggs
5   cups flour
2   pounds Romano cheese, grated
1   cup oil, olive or corn
    pinch black pepper and salt

Mix yeast in lukewarm water and let stand. Mix eggs and milk into flour (after making a pocket in middle of flour), gradually adding grated cheese a little at a time and the oil. Add more flour as needed to keep firm but not sticky. Combine with yeast and let rise twice by covering dough and putting in a warm place.

Preheat oven to 400° and bake for 30 to 40 minutes. Beat 2 egg yolks and paint top of bread if you want a glossy top—both before and during the baking.

ALEX SANTILLI
BRIDGEWATER, MASSACHUSETTS

High-Fiber Bread

4½ cups warm water
2   packages dry yeast
4   tablespoons sugar
4   teaspoons salt
1½ cups oatmeal
1   cup dry potato flakes
1   cup toasted wheat germ
10 to 12 cups sifted flour
1   cup dry milk
3   eggs
4   tablespoons oil

Dissolve yeast in warm water. Add sugar and let stand for 5 minutes. Then add salt, oatmeal, potato flakes, and wheat germ and let stand. Into a large bowl, resift flour with dry milk. Add to it the yeast mixture, eggs, and oil. Stir together and turn out onto a pastry board dusted with 1 cup of the flour. Knead flour gradually into dough. When all flour is incorporated, continue to knead for 8 to 10 more minutes, or until the dough is nice and elastic. Turn into a large greased bowl and let rise in a warm place until double in bulk, approximately 2 hours. Punch the dough down and divide into 4 equal parts. Form into loaves and place in well-greased bread pans. Again let rise until almost double in bulk. Bake at 350° for 45 minutes. When baked turn out of the pans immediately and cool on racks.

Dave's note: What fantastic toast!

ELEANOR WILSON
BOOTHBAY, MAINE

Nisu

(Finnish Coffee Bread)

This is an old Finnish recipe. Finnish folks make it for holidays and church fairs. When we were small, we could smell the aroma all through the house and could not wait for it to cool. It's a good recipe for large families.

½ cup milk, scalded
½ cup butter
½ cup sugar
½ teaspoon salt
1 package dry yeast, softened in ½ cup warm water
2 eggs, beaten
3½ cups flour
1 teaspoon powdered cardamom seeds
¼ cup hot coffee, sweetened

Combine milk, butter, sugar, and salt. cool to lukewarm. Add yeast, eggs, flour, and cardamom. Mix with large spoon until smooth. Cover and let rise in a bowl in a warm place until dough is double in bulk. Punch down with a spoon and let rise for 30 minutes more. Divide dough into two equal parts, then separate each part into 3 balls (for forming a braid). Roll balls into ropes and braid them. Set the braids into buttered pans, cover with a light towel, and allow to rise in a warm place until double (an hour).

Bake at 375° for 25 to 30 minutes, until the braids sound hollow when tapped with a finger. Remove from the oven and brush with coffee. Sprinkle immediately with more sugar.

Dave's note: Cardamom adds such a great plus. I grilled this with butter and fought everybody off.

MRS. EVA PELLETIER
PEABODY, MASSACHUSETTS

Soft Mandel Bread

I've had this recipe in a simplified version for over thirty years, and somewhere along the line I added the cherries and nuts and we love it. It's been a big hit at PTA meetings and at cake sales. I sometimes even add raisins or chopped dates.

3 cups flour
1½ teaspoons baking powder
1 cup sugar
3 eggs
½ cup oil
1 teaspoon vanilla
1 teaspoon almond extract (optional)
¾ cup nuts, chopped
1 small jar maraschino cherries, drained
¾ cup coconut

In a large bowl, combine flour, baking powder, and sugar. Add eggs, oil, vanilla, and almond extract, and mix well. Add nuts, cherries, and coconut. Form into two or three bread rolls on a foil-lined cookie sheet. Flatten top slightly if too high. Bake at 350° for 30 minutes, or until done. Cut into ¾-inch slices when cool. Freezes well.

MRS. BESS NOTKIN
CHELSEA, MASSACHUSETTS

Currant or Speckled Bread

(called "Bara Brith" in Welsh;
it means bread currant)

This recipe was handed down by my
Welsh maternal grandmother from
Swansea, Wales back in 1810. It's for
the national bread of Wales and gets
passed down over the centuries through
every native Welshman. Not a fancy
dish, but oh, so delicious with a cup of
tea.

1   ounce yeast
½   cup warm milk
¾   pound lard or butter or mixture of
    both
3   pounds flour
¾   pound brown sugar
1   pound raisins
1   pound small seedless raisins
1   pound currants
¼   pound candied orange peel
½   teaspoon pudding spice
1   teaspoon salt
2   eggs

Mix yeast with warm milk. Combine
shortening with flour, then mix in rest
of dry ingredients. Make a well in the
center and add yeast and eggs.
Mix into a soft dough. Then cover and
let rise in a warm place for 1½ hours,
or until twice its original size. Turn
onto a floured board, then place in
greased loaf pans; let stand again in a
warm place for about 20 minutes.
Bake at 350° for 1 to 2 hours
(test after first hour by inserting
a toothpick.) Cut when cold.

PEGGY EDWARDS GLUCK
HARRISBURG, PENNSYLVANIA

Grandma's Bran Bread

This really has no family tradition that
I know of except that my boys ask me
to make Grandma's Bread so I do just
that—it is delicious.

1½   cups potato water, boiling
3   tablespoons margarine
3   tablespoons dark brown sugar
2   tablespoons molasses
2   teaspoons salt
1   cup whole bran
1   package dry yeast
½   cup warm water
5   to 5½ cups sifted flour

In a large bowl, pour boiling water
over margarine, sugar, molasses, salt,
and bran. Blend well and set aside to
cool to lukewarm. Meanwhile soften
yeast in warm water; let stand 5 to 10
minutes. Beat 1 cup of flour into
bran mixture. Add softened yeast and
beat until smooth. Continue beating
while adding about ½ of remaining
flour. Beat in enough remaining flour
to make a soft, smooth dough. Turn
into a greased bowl and lightly
grease surface of dough. Cover with
waxed paper and a towel. Let rise
in a warm place until doubled, about
2 hours. Turn onto a lightly floured
surface, divide into two portions,
and shape dough into loaves. Put into
two greased 8½ x 4½ x 2½-inch loaf
pans. Cover and let rise in a warm
place until almost doubled. Bake at
325° (not preheated) 50 to 55 minutes. Remove from the oven and lightly
brush tops of loaves with melted
butter. I generally add about ½ cup
raisins to the dough. Makes 2 loaves.

*Dave's note: I loved it. Good plain
and toasted—sensational!*

MRS. ROGER J. DOOLEY
LA SALLE, ILLINOIS

Nana's Oatmeal Bread

My grandfather says he used my grandmother's first batch of biscuits to hammer a nail in the wall to hang a picture
in their first home. He knew she needed help baking and enlisted the aid of
his Aunt Mary, who gave this recipe
to my grandmother in the early 1900s.
Since that time everyone has enjoyed
Nana's Oatmeal Bread.

1   cup rolled oats
2   cups boiling water
1   tablespoon butter
½   teaspoon sugar
1½   teaspoons salt
2   packages yeast mixed with ½ cup
     lukewarm water
½   to 1 cup molasses
8   cups flour

Mix rolled oats, boiling water, butter,
sugar, and salt; cool to lukewarm. Add
yeast mixture and molasses; stir well.
Add flour and mix. Cover with greased
wax paper. Let rise in a warm place
until dough doubles in size. Flour
hands and knead bread until elastic.
(Take a ball of dough; put in a
greased pan for rolls, or put dough in
greased loaf pans for bread.) Let rise
until double. Preheat oven to 425°
and bake for 15 minutes; then lower
oven to 400° for 15 minutes more.

*Dave's note: The best thing I can
say is—it's as good as mine.*

MIRIAM BIBBO
FRAMINGHAM, MASSACHUSETTS

Grandma's Yummy Homemade White Bread

Our whole house smells so good when
this bread is baking!! This is an old
recipe that makes four loaves very
cheaply (all for under forty cents as of
this writing).

2   cups lukewarm water
⅓   cup shortening (chicken fat, bacon
     fat, margarine, or lard), melted
⅓   cup white sugar
1   cake (or tablespoon of dry yeast),
     softened in ½ cup lukewarm water
1   tablespoon salt
7   cups flour to make dough you can
     knead (add more if necessary)

Combine all ingredients and knead
dough on a floured surface until smooth
and elastic. Brush top of bread with oil
or butter before rising to prevent bread
from cracking and drying. Allow to
rise until double in volume, then divide
into loaves. Either shape bread into a
free-form loaf, or place in a greased
loaf pan. Let rise at 350° to "puff" the
bread, then reduce heat to 325° for
about 45 minutes.

To make a richer bread, use 2 cups
warm milk instead of water. To prepare yeast, use ½ cup of warm milk.
The rest of the milk is combined with
the other ingredients. Add yeast mixture
when ready, then follow the same directions as above. The bread costs a
bit more when made this way, but
milk lends it a fuller taste.

MRS. DOROTHY B. HIGGINS
KINDERHOOK, NEW YORK

Cheese Bread

I found the following bread recipe in a food column many years ago, and have made it often since. It's quicker to make than most other breads, because it requires no kneading and must rise only once. I sometimes cut down on the time further by using a presifted flour. I think the bread is delicious.

2 packages dry yeast
2 cups very warm water (105° to 115°)
½ cup dry milk
5 to 6 cups flour, sifted
2 tablespoons sugar
2 teaspoons salt
2 tablespoons vegetable oil
1½ cups Gouda cheese, grated

Dissolve yeast in warm water, then beat in dry milk and 2 cups flour. Add remaining ingredients and beat again. Cover bowl. Let rise in a warm place about 45 minutes or until dough doubles in bulk. Stir the dough down, and stir again 5 times. Put into a well-greased tube pan. Bake at 350° for 70 minutes. It will sound hollow when done. Sesame seeds are a nice addition: Spread top of uncoooked bread with beaten egg yolk, then add seeds.

Dave's note: For a ham sandwich or fried egg, this is the best.

MRS. CHARLES V. KNOX
CHRISTMAS COVE, MAINE

Great-Grandma Flagg's Shredded Wheat Bread

This recipe has been used for four generations of "Flagg" women whose names all began with the letter "L" — Lucina, Lorraine, Louise, and Lucille (me). One of my sons, who has lived in Alaska for thirteen years, was at first intrigued by sourdough bread, but soon wrote home for the shredded wheat bread recipe. This recipe is a cinch to make and is delicious and nourishing.

4 shredded wheat biscuits
1 teaspoon salt
2 tablespoons shortening
1 cup molasses
2 yeast cakes
2 teaspoons sugar
8 cups flour

Soak shredded wheat biscuits in 1 quart boiling water to which salt has been added. Add shortening and molassses. Dissolve yeast cakes in 1 cup warm water plus sugar. Add enough flour to make fairly stiff (about 8 cups). Combine with biscuit mixture. Let rise in warm place until double in size. Knead and let rise again for 1 hour. Bake until nicely browned, at 350°. Makes two loaves of bread and one pan of biscuits.

Dave's note: One night while baking this, I threw in a lot of different leftover cereals (nonsweetened). It turned out pretty well — the bread tasted good, my cupboards were neater, and I saved money.

LUCILLE B. FLAGG
ELMWOOD, MASSACHUSETTS

What a memorable occasion. The scene: Buzzards Bay, Massachusetts. The date: January 1, 1973. The time: 4 P.M. Cold — boy was it cold and who noticed? Not me. I was getting my first shellfishing lesson in armpit waders from Rocky. How to sweep scallops. How to tell a quahog from a rock with the metal tip of a scallop rake. How not to lose your cool when you bring up a spider crab or step on a sleeping flounder who slithers out from under your foot. I learned how to lie artfully when asked by other shellfish seekers how many I'd gotten so far. Rocky had it down pat. The combination of a blasé look and "It's really not too good here!" Then the master stroke of getting the wives to shuck the scallops and clams while we got warmed up, inside and out.

Here's an old Portuguese fish tip that I've turned into rhyme:

> *If head, tail and fin*
> *do not make the pot,*
> *your chowder is blah*
> *for stock you'll have not.*

—Dave

Fish and Shellfish

Ambrosia from the Sea
(Baked Stuffed Seafood)

6 cloves garlic, minced
3 tablespoons onion, diced
1 tablespoon parsley, minced
¾ cup Italian-flavored bread crumbs
6 tablespoons olive oil
⅜ teaspoon salt
1 can minced clams
1 can shrimp, drained
1 can crabmeat, drained and flaked
  Parmesan cheese, grated

Sauté garlic, onion, parsley, and bread crumbs in olive oil for 2 minutes, mixing thoroughly. When onion and garlic start to brown, remove mixture from frying pan and mix with clams (with liquid), shrimp, crabmeat, and salt. Spoon into serving shells, and sprinkle lightly with bread crumbs and Parmesan cheese. Place on baking sheet in 375° oven for 25 to 35 minutes, or until golden and crusty on top.

Dave's note: This is one delectable filling for Cheryl's cream puffs in "Appetizers."

CHERYL M. HOFFMAN
ITHACA, NEW YORK

Scalloped Scallops

This recipe was acquired from a friend over twenty years ago. She brought the dish to a potluck choir party. It was relished by all and requested for all future parties.

1 pint (or pound) scallops
½ cup butter
1 cup saltines, crumbled
½ cup bread crumbs
⅔ cup light cream
  salt
  pepper

Wash scallops. If you use large scallops, cut into smaller pieces. Melt butter and mix with all crumbs. Alternate layers of scallops with crumbs in buttered, shallow ovenproof dish. Pour cream over top. Bake at 350° for 25 minutes. Serves 4 to 6.

Dave's note: Good and easy to prepare. Do on individual shells and serve as a first course.

EUGENE K. SCHMIDT
RUMFORD, RHODE ISLAND

Seafood in a Package

This delicious gourmet "cookout" recipe takes only a few minutes to prepare and is guaranteed to produce rave reviews from seafood aficionados! I heartily recommend martinis before—garlic bread and tossed green salad with—and fresh strawberries for dessert.

1 pound shrimp, peeled
1 pound scallops
1½ pounds fresh mushrooms
½ pint heavy cream
1 jigger brandy
  salt and freshly ground pepper

Cut heavy-duty foil into 4 rectangles, about 12 x 18 inches each. On each, spread ¼ of the shrimp, scallops, and mushrooms with the tough part of the stems removed. Mix cream and brandy and pour ¼ onto each package, being careful to fold sides up first. Add salt and pepper and fold up each package, using a double fold down the middle. Tightly press each end.

Chill for ½ hour before cooking. To cook, lay the packages over a charcoal fire, or in the ashes of an open fire, and bake for about 10 to 12 minutes, turning them while they cook. Serve one package to a person.

Dave's note: You're right, Mary! Garlic bread and tossed green salad made it a great meal and I didn't even need the martini.

MARY S. FIELD
MARBLEHEAD, MASSACHUSETTS

Salmon Loaf Surprise

1 15½-ounce can salmon, flaked
⅓ cup milk
¾ cup soft bread crumbs
2 eggs
2 tablespoons onion, minced
1 tablespoon lemon juice
1 tablespoon parsley, minced
¼ teaspoon salt
   dash pepper

Drain salmon and reserve liquid. Pour milk over bread crumbs and let stand for 5 minutes. Add flaked salmon, liquid, eggs, onion, lemon juice, parsley, and seasoning and mix them well. Spoon into loaf pan. Bake at 350° for 40 to 50 minutes, or

until firm. Unmold; serve plain or with a white sauce with a little snipped dill (or you could make a volute if fish stock is available). Makes 4 to 6 servings.

Dave's note: Very easy to do. Served for a summer luncheon with, perhaps, a lettuce salad, and you'd have something plain and yet fancy.

E. THOMAS
SOLON, OHIO

Baked Oysters and Bacon

This recipe was copied from a cookbook my mother-in-law had. I copied it fifty-two years ago, so I really can't say how old it is. I have used it many times and have had many compliments.

4 tablespoons butter, melted
1 cup bread crumbs
1 pint small oysters
6 strips bacon
¼ teaspoon salt
¼ teaspoon Worcestershire sauce
   (optional)
⅛ teaspoon paprika
1 teaspoon parsley, finely chopped

Mix butter and bread crumbs and sprinkle over oysters, which have been placed in a greased, shallow pan. Add bacon in a layer. Mix seasonings and sprinkle over bacon. Bake 20 minutes in a moderate oven—300°. Serves 6.

Dave's note: Why small oysters—If you can get them big, take them.

MRS. HELEN ENDERLE
COLUMBUS, OHIO

Codfish Surprise

In the old days, Friday was always "fish day," and at one time, we New Englanders were urged to eat fish on Wednesdays too! When the family was growing and if their small friends came along, I'd always find Codfish Surprise adequate for an extra or so.

1 pound frozen cod fillet
1 small onion
1 large bay leaf
4 whole allspice
1 teaspoon salt
1 teaspoon sugar
2 carrots, thinly sliced
2 outer stalks celery, coarsely chopped
2 eggs
1½ cups milk

Remove fish from freezer and bring 1½ quarts of water to boil in a flat 2½-quart pan. Peel and slice onion in thin rings; place in water together with seasonings. Cook 5 minutes, then add carrot and celery. Cook 5 minutes. Add fish and cook, covered, for 10 more minutes, or until fish flakes. Be sure to keep burner on high to maintain boiling throughout. Drain. Remove bay leaf and distribute mixture evenly with a fork in an 8 x 8-inch glass dish that has been well buttered. In a bowl, beat eggs slightly, then add milk and ½ teaspoon salt. Pour carefully over fish and vegetables. Place in preheated 400° oven. Reduce heat to 325° and bake 45 minutes, or until eggs are set. Sprinkle with chopped parsley or paprika before serving. An economical dish with fish so high in price. Quartered hard-boiled eggs could be added to stretch this even further.

ENID CANTOREGGI
NORFOLK, MASSACHUSETTS

Eulalie's Oyster Patties

This recipe was given to me by my niece from Vicksburg, Mississippi, and has been in the family many years. Anyone liking oysters will like Eulalie's Oyster Patties. They are delicious.

1½ sticks butter
1 cup flour
1 cup celery, finely chopped
1 cup green onions, finely chopped
¾ cup parsley, finely chopped
3 pints oysters
juice of 2 lemons
1 dash Worcestershire sauce
2 dashes hot pepper sauce

Melt butter in skillet and sauté celery, onions, and parsley. Add flour, stirring constantly. Drain juice off oysters into a small bowl and cut up oysters. Combine juices and oysters in a stew pan and heat, but do not boil. Pour oysters and liquid into skillet with sautéed ingredients and let simmer slowly for 20 minutes. Mixture must be thick, but if too thick, add a cup or more of hot water. Season with lemon juice, Worcestershire sauce, and hot pepper sauce. Put in patty shells. Bake at 350° and get steamy hot before serving. Serves 6 to 8.

Dave's note: To this recipe I added salt, pepper, and a little white wine to avoid any paste-like consistency.

MRS. LIDA CAMPBELL
ELSIE, MICHIGAN

Northern Pike in Wine

2 pounds pike fillets
1 cup white wine
   salt and pepper

Sauce:

1½ tablespoons butter
1½ tablespoons flour
1 egg yolk, beaten
1 cup wine including juice of fish
   (from above)
   salt and pepper

Place fish and white wine in a saucepan and simmer gently until fish is tender. Remove from pan and keep warm until sauce is made. Season. Save liquid for sauce.

To make sauce, melt butter, then add flour, stirring to make smooth paste. Add enough wine to the liquid in which fish was cooked to make 1 cup. Add to butter and flour and cook over low heat until mixture thickens. Cool slightly and add egg yolk. Season to taste. Pour sauce over fillets and serve with slices of onion and boiled potatoes. Garnish with parsley and lemon. Serves 4 to 6.

ALEXANDRIA BATES
WEBSTER, MASSACHUSETTS

Kennebec Scalloped Clams

From the kitchen of "Baba" Stevens.

1½ cups cracker crumbs
1½ cups milk
2 cans minced clams and juice
½ cup butter, melted
¼ teaspoon Worcestershire sauce
1 teaspoon green pepper, minced

2 tablespoons onion, chopped
   salt
   pepper
2 eggs, beaten

Soften cracker crumbs in milk. Combine all ingredients, adding eggs last. Place in greased casserole inside a pan of hot water. Bake at 350°, uncovered, for about 40 minutes. Serves 4.

CAROL BURKE
AUGUSTA, MAINE

Scrambled Scallops

It was through my husband that I obtained this recipe when we first were married (1935). I didn't even know how to boil water at that time. He loved fish (being born in Nova Scotia), and I didn't. Gradually I became accustomed to seafood, and furthermore did develop into a good cook through the purchase of many cookbooks and saving hundreds of recipes throughout those forty-five years.

1 cup scallops
2 eggs, beaten
2 tablespoons milk
  salt and pepper

Boil scallops in enough water to cover until they begin to shrink. Drain. Break into small pieces and place in greased frying pan. Add eggs, milk, and salt and pepper to taste. Cook, stirring constantly, until egg is set. Serve on buttered toast. Serves 4.

Dave's note: Until I tried this recipe, I had never boiled a scallop for any reason.

MRS. JULIE F. CURTIS
WESTWOOD, MASSACHUSETTS

Shrimp Pie

3 pounds shrimp
3 large onions
¼ pound butter
1 large can tomatoes
2 pinches salt
1 quart cooked rice
6 strips bacon
½ teaspoon cayenne or paprika
1 teaspoon Worcestershire sauce

Gently saute shrimp and onions in butter. Add tomatoes once the shrimp turns pink. Combine with dry, fluffy rice and seasonings, and place in a greased casserole. Cover with bacon strips. Bake at 350° for 45 minutes. Cover and keep over low heat until ready to serve. Serves 6 to 8.

MRS. H. STEWARD DeTURK
TEMPLE, PENNSYLVANIA

Scallops Luigi

1 pound sea or bay scallops
1 pound mushrooms
1 cup butter, melted
½ cup sweet vermouth
1 cup seasoned bread crumbs

Wash scallops and drain for 5 minutes. Wash mushrooms and remove stems. Place scallops and mushrooms in pizza pan. On tops distribute melted butter and vermouth. Then sprinkle with bread crumbs and garnish with favorite seasoning and/or cheese. Broil for 10 to 12 minutes. Serves 4.

Dave's note: Use your imagination with the seasonings—an herb one time, a spice the next.

LOU GILARDI
BOSTON, MASSACHUSETTS

Shrimp and Mushrooms en Casserole

1 cup well-seasoned chicken broth
⅓ cup mushroom liquid
   few sprigs celery leaves
1 slice onion
3 tablespoons cornstarch
   dash powdered ginger
4 tablespoons chicken fat
2 egg yolks
2 cups whole shrimp, cooked
1 4-ounce can (⅔ cup) button mushrooms, drained
   paprika

In a saucepot, combine chicken broth and mushroom liquid and stir. Add celery leaves and onion slice and simmer, covered, for 5 minutes. Remove from heat. Blend together cornstarch, ginger, and chicken fat and add to broth. Cook, stirring constantly, until mixture thickens. Beat egg yolks. Add a little hot mixture to egg yolks, then stir egg into hot sauce. Remove black veins from shrimp. Add button mushrooms. Heat thoroughly. Place in individual casseroles. Garnish with paprika. Serve immediately. Serves 4.

Dave's note: Ethel May strikes again.

E. THOMAS
SOLON, OHIO

German Fish Dinner

This recipe came from Germany via my grandmother, who gave it to my mother. It's a favorite meal to serve to first-time guests. It's different, unusual, and delicious.

3   pounds cabbage, finely chopped
10 strips bacon
2½ medium onions, finely chopped
2   tablespoons sugar
2   tablespoons vinegar
    salt
6   to 8 peppercorns
¼   pound butter or margarine
2   bay leaves
6   to 8 medium potatoes, peeled
3   pounds haddock, skinned

Slice cabbage very fine. Add to enough boiling, salted water to cover. Cover. When boiling again, uncover and boil vigorously for 8 minutes. Meanwhile, dice bacon and 2 onions into about equal amounts of small bits. Saute bacon and remove from fat; add onions to bacon fat and saute until transparent; then saute about 5 minutes more. Drain cabbage and place back in pot. Add bacon and onions. Season to a sweet-sour taste with the sugar, vinegar, salt, and pepper. Simmer until heated through.

Brown butter or margarine over medium-high heat by bringing it to a fast, intense boil (it should be well browned but not black). Stir. Bring again to a foamy, high boil. Stir, then boil again. Stir down. Set aside on low flame and boil potatoes—do not burn. Drain.

Put 2 inches water in a large pan. Add bay leaves, peppercorns, ½ onion, vinegar, and salt. Bring to boil and add fish. Boil for 15 minutes, covered. Add several teaspoonfuls of fish liquor to browned butter to increase both amount and flavor of the butter. Serve butter at table to be added liberally to both fish and potatoes. Serves 6.

Tips: Cabbage, bacon, and onions can be prepared a day ahead, and then cooked the next morning and allowed to simmer or just sit until dinnertime. I plan on a bit less than ½ pound of cabbage per person and over ½ pound of fish for each.

Dave's note: Serve cabbage, potatoes, and fish separately. Potatoes could be tossed in some of the browned butter before serving. Aces for a stormy day.

MRS. PHILIP A. JENKIN
YARMOUTH PORT, MASSACHUSETTS

Haddock in Shells

This recipe is a result of my seeking out the recipe of a friend's mother. Since it wasn't written down, I decided to experiment. We knew only that it was an old New England recipe that consisted of a thick white sauce and haddock. After many trials, this is the result. My friend and I agree that this is just like her mother's recipe. Enjoy!

3½ to 4 pounds haddock
10   tablespoons butter
⅔   cup flour
1   teaspoon salt
    dash pepper
1   teaspoon paprika
3   shakes cayenne
1   quart warm milk
9   or 10 scallop shells (5 inches across), buttered

Crumb mix:

5   slices bread
6   tablespoons butter
1   cup sharp cheddar cheese, grated
    paprika to taste

Cover haddock with cold water and bring to a boil. Simmer until haddock flakes and turns white. Do not over-cook. Remove skin and bones. Leave haddock in good-sized pieces.

To make sauce, melt 10 tablespoons butter, add flour, salt, pepper, paprika, and cayenne. Add warm milk slowly. Bring just to a boil, stirring constantly. If lumpy, strain. Add fish to sauce. Spoon into scallop shells. Top with crumb mix.

To make crumb mix, toast bread lightly and slice into small cubes. Melt 6 tablespoons butter, add cubes and cheddar cheese, and mix well.

Place shells on a foil-lined cookie sheet and bake at 350° until bubbly (about 20 minutes). Freezes well. Serves 4 to 6.

Dave's note: We did this on television together and received over 2,000 requests for the recipe. Use ramekins if you have no shells.

BARBARA FRENCH
WOBURN, MASSACHUSETTS

Baked Stuffed Shrimp

My baked stuffed shrimp recipe really does have an interesting history. It came from the chef at a hotel in Rock-land that has been standing here and open as a hotel for more than a hun-dred years. For a long time various local people tried unsuccessfully to get the recipe for this ever-popular but seldom-published New England deli-cacy. Finally, near the end of his tenure at the hotel, the chef gave the recipe to a Rockland woman who in cluded it among a collection for a local service group. I have altered it to its present form to make it as simple and foolproof, but elegant, as possible. This is authentic coastal Maine fare.

12 jumbo shrimp (about 4 inches long)
½   pound butter
½   cup green peppers, diced
½   cup onion, diced
6   or 7 slices white bread
    salt and pepper
    paprika

Peel shrimp shells and remove the black veins from shrimp. In butter saute green peppers and the onion over medium heat. Tear up white bread (homemade is best) and toss lightly in pan with peppers and onion. Add salt and pepper to taste. Preheat oven to 350°. Arrange shrimp on the bottom of two or three buttered bread pans (5 x 9 inches). Cover with stuffing. Pour on some of the melted butter and sprinkle with paprika. Bake 20 minutes. Serve with additional melted butter. Serves 4.

Dave's note: I would suggest a simple salad that includes raw onion. This cuts down the cholesterol level of any dish—even those that include as much butter as this one.

B. R. HARDEN
ROCKLAND, MAINE

Salmon Mousse

This elegant but easy mousse looks super served with a garnish of watercress. I serve it in a fish-shape mold. It holds up well through a dinner, but I wouldn't take it to the beach.

1   envelope unflavored gelatin
2   tablespoons lemon juice
1   small slice onion
½   cup boiling water
½   cup mayonnaise
1   1-pound can salmon, drained
¼   teaspoon paprika
1   teaspoon dill weed
1   cup heavy cream

Empty gelatin into food processor bowl (a hand-held mixer is okay too—just beat longer), and add lemon juice, onion, and water. Blend well. Then add mayonnaise, salmon, paprika, and dill weed. Blend until consistency is smooth. Gradually pour in cream, again beating until smooth. Pour into 4-cup mold and chill until set. Serve topped with sour cream mixed with dill. Serves 3 to 4.

INGE MUENCH
MARBLEHEAD, MASSACHUSETTS

Dilled Shrimp in Beer

This recipe can be found all over Kentucky. My family has used the dilled shrimp because it keeps well when chilled or frozen. The recipe probably developed when fresh seafoods were hard to come by in Central Kentucky. With a simple cooler, the shrimp could be brought by car from the East Coast, where our relatives lived. Our best, largest shrimp was sent by rail from Louisiana, packed in ice.

2   pounds medium or large shrimp, unpeeled
2   12-ounce cans beer
1   tablespoon lemon juice
1   celery stalk, cut in four or five pieces
1   small onion, quartered
1   teaspoon dried dill and herb salt
    pepper to taste
    melted butter
    lemon wedges

If desired, peel and devein shrimp, leaving tails intact. Place beer, lemon juice, celery, onion, dill, herb salt, and pepper in a saucepan and bring to a boil. Add shrimp, then cover and simmer for 3 to 5 minutes, depending on the size of shrimp; the shrimp are done when they turn pink. Do not overcook. Drain the shrimp, pile them into a large serving bowl, and serve with melted butter and lemon wedges. Serves 6.

Dave's note: Don't forget to peel and devein shrimp before cooking.

RUTH COMBS SPURLOCK
RICHMOND, KENTUCKY

Fish and Shellfish 59

Mushroom and Scallop Dish

I found this recipe in my mother's handwritten cookbook, which she filled with rich and fattening recipes. I am quite sure they were passed along by my grandmother, so they are old. My mother didn't have to cook after she was married; however, she had this dish served often for formal luncheons and it was good.

1 pint scallops, cut up
1 tablespoon butter
2 tablespoons oil
1 tablespoon onion, chopped
2 cups mushrooms, sliced
4 tablespoons butter
4 tablespoons flour
½ pint medium cream
½ cup scallop juice, derived from simmering scallops
  salt and pepper
  bread crumbs

Simmer scallops in enough water to cover. Sauté onions and mushrooms in butter and oil for 3 to 4 minutes. Melt butter in saucepan and blend in flour. Slowly add cream and juice, blending well. Add scallops and mushrooms and season with salt and pepper. Place in a baking dish and lightly cover with bread crumbs. Heat in a slow oven (325°) until bubbly. Serves 4.

MRS. C. H. BARTON
IPSWICH, MASSACHUSETTS

Clam Whiffle

12 saltines, crumbled
1 cup milk
1 can minced clams
1 teaspoon green pepper, chopped
½ cup butter, melted
¼ teaspoon Worcestershire sauce
2 teaspoons onion, minced
2 eggs, beaten

Soak saltines in milk until softened. Add other ingredients, ending with eggs. Pour in buttered, shallow casserole dish set in pan of hot water. Bake at 350°, uncovered, for 40 minutes. Serves 2 to 4.

MAUDE P. CONANT
PORTLAND, MAINE

Seafood Casserole

This recipe started when unexpected callers arrived at mealtime and I had no meat in the refrigerator.

2 cups elbow macaroni, cooked
1 cup fresh bread crumbs
1 cup American cheese, grated
1 cup light cream or evaporated milk
½ cup butter, melted
3 tablespoons parsley, chopped
3 tablespoons pimiento, chopped
3 eggs, beaten
1 or 2 cans lobster, shrimp, tuna, or crabmeat

Mix ingredients in order given. Place in greased casserole dish. Bake at 325° for about 45 minutes. Serves 6 to 8.

HARRIET BEATON
ROCKLAND, MAINE

Clara's Stuffed Quahogs or Clams

This recipe has been in the family for years. I remember my uncles going to the beach after a storm and picking quahogs. All my aunts would help clean them. We would then stuff them and cook. They were delicious.

24 large quahogs (or large clams)
1½ cups seasoned bread crumbs
2 teaspoons parsley
2 cloves garlic, minced
1 teaspoon dry basil
1 tablespoon Parmesan cheese, grated
½ teaspoon red pepper seeds
¾ cup oil
⅔ cup tomatoes, crushed

For this recipe I usually buy quahog meat by the pound all cut up. Mix 1 pound of quahog meat, bread crumbs, parsley, garlic, basil, cheese, and pepper seeds. Add oil and mix all together until very moist. Then stuff clam shells, and top each shell with about 1 teaspoon crushed tomatoes. Set shells in a shallow 12 x 16-inch baking pan into which a little bit of water—enough to cover bottom of pan—has been poured. Bake in preheated oven at 350° for about 25 minutes. Serves 6 to 8.

Dave's note: I cover the bottom of the pan with rock salt. It seems to have more of a sea-flavor to me. If shells are unavailable, use a buttered pan—not as attractive, but the same flavor.

C. CATALDO
REVERE, MASSACHUSETTS

Lobster and Beer Dressing

All I can say is that it is delicious, delightful, and expensive now, but was not fifty years ago.

1 lobster, cleaned and parboiled
2 tablespoons butter, melted
2 tablespoons celery, minced
1 teaspoon onion, minced
½ cup bread crumbs
¼ teaspoon salt
⅛ teaspoon rosemary
⅛ teaspoon thyme
¼ cup beer
parsley

Remove and chop meat from tail of lobster. Heat butter in skillet and add celery and onion, sautéing until tender but not brown. Toss with bread crumbs, salt, rosemary, and thyme. Stir in beer over low heat until stuffing is compact but not dry. Toss with chopped lobster tail meat. Fill lobster tail with stuffing. Dot with butter. Place lobster in foil or shallow pan. Broil in preheated broiler for about 5 minutes. Garnish with parsley. Serves one. Serve with tossed salad, french bread, and tall mugs of beer.

Dave's note: Herbs and beer work very well together in this recipe.

CLARA DENZER
ALLSTON, MASSACHUSETTS

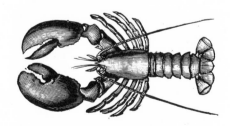

Crabmeat Casserole

One evening I prepared this and served it to my guests. My first mouthful told me I had forgotten something in making the recipe. The casserole was very dry, extremely dry. Just then my husband, Richard, announced, "Well, honey, your cooking's improved, you gave sawdust a crabmeat taste." To my horror, I realized I forgot to add the milk when preparing the recipe. You can bet I'll never make that mistake again.

1 14-ounce package frozen crabmeat or 2 cans crabmeat
1 cup milk
1 egg, beaten
2 tablespoons butter, melted
1 tablespoon vinegar
½ teaspoon prepared mustard
¼ teaspoon pepper
½ teaspoon salt
½ teaspoon onion, chopped
1 cup bread crumbs

Mix together crabmeat, milk, egg, butter, vinegar, mustard, pepper, salt, and onion. Toss well. Put into buttered quart casserole. Cover with bread crumbs. Bake at 350° for about 30 minutes. Serve warm. Serves 4.

Dave's note: Can easily take a little more onion. And a dash of paprika. Serve on toast points garnished with lemon.

ALEXANDRIA BATES
WEBSTER, MASSACHUSETTS

Deviled Scrod

1½ to 2 pounds scrod or small haddock
¼ cup green pepper, chopped
¼ cup onion, minced
1 tablespoon prepared mustard
1 teaspoon Worcestershire sauce
⅛ teaspoon hot pepper sauce
3½ tablespoons lemon juice
½ cup butter or margarine
2 cups fine, soft bread crumbs
2 tablespoons Parmesan cheese, grated
2 tablespoons butter

Wipe scrod with a damp cloth; cut into 4 portions. Combine green pepper, onion, mustard, Worcestershire sauce, hot pepper sauce, and lemon juice. Melt butter or margarine and stir in bread crumbs; add to vegetable mixture, blending well. Season scrod with salt and pepper, dot with additional butter or margarine, and place on foil-lined broiler rack with surface about 4 inches below source of heat. Broil 5 minutes, then remove from broiler. Turn scrod; top with bread mixture. Return to broiler. Broil 5 to 7 minutes, or until fish flakes easily with a fork. Sprinkle with cheese. Broil 1 minute longer. Serves 4.

Dave's note: Use less bread crumbs as crumbs tend to brown too quickly and vegetables don't cook as well. Make sure pan is buttered.

MRS. F. KORVARC
ROCHESTER, NEW YORK

Tuna Spinach Puff

This Scandinavian dish is a delectable main-dish pudding with the traditional dill. It's an easy recipe. Your blender does much of the work. It's not risky, as is a soufflé, yet its texture is lighter than a pudding.

2   7-ounce cans tuna, packed in vegetable oil
2   tablespoons capers, drained
½   teaspoon dry mustard
1   10-ounce package frozen chopped spinach, thawed and well drained
1   teaspoon dried dill
2   teaspoons lemon juice
½   teaspoon salt
⅛   teaspoon nutmeg
⅛   teaspoon hot pepper sauce
2   eggs
3   tablespoons butter or margarine
3   tablespoons cornstarch
1   cup milk
2   egg whites

Place tuna, capers, dry mustard, spinach, dill, lemon juice, salt, nutmeg, hot pepper sauce, and eggs in the container of an electric blender. Cover and process at low speed until thoroughly mixed and smooth. Melt butter in a medium saucepan and blend in cornstarch. Stir in milk slowly. Cook, stirring constantly, until mixture thickens and comes to a boil. Remove from heat.

Beat egg whites until stiff peaks form. Fold into tuna mixture. Turn into a buttered 1-quart casserole and bake at 350° for 1 hour and 15 minutes, or until a knife inserted in the center comes out clean. Serves 4.

Dave's note: I loved it.

L. S. MORIN
BRADFORD, MASSACHUSETTS

Broiled Sardines Parmesan

6   whole large sardines, split in two (the big fat Portuguese ones)
12 pieces of thin toast, cut in size and shape of sardines
6   tablespoons Parmesan cheese, grated
½   teaspoon dry English mustard sardine oil

Place in a mixing bowl 4½ tablespoons of grated cheese, mustard, and some of the oil from sardines. Mix well into soft paste. Spread paste on toast. Arrange sardines on top. Sprinkle the remaining cheese on the sardines. Place under broiler, not too close to flame, and brown lightly. Serve hot with small wedges of lemon and sprigs of parsley.

DAVE

Fish and Shellfish 63

Soong Scallops

I was told to call a Chinese-type dish
Soong — if I couldn't think of anything
else.

2   pounds scallops, fresh or frozen
1   7-ounce package frozen pea pods
¼   cup butter or margarine
2   tomatoes, cut into eighths
1   cup water
2   tablespoons cornstarch
1   tablespoon soy sauce
½   teaspoon salt
⅛   teaspoon pepper
3   cups hot cooked rice
¼   cup sherry

Thaw pea pods and scallops, if frozen.
Rinse scallops with cold water. Cut
large scallops in half crosswise. Drain
pea pods. Melt butter in a 10-inch fry
pan. Add scallops and cook over low
heat for 3 to 4 minutes, stirring frequently. Add pea pods and tomatoes.
Combine water, cornstarch, soy sauce,
sherry, salt, and pepper. Add to scallop mixture and cook until thick, stirring constantly. Cook rice separately and
serve with soy sauce topped with the
vegetables. Serves 6.

DAVE

Me, the trivia expert, and I can't remember the president who promised "a chicken in every pot." No matter — during the Depression years when I was a small boy, the only way I remember having chicken was fricasseed with dumplings in a big pot with lots of gravy to serve on bread for the second or third helping. Boy, I really grew to loathe it.

Today, chicken and I are great pals, both on the stove and on the plate. It's fairly cheap, quick to fix, takes on other flavors nicely — what more do you want?

Ever added it to pizza? Add it in the final minutes of cooking so it won't get too dry, and it's delicious. As part of a Japanese tempura meal? Try small pieces dipped in that special batter and deep fried in peanut and sesame oil for about two minutes. Oh momma! Or fancier, with veal glaze and lightly sautéed mushrooms.

Oh yes, we should all be chicken fans. If they ever nominate Frank Perdue for president, I may even vote for him. —Dave.

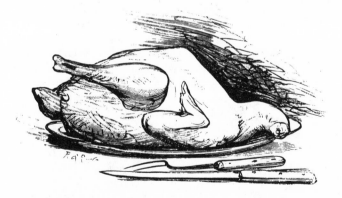

Poultry

Roman Chicken Cacciatore

When we were kids, we lived on Federal Hill, the ethnic section of Providence (mostly Italian, Irish, Armenian, Greek, Syrian, etc.). One of my brothers worked in a poultry store (in those days we worked from age eight). He brought home chicken and chicken parts, and my mother cooked everything he brought home. We were lucky to get all that chicken!

One day my father went hunting. He couldn't bring home any game (no luck!), so he picked mushrooms instead. One of my neighbors suggested cooking chicken with the mushrooms and tomatoes. My mother did, and *voila*! We have feasted on Chicken Roman Style for over fifty-five years. When I cook it, it brings back fond memories of my family working together to help our parents and all the love we shared with our neighbors and friends.

2 to 2½ pounds chicken, cut up
¼ cup olive or salad oil
1 large onion, minced
2 cups tomatoes, peeled and crushed
1 clove garlic (optional)
1 pound mushrooms, sliced
½ teaspoon oregano (optional)
1 teaspoon fresh parsley
  salt and pepper to taste
¾ cup sherry or white wine

Brown chicken pieces in hot oil over medium heat, and set them aside until needed. Sauté onion and garlic in remaining oil until soft. Add tomatoes, simmer for 5 minutes, then add chicken, mushrooms, and seasonings. Cover pan and simmer until chicken is tender (about 25 minutes). Turn occasionally.

Add wine or sherry. Cook for five more minutes. Serve with hot, crusty bread. Serves 4.

Dave's note: You may want to add a little tomato paste to the tomatoes for a thicker sauce.

MRS. WILLIAM E. CIPRIANO
CRANSTON, RHODE ISLAND

Baked Chicken

I submitted this recipe to a contest in the *Worcester Telegram and Gazette* two years ago and it won an Honorable Mention.

1 3-pound chicken, cut up
2 tablespoons butter
½ teaspoon ginger
1 lemon
2 tablespoons brown sugar
1 teaspoon Worcestershire sauce
 ½ teaspoon dry mustard
2 medium apples, cored and sliced into rings
⅓ cup bourbon
  salt and pepper to taste

Arrange chicken pieces in a baking dish and dot with butter. Sprinkle with ginger, salt, and pepper. Bake at 350° for 1 hour or until done. Meanwhile, in a skillet over low heat, combine juice and rind of lemon, brown sugar, Worcestershire sauce, and mustard. Stir until sugar melts. Add apple rings and simmer until they are soft. Add bourbon. Arrange chicken and apples on platter. Pour hot sauce over both. Another idea is to prepare the dish and refrigerate overnight. Heat the next day and serve. Serves 4 to 6.

JESSICA MacNEIL
WHITINSVILLE, MASSACHUSETTS

Old-Fashioned Chicken Pot Pie

This was one of our favorite dinners as children on the farm, which was twenty-five miles east of Baltimore. My father owned all kinds of animals — cows, horses, sheep, pigs, turkeys, and, of course, chickens. When he found an extra-heavy hen in his flock or too many roosters for his brood, we would have chicken pot pie, which my mother prepared with great delicacy. Each member of the family requested their favorite piece. This required some digging, but all in good fun.

1 3½-pound chicken, cut up
5 to 6 potatoes, cut up
½ pound ham or salt pork (if desired)
   pastry shell and bits

Line the bottom and sides of a deep pot with a good, rich pastry, reserving enough for a top crust and for the small square bits to be scattered through the pie. Butter the pot very lavishly to avoid sticking. Put in a layer of ham, chicken, and pastry squares, add potato layer, sliced or diced. Repeat layers until chicken is used up. Cover with pastry rolled out quite thinly. Make a slit in the middle. Set pan in another pan of water in oven and boil/bake for 2 hours at approximately 275°. Serves 4 to 6.

HANNAH F. HANWAY
BEL AIR, MARYLAND

Chicken Paprikash

This recipe was given to me by a Hungarian woman who before she came to America was the cook for a baron in Hungary. It has been a favorite in our family for many years.

1 large onion, chopped
2 tablespoons butter
1 3½- to 4-pound frying chicken, cut in pieces
1 small can tomato sauce
2 cans water
   salt and pepper to taste
1 teaspoon sugar
2 tablespoons paprika
4 to 5 teaspoons flour

Noodles:

2 eggs
1½ cups flour
½ cup sour cream

In a cooking pot, sauté onion in butter until golden brown and then add chicken. Add tomato sauce, water, salt and pepper, sugar, and paprika. Simmer uncovered until chicken is done. When done, thicken sauce with paste made by melting 4 or 5 teaspoons of butter, into which flour has been added. Cook roux until golden brown in color, then add 1 cup water. Stir until blended and add to chicken. Let it come to a boil, stirring constantly.

To prepare noodles, beat eggs and combine with flour and sour cream. Beat until blended, then drop by teaspoonfuls into boiling salted water. Cook for about 5 minutes. Drain.

Serve the chicken over the homemade noodles, topped with a dollop of sour cream. Serves 4 to 6.

MRS. EDNA M. WOLFRAM
SOUTH DEERFIELD, MASSACHUSETTS

Clam and Chicken Pie

1 dozen small white onions
2 tablespoons butter
2 dozen clams, chopped
1 cup cooked chicken, diced
2 hard-cooked eggs, diced
1 cup cooked potatoes, diced
½ cup celery, chopped
1 teaspoon salt
½ teaspoon pepper
¼ cup sherry
1 tablespoon flour
½ cup light cream
    pastry for 1-crust pie

Sauté onions in butter until soft. Add clams, chicken, eggs, potatoes, celery, seasonings, and sherry. Simmer for about 5 minutes. Mix flour and cream into a paste and blend in. Simmer for another 5 minutes. Pour into a baking dish and cover with pastry, rolled thinly, and slash to let steam escape. Bake for 15 minutes at 400°. Lower heat to 350° and bake an additional 15 to 20 minutes. Serves 4.

MRS. A. J. McLEAR
SWANSEA, MASSACHUSETTS

Chicken with Asparagus

2 pounds fresh asparagus or 2 packages frozen asparagus
½ cup butter or margarine
2 chicken breasts, cooked and sliced
1½ teaspoons salt
¼ teaspoon pepper
¼ teaspoon powdered thyme
2 eggs, separated
¼ cup sour cream
½ cup milk

Cook asparagus in salted water until just tender. Drain and arrange in a 12 x 8 x 2-inch baking dish. Melt butter or margarine in a skillet and sauté chicken until hot. Add salt, pepper, and thyme. Arrange chicken evenly over asparagus. Blend egg yolks with sour cream and milk. Fold in stiffly beaten egg whites. Spoon over chicken. Bake 20 minutes at 375°, or until golden brown. Serves 4.

Dave's note: Much tastier with fresh asparagus.

ESTHER M. SAMSON
LEXINGTON, MASSACHUSETTS

Thirteen-Week Chicken

13 pieces chicken breast, boned and skinned
1 cup maple syrup
1 tablespoon olive oil
¼ cup white wine vinegar
1 tablespoon soy sauce
1 cup tomato sauce
2 teaspoons curry powder
1 teaspoon powdered marjoram
4 cloves, crushed
    salt and pepper
¼ cup sherry
2 cups celery, finely chopped
1 green pepper, finely chopped
6 medium mushrooms, cut up
1 small onion, finely chopped
2 ounces raisins
2 ounces almonds, chopped

In a large pot, combine chicken, maple syrup, oil, vinegar, soy sauce, tomato sauce, curry powder, marjoram, cloves, salt and pepper, and sherry. Simmer, covered, for 30 minutes. Then add celery, green pepper, mushrooms, onion, raisins, and almonds. Cover and cook for 30 minutes more. Serves 4 to 6.

Dave's note: If you wonder what's going on with this dish, don't worry. It turns out to be a wonderfully flavored Middle-Eastern type of dish, and one that is well complemented by plain rice!

MRS. ELINOR T. MURTHA
YORK HARBOR, MAINE

Japanese Chicken Dinner

I am a displaced person and my grand-parents spoke only Norwegian. While I knew them years ago, I didn't much care for ludafish or lefsa, and heaven forbid they would ever serve Swedish meatballs. I grew up believing that a Swede was a Norwegian with his head cut off.

1 chicken breast
1 package frozen Japanese-style vegetables
1 tablespoon water
1 tablespoon soy sauce
dash of Chinese five-spice powder
Chinese noodles

Broil chicken breast for 10 minutes on each side. When done, let sit for 10 minutes to seal juices. Cook Japanese-style vegetables, but instead of following the package directions, put the seasoning envelope aside and save. Cook the vegetables very rapidly in 1 tablespoon water and soy sauce for 1 minute. Remove from heat, drain, and cover. Save the juices. Then skin and bone chicken and slice thinly. Again,

save any juice and combine with juice from the vegetables. Sprinkle half of the seasoning from the Japanese-style vegetables and dash of Chinese five-spice powder over the chicken. Let stand for a couple of minutes. Add all the saved juices and vegetables. Heat rapidly and serve over rice. Add Chinese noodles. Serves 2.

Dave's note: I stock up on Chinese and Japanese staples three or four times a year. You'll use them in many ways.

MARGE WRIGHT
GREENSBORO, NORTH CAROLINA

Sweet and Smoky Chicken

2 large onions, sliced
1 3- to 4-pound chicken, cut in serving pieces
2 teaspoons hickory-smoked salt
¼ teaspoon pepper
½ cup catsup
¼ cup vinegar
2 tablespoons prepared mustard
½ cup maple syrup

Place onion slices in the bottom of a shallow baking pan. Place chicken in a single layer, skin side up, on top of onions. Sprinkle with hickory salt and pepper. Combine remaining ingredients and pour over chicken. Bake uncovered at 350° for approximately 1 hour, or until done. Serves 4.

Dave's note: Get the hickory-smoked salt if you have to hunt for it. It's the most important ingredient in the recipe.

MRS. PAUL D. BLOIS
WESTBOROUGH, MASSACHUSETTS

Poultry 69

Chicken Sesame

I learned to spell *sesame* writing out this recipe after sixty-three years. Ha!

¼ cup whole wheat flour
1 teaspoon salt
¼ teaspoon pepper
1 frying chicken, cut up
1 egg, slightly beaten
½ cup bread crumbs
½ cup sesame seeds
½ cup butter

Mix flour, salt, and pepper. Roll each chicken piece in seasoned flour, dip in egg, and roll in bread crumbs mixed with sesame seeds. Melt butter in a frying pan and sauté chicken until brown. Cover and simmer for 30 minutes. For the last 10 minutes, remove the cover in order to crisp the chicken. Serves 4.

MRS. THADDEOUS W. SHORE, JR.
BOONVILLE, NORTH CAROLINA

Chicken Waikiki Beach

I have had the Chicken Waikiki Beach recipe for many years. While sitting in a doctor's waiting room, I came across this recipe in one of the magazines. Now I carry a writing pad whenever I go to a doctor or dentist. I've gotten many recipes this way.

2 whole chicken legs and 2 whole chicken breasts
½ cup flour
⅓ cup salad oil or shortening
1 teaspoon salt
½ teaspoon pepper

Sauce:

1 1-pound, 4-ounce can sliced pineapple
1 cup sugar
2 tablespoons cornstarch
¾ cup cider vinegar
1 tablespoon soy sauce
¼ teaspoon ginger
1 chicken bouillon cube
1 large green pepper, cut crosswise in ¼-inch circles

Wash chicken and pat dry with paper towels. Coat chicken with flour. Heat oil in a large skillet. Add chicken, a few pieces at a time, and brown on all sides. Remove as browned to a shallow roasting pan, arranging pieces skin side up. Sprinkle with salt and pepper. Meanwhile preheat oven to 350°.

To make the sauce, drain the sliced pineapple, pouring syrup into a 2-cup measure. Add enough water to make 1½ cups. In a medium saucepan, combine sugar, cornstarch, pineapple syrup, vinegar, soy sauce, ginger, and bouillon cube, and bring to a boil, stirring constantly. Boil for 2 minutes, then pour over chicken. Bake, uncovered, at 350° for 30 minutes. Add pineapple slices and green pepper; bake for 30 minutes more, or until the chicken is tender. Serve with fluffy white rice. Serves 4.

Dave's note: An attractive and relatively easy dish to prepare. It's a sweet-and-sour kind of dish.

ANN WOODS
MORGANTOWN, WEST VIRGINIA

Chicken Florentine

3 pounds chicken breasts, cooked
   and boned
1 4-ounce can mushrooms, drained
¼ cup chives, chopped
1 cup white sauce
1 cup creamy chicken mushroom
   soup, undiluted
1 package frozen spinach, thawed
   and drained
   Parmesan cheese, grated
   bacon, fried and crumbled

Place chicken, mushrooms, and chives in a 9 x 13-inch pan. Combine white sauce with soup and place in pan. Add spinach to pan. Spinach should be spread evenly over liquid. Sprinkle with Parmesan cheese and bacon to taste. Bake at 350° for 25 minutes. Serve over hot, fluffy white rice. Serves 4 to 6.

Dave's note: Original chicken florentine recipes usually call for the chicken to be served on a bed of spinach, which I prefer. However, this is interesting, delicious, and great for getting spinach into the stomachs of children before they realize what they're eating.

MRS. W. J. BISDEE
ESCANABA, MICHIGAN

Brandied Chicken Breasts

Tastefully flavored with the fruit of the cordial... takes the boredom out of chicken dishes. Tasters commented, "The liqueur added a new and delightful flavor."

2 whole chicken breasts
3 tablespoons butter, clarified
6 mushroom caps
½ cup onions or scallions, chopped
6 artichoke hearts
½ lemon, thinly sliced
½ lime, thinly sliced
½ cup apricot-flavored brandy
   salt and pepper to taste

Cut chicken into bite-sized pieces and sauté in butter. Add mushrooms, onions or scallions, artichokes, and lemon and lime slices. Cook 5 minutes covered, then add brandy. Heat 1 minute more, season with salt and pepper to taste, and serve. Serves 4.

RACHEL DiBENEDETTO
HYANNIS, MASSACHUSETTS

Sour Cream Baked Chicken

Sour Cream Baked Chicken is a recipe that I made up one day just to give chicken a different taste. I had some sour cream and chicken breast and put them together. Now I'm using seasoned chicken stuffing, run through my blender for crumbs. They are nicely flavored. I'm sorry, but I can't seem to come up with a better name.

1 3-pound broiler-fryer, cut into
   serving pieces
1 cup sour cream
2 cups bread crumbs
1 teaspoon salt
¼ teaspoon pepper
¼ teaspoon sugar
1 teaspoon dried thyme
⅛ teaspoon paprika
⅓ cup butter, melted

Remove skin from chicken. Spread sour cream in a shallow baking pan; dip chicken pieces in sour cream. Let stand in a pan for about 20 minutes.

Meanwhile prepare seasoned bread crumbs. Mix together bread crumbs, salt, pepper, sugar, dried thyme, and paprika (or use stuffing crumbs with additional seasoning to taste). Roll chicken pieces in bread crumbs, coating them thoroughly. Place on a well-greased baking sheet. Drizzle melted butter over each piece. Bake in a preheated 375° oven for 45 minutes, turning chicken pieces after 25 minutes cooking time. Serves 4.

Dave's note: Any vegetable and a salad would complement this subtle and tasty chicken dish.

MRS. PAUL A. DAVIS
AKRON, OHIO

Grandma's Old-Fashioned Chicken and Stuffing
(Czechoslovakian Style)

My father said his grandmother used to make this simple, unique recipe; instead of the stuffing being in the chicken, the chicken is in the stuffing.

1 3-pound broiler-fryer, cut up
¼ cup butter

Stuffing:
4 to 5 cups day-old Italian bread,
   cubed
1 cup milk
1 teaspoon poultry seasoning
1 teaspoon salt
½ teaspoon ground black pepper
½ cup parsley, chopped
2 eggs
8 tablespoons butter or margarine

To make the stuffing, place bread cubes in a medium bowl and soak in milk for 1 hour. Add poultry seasoning, salt, pepper, parsley, and eggs and mix well. Set aside. In a large skillet, melt 4 tablespoons butter or margarine. Add chicken pieces and brown on both sides. When browned, cover and cook over low heat for 30 minutes.

To bake the chicken, place chicken pieces in a shallow baking dish and spread stuffing on top. Bake, uncovered, at 375° for 30 minutes, or until stuffing turns golden brown. Baste with 4 tablespoons melted butter from time to time to bring out the highlights of golden-brown color. Makes 4 servings.

LOUISE MORIN
BRADFORD, MASSACHUSETTS

Country-Style Chicken Kiev

My Chicken Kiev recipe came about purely by accident. I was newly married and not a very good cook. After doing everything I could with hot dogs and hamburg, I began experimenting with chicken. This recipe was modified several times to the point where it is now. After several compliments, I titled it and put it in my recipe box. The recipe is now five years old and on its way to being a Secret Family Recipe.

⅔ cup butter
½ cup fine, dry bread crumbs
2 tablespoons Parmesan cheese, grated
1 teaspoon each basil and oregano
½ teaspoon garlic salt
¼ teaspoon salt
2 chicken breasts, split
¼ cup dry white wine or apple juice
¼ cup green onion, chopped
¼ cup parsley, chopped

Preheat oven to 375°. In a heavy 2-quart saucepan, melt butter. Meanwhile, on a piece of waxed paper combine bread crumbs, Parmesan cheese, basil, oregano, garlic salt, and salt. Dip chicken breasts in melted butter, then roll in crumbs to coat. (Remaining butter should not be discarded.) Place skin side up in an ungreased 9-inch-square baking dish. Bake near center of 375° oven for 50 to 60 minutes, or until chicken is brown and tender. Meanwhile add wine or apple juice, onion, and parsley to remaining melted butter (about ½ cup). When chicken is golden brown, pour butter sauce mixture around and over. Return to oven for 5 minutes more, until sauce is hot. Serve with sauce spooned over. Serves 2 to 4.

Dave's note: If you've often worried about making Chicken Kiev, don't. This is easy and delicious!

MRS. PAT BRENDLE
HUDSON, NEW HAMPSHIRE

Chicken à la Joan

I made this dish in very small portions the first time. I first served it in January 1978 to a group of twenty scientists gathered to discuss unidentified flying objects. I've made it often since; it is best made in a cast-iron Dutch oven!

1 3½-pound chicken, boned, skinned, and cut in strips
6 tablespoons butter
4 teaspoons salt
1 teaspoon pepper
1½ cups green onions, sliced
½ cup onion, chopped
3 8-ounce cans mushrooms, with liquid
3 cups green pepper, chopped
1 red pepper, chopped
6 fresh tomatoes, peeled and cut into eighths
1½ cups dry white wine
2 cans cream of chicken soup
3 cups fresh or frozen green beans or peas or both (should be blanched if fresh)
dash of curry
½ teaspoon curry
selection of several different rices

Brown chicken in butter and season with salt and pepper. Add onions, mushrooms, and peppers. Cook for 3 to 4 minutes. Then mix soup, wine, and ½ of the mushroom liquid and add slowly, stirring well. Stir in drained
(Continued)

green beans and/or peas. Cover and simmer for 15 to 20 minutes, stirring occasionally. Add tomato sections and cook uncovered for about 5 minutes.

Prepare several different rices, long-grain and wild rice, rice pilaf, plain rice, rice with curry—about 3 cups of each —to serve as a bed for the chicken. Serve with a crisp mixed green salad and assorted breads and/or rolls. Good any time of the year, but best on cold, blustery winter days. Serves about 15 and allows for second helpings.

JOAN JEFFERS
BRADFORD, PENNSYLVANIA

Chicken Stroganoff

I have had this recipe so long I think I was born with it in my hand. It is so easy to fix and always a hit at a dinner party. One just needs a salad, garlic bread, and depending on the season, fresh vegetables and fruit or whatever one chooses for a gathering of friends at the table.

I wish I could remember where and how I got it, but it seems I've used it since the wheel was discovered. And the platter has been licked clean whenever it's been served.

The plain old name of Chicken Stroganoff is all I can think of for a title. I could go down in history with Chicken Stroganoff à la Pels.

¼ cup flour
1 teaspoon salt
½ teaspoon pepper
1 3-pound frying chicken, cut up
  chicken fat or oil for browning
1 medium onion, chopped

1 clove garlic, minced
3 tablespoons lemon juice
1 chicken bouillon cube dissolved in
  1 cup boiling water
2 4-ounce cans mushrooms, sliced
½ 4-ounce package egg noodles
1 cup sour cream
¼ teaspoon paprika

Combine flour, salt, and pepper in a large paper bag; shake chicken pieces in bag until well coated. Heat fat in a large frying pan. Brown chicken, a few pieces at a time, then drain on absorbent paper. Pour off any fat left in the pan. Return chicken to the pan. Add onion, garlic, lemon juice, water and bouillon cube, and mushrooms with liquid. Cover and simmer for 20 minutes. Add noodles and cook 10 minutes more. Just before serving, fold in ¾ cup sour cream. Stir in paprika. Top with rest of sour cream. Serves 4 to 6.

Dave's note: What a different way to serve stroganoff (instead of using beef)! The chicken lends a light and delicate taste to the dish. You may want to skin and debone the chicken and cut into small bite-sized pieces.

PATTY PELS
NORFOLK, MASSACHUSETTS

Martha's Vineyard Honey-Rum Chicken

This recipe came from a friend Linda who got it from another friend Cathy. Linda tells me she's added to and omitted from it to make it the tasty dish that it is. The kids all think that they will get drunk by eating chicken with rum.

1 carrot, diced
2 onions, diced
1 celery stalk, diced
¼ cup butter
1 3½-pound chicken (or chicken pieces)
½ cup honey
¼ to ½ cup rum
1 tablespoon paprika
1 to 2 teaspoons salt

Sauté carrot, onions, and celery in butter. Bake chicken in a shallow dish at 350°, uncovered, with sautéed vegetables strewn on top. Combine honey, rum, paprika, and salt and use to baste chicken from time to time until done. (I baste every 20 minutes or so.) Serves 2 to 4.

Dave's note: This is a colorful and slightly sweet chicken dish.

RITA PELISSIER
BARRINGTON, RHODE ISLAND

Baked Chicken Thermidor

This is not an old family recipe, but one I received through my sorority alumnae group. Once a year we have a covered-dish dinner with our husbands, who look forward to this annual affair more than we do because they know the food will be a gourmet's delight. At least, that's what they tell us!

I have served this at family get-togethers, luncheons, and buffet dinners, and each time I have been asked for the recipe. To me, that is proof of the goodness of any dish, so that is why I wanted to share this with your cookbook readers.

1 10-ounce package frozen peas
2 cups cooked chicken, cut up
1 cup celery, diced
1 5-ounce can water chestnuts, thinly sliced
½ cup sliced almonds, toasted
2 tablespoons green peppers, chopped
1 tablespoon onions, grated
2 tablespoons pimientos, chopped
2 tablespoons white wine
1 tablespoon lemon juice
½ teaspoon salt
½ cup milk
1 can cream of chicken soup
2 slices white bread
1 tablespoon butter
1 cup sharp cheddar cheese, grated

Cook peas and drain. In a 2-quart buttered casserole dish, combine peas, chicken, celery, water chestnuts, almonds, green pepper, onions, and pimiento. Sprinkle with wine, lemon juice, and salt. Toss gently to mix well. In a small pan, combine milk and soup. Heat to boiling, stirring. Add to casserole dish, combining well. Trim crusts from bread, cutting the bread first in narrow strips, then again in the opposite direction. Each cube should be just under ½ inch. Melt butter in a skillet and add bread cubes. Quickly toss to coat bread cubes with butter. Then sprinkle onto casserole.

Bake for 20 minutes in preheated oven (375°), or until sauce is bubbly and bread cubes are toasted. Sprinkle with cheese and bake for 5 more minutes, or until cheese is melted. Serve hot. Serves 6.

Dave's note: This casserole is loaded with plenty of good things. No need for any other vegetables. Just dig in and enjoy!

ELAINE STONNEGER
MORGANTOWN, WEST VIRGINIA

Buckeye Baked Chicken

6 to 8 whole chicken breasts
¾ cup flour
¼ cup vegetable oil
1 4-ounce can mushrooms
1 can mushroom soup
1 envelope onion soup mix
1 pint sour cream

Roll chicken in flour, then brown in oil for about 15 minutes, or until nicely browned. Place chicken in a casserole dish. Mix mushrooms with liquid, add remaining ingredients, and pour over chicken. Bake at 300° for 1½ hours. Serves 8 to 10 people.

Dave's note: Delightful taste and a great crispy crust.

MRS. DONALD E. TRACY
CONTINENTAL, OHIO

Chicken Basque

¼ pound bacon, diced
1 3-pound chicken, disjointed, OR chicken legs and breast
1 medium green pepper, diced
2 or 3 carrots, diced
1 medium clove garlic, minced
1 medium onion, diced
2 tomatoes, chopped and peeled
1 bay leaf
  basil to taste
1 cup chicken bouillon or stock (more if needed)

Fry bacon in a skillet until crisp, then drain on absorbent toweling. Reserve bacon drippings. Brown chicken in bacon drippings and remove from the pan. Sauté green pepper, carrots, onion, and garlic until lightly browned, then place in a casserole dish. Arrange chicken pieces over green pepper mixture and sprinkle tomatoes over top. Crumble bacon and sprinkle over tomatoes. Add bay leaf and basil. Pour bouillon over top until chicken is covered. Bake in preheated oven at 375° for about 1 hour, or until chicken is tender. Serve over rice cooked with curry powder or orange juice if desired. Serves 6.

Dave's note: If you like to serve chicken in a different way, this recipe is relatively easy, good eating, and great served in a beret!

VERONICA McKINNON
KIRKLAND LAKE, ONTARIO, CANADA

Scalloped Chicken

This recipe goes back to those Depression days prior to television and a lot of modern kitchen conveniences, when a hand-driven meat chopper was king. Six or so couples would gather on Friday and Saturday evenings at someone's house, play bridge, talk, and eat — scalloped chicken was just the thing for the times.

Chicken:

1 5-pound chicken
1 carrot, diced
1 onion, sliced
2 teaspoons salt
2 quarts boiling water

Stuffing:

1½ loaves 2-day-old white bread
½ cup butter
6 sprigs parsley
6 scallions, with tops, OR 1 medium onion
2 large pieces celery, with tops
1 teaspoon salt
1 teaspoon poultry seasoning
1 dash white pepper
6 tablespoons chicken broth (from cooked chicken)

Sauce:

butter (as needed)
4 cups chicken broth (from cooked chicken)
1 cup milk
1 cup sifted flour
2 teaspoons salt
4 eggs

Place chicken in a large pot with carrot, onion, salt, and boiling water. Cook very slowly for 2½ hours or so, or until meat begins to leave bones. Let bird cool in its own liquid. When cool, take out chicken. Pull meat off bones, reserving skin. Put skin through the meat chopper and cook giblets in salted water until tender.

While the chicken cooks, prepare the stuffing. Crumble up bread (don't use crusts). Melt butter in a very heavy skillet. Chop parsley and then scallions and celery together. Cook in melted butter over low heat for 5 minutes. Then lightly mix the vegetables into bread crumbs with a fork to keep the stuffing fluffy. (Reserve 1 cup of crumbs for baking later.) Mix in cooked giblets. Add salt, poultry seasoning, and a good dash of white pepper. Finally,

mix in chicken broth (but no more than 6 tablespoons or the dressing will be heavy).

To make the sauce, skim the fat off the top of chicken broth and melt 1 cup in a large, heavy saucepan. If you don't get that much fat to make a roux, you can make up the difference with butter. In a separate pan, heat 4 cups chicken broth and milk together, but do not boil. Stir flour into melted fat until smooth. Add broth and milk mixture gradually, stirring constantly. Then add salt and cook until very thick, stirring constantly. Beat eggs slightly and mix in a little of the sauce (this is to keep eggs from cooking). Then combine the rest of the sauce and eggs, and cook over low heat for another 3 or 4 minutes. Keep stirring. Add chicken skin when you remove the sauce from the stove.

To bake, grease 1 very large or 2 small casserole dishes. Carefully spread stuffing along the bottom. Pour half of the sauce over it. On top of this, cut up the chicken meat into pieces with scissors. Add the remaining sauce. Take 1 cup dry bread crumbs and toss in 4 tablespoons melted butter. Sprinkle on top. Bake at 375° for 20 minutes, or until crumbs are golden brown and scalloped chicken is piping hot through and through.

Note: I do this all in steps: cook the chicken one day, make the sauce the next, and finish the job, except for the final cooking. All this can be put in the freezer and kept until you need it or kept in the refrigerator overnight if you want to put it in the oven the next day. Serves 4.

CHARLES CHRISTMANN, JR.
HAMBURG, NEW YORK

Chicken Cashew Casserole

This recipe came from a very dear aunt. She loved to cook this casserole when she had the *girls* in for lunch.

½ cup onion, chopped
1 cup celery, diced
1 tablespoon butter
1 can cream of mushroom soup
  black pepper
⅓ cup chicken broth
1 tablespoon soy sauce
3 drops hot pepper sauce
2 cups cooked chicken, diced
⅓ cup cashews, chopped
1 small can crisp noodles

Fry onion and celery in butter. Add mushroom soup, black pepper, chicken broth, soy sauce, and hot pepper sauce. Add chicken and simmer for a few minutes. Pour into a 1-quart casserole dish and sprinkle with cashews and noodles. Bake at 350° for 20 minutes. Serves 4.

Dave's note: The cashews in this dish add a surprising crunchy flavor to the chicken. Hope you don't have to take a bank loan for the nuts.

MRS. LEON BEAULIEW
WEST BRIDGEWATER, MASSACHUSETTS

Ginger-Peachy Chicken Bake

Both Mama and Daddy were Swedish immigrants. They came from different parts of Sweden, but met and married in Boston. Like many other Depression kids, we never knew we were poor because we were kept well fed and happy by Mama's ingenious cooking and Daddy's sense of humor.

Daddy raised his own chickens for our table, so we had to eat a lot of it, but Mama had so many varieties of chicken dishes, we never complained.

1 4-pound chicken
1½ quarts water
1½ tablespoons salt
1 cup celery, chopped
1 tablespoon instant minced onion
  OR 1 small onion, minced
⅔ cup butter or margarine
⅔ cup flour
¼ teaspoon pepper
½ teaspoon fines herbes
1 cup sliced mushrooms or canned
  stems and pieces
1 package frozen green peas,
  blanched
1 cup biscuit mix
⅓ cup milk
  powdered or ground ginger
1 1-pound can cling peach halves
6 tablespoons apple-mint jelly

Place chicken in a pot with water to cover, 1 teaspoon salt, celery, and onion. Simmer about 2½ hours, more or less, until chicken is tender. Remove meat from bone and cut into bite-size pieces. Add enough water to broth, if necessary, to measure 3 cups. Melt butter or margarine in a large pan. Add flour, pepper, and remaining salt. Stir until blended. Add broth and cook over low heat, stirring constantly until mixture thickens. Add fines herbes, mushrooms, peas, and chicken. Stir together biscuit mix and milk. Pour chicken mixture into an 8-inch-square pan or baking dish. Lightly sprinkle with ginger. Arrange peaches, cup side up, on top of chicken mixture, and place dollops of biscuit dough around the peach cups. Bake at 450° about 20 minutes. Bake any remaining dough on cookie sheet to serve as biscuits.

Just before serving, spoon 1 tablespoon mint jelly into each peach
half. Serves 6.

*Dave's note: We did this one on
television and got over 1,000 requests
for it.*

VIOLET M. BROWN
MALDEN, MASSACHUSETTS

Saltimboca

3 whole chicken breasts
6 slices smoked Virginia ham
1 cup Parmesan cheese, grated
¼ cup all-purpose flour
1 teaspoon salt
½ teaspoon sage
¼ teaspoon pepper
½ cup olive oil
½ cup dry white wine
1 can chicken broth

Prepare chicken breasts (you must
have 12 thin, thin cutlets). Sandwich a
ham slice between 2 cutlets and fasten
together with toothpicks.

In a bowl mix cheese, flour, salt,
sage, and pepper. Dip cutlets in mixture and press firmly to coat both
sides. Shake off excess. Chill. Reserve
¼ cup coating mixture.

In a large skillet, heat oil and sauté
cutlets, 2 at a time for 4 to 5 minutes
over medium heat to keep them from
burning. Drain cutlets on paper towels
and keep warm until all are cooked.

Pour ¼ cup pan drippings into a
separate saucepan and add reserved
coating mixture. Blend in chicken
broth and white wine, and cook over
low heat until sauce bubbles and thickens, stirring constantly.

Place cutlets on a bed of hot fresh
spinach leaves and pour sauce over

top. Sprinkle with Parmesan cheese.
Serves 6.

*Dave's note: If you forget to remove
the toothpicks before eating, it will
ruin your meal*

DAVE

Chicken and Broccoli Loaf

1 pound broccoli, trimmed, separated
   into flowerettes; peel and dice stalks
   water
½ teaspoon salt
½ cup bechamel
¼ cup Parmesan cheese, grated
6 eggs, slightly beaten two at a time
2 cups cooked dark chicken meat,
   ground
1½ cups veloute sauce
2 cups cooked white chicken meat,
   ground
   salt and pepper

Steam broccoli for 8 to 10 minutes in
salted water. Rinse under cold water.
Chop. Combine broccoli, bechamel,
Parmesan cheese, and 2 eggs. Combine dark meat with ½ the veloute
sauce and 2 more eggs. In another
bowl, combine the light meat with the
rest of the veloute and final 2 eggs.
Season each bowl of ingredients with
salt and pepper. Butter an 8 x 4 x 2-
inch loaf pan. Put in a layer of dark
meat, then a layer of broccoli mixture,
then a layer of white meat. Cover with
aluminum foil. Place in a pan of hot
water, having water reach ⅔ to ¾ of
the way up. Bake at 350° for 1½ hours.
Remove from oven, let cool on rack
for 5 to 10 minutes. Loosen with knife.
Invert onto serving platter.

DAVE

It's a good thing for all of us that so many new studies have damned beef for one reason or another—a good thing in the sense that, at the same time, prices on this most popular meat have risen to out-of-sight levels. A great jazz musician once said, in commenting on the size of a lady pianist's hands, "They're about the size of $3 worth of ribs in 1937." If we updated the remark to the present time, gone would be any trace of humor. For $3 in some stores, you can buy a pound of cheap hamburger and maybe some beef bones to give your kitchen a beef aroma.

Except for a few cases, the recipes in this section use less expensive cuts of meat. I guess this is because when the recipes were devised, times were poorer and folks kept experimenting with their cooking to make plain food taste better.

Do you think we're going back to those times? I think perhaps it wouldn't be so horrible after all. —Dave

Beef

Florence's Meat Loaf

2 cups seasoned bread crumbs
¼ cup green peppers, chopped
¼ cup Parmesan cheese, grated
¼ heaping teaspoon rosemary
¼ heaping teaspoon basil
   Worcestershire sauce to taste
2 medium onions, minced
2 eggs, beaten
2 pounds ground beef
1 tablespoon salt
¼ tablespoon oregano
1 cup canned or stewed tomatoes

Preheat oven to 400°. Combine all ingredients, mixing thoroughly. Shape mixture into a loaf and place in a loaf pan. Bake at 350° for 50 minutes or until done. Serves 6.

MRS. CHRISTINE FORSYTHE
BALLARDVALE, MASSACHUSETTS

Steak Roll-Ups

I have used this for some thirty-seven years. My husband was in World War II and spent a year in Germany as a cook while in the 99th Infantry Division. They took over private homes and set up kitchens. The lady of the house would come daily and tidy up their home. Coffee was very hard to come by. My husband would save the coffee grounds. This German lady cooked this dish for them. Everyone was fond of it. This was in Bruckenaw near Wurzburg. Her son Heintz is in the import business now. How fast the years pass by.

2 pounds round steak or flank steak, thinly sliced
2 cups bread stuffing

2 tablespoons shortening
1 can condensed cream of mushroom soup
½ cup water
½ cup sour cream (optional)

Pound steak with a meat hammer or with the edge of a heavy saucer. Cut steak into 8 pieces that are long enough to be made into rolls. Place about ¼ cup stuffing near the center of each piece of steak; roll, pinwheel fashion, and fasten with a toothpick or skewer. In a skillet, brown the roll-ups in shortening. Add soup and water. Cover and cook over low heat for about 1½ hours, or until tender. Spoon the sauce over the meat occasionally during the cooking. Remove the roll-ups from the pan. Stir sour cream into the sauce. Heat and serve. Serves 4 to 6.

MRS. ROBERT FISHER
COLUMBUS, OHIO

Spicy Steak Strips

I first tried this unusual recipe for some in-laws that I wasn't too fond of and wanted something that wasn't very expensive. It was such a success that I have served it for company many times since. I even got to like the in-laws. I serve this with fluffy rice.

1½ pounds round steak
2 tablespoons butter
1 clove garlic, mashed
¼ teaspoon pepper
¼ teaspoon chili powder
¼ teaspoon cinnamon
¼ teaspoon celery seed
2 tablespoons prepared mustard
1 tablespoon instant minced onion
⅛ teaspoon cayenne
1 cup beef broth or bouillon

Cut steak into strips about ½ inch wide and 2 inches long. Brown on both sides in butter. Mix remaining ingredients and pour over meat. Cover and simmer for 30 to 35 minutes, or until meat is tender. Serves 3 to 4.

IDA NILES
HASLEH, MICHIGAN

One-Dish Depression Meal

3 carrots, cubed
1 stalk celery, chopped
3 potatoes, cubed
1 package chipped beef, shredded
   medium white sauce
   biscuit dough (refrigerated or
   prepared mix)

Cook vegetables in a small amount of water until tender. Combine with shredded beef and white sauce. Place in a casserole dish and cover with your favorite biscuit dough. Bake at 350° until top is golden brown. Any other cooked meat could be substituted, but I only recall having it with chipped beef, which must have been cheap in the 1930s. Serves 2.

Dave's note: How I remember chipped beef as a youngster — hated it. Not bad now though.

MRS. LOU IANNOTTI
WATERTOWN, NEW YORK

German Schnitzel

In lean times we use almost any meat combination, and it always tastes fine. It can even be frozen for later use.

2 pounds ground beef
3 tablespoons dried onion (or 2 tablespoons onion soaked in ½ cup water)
½ teaspoon paprika
½ to 1 teaspoon salt
2 eggs, beaten
1 tablespoon soy sauce
½ cup dried bread crumbs
   peanut oil or clarified butter

Break up meat in a large bowl and sprinkle with onion. Use hands to mix well. Add paprika, salt, eggs, soy sauce, and bread crumbs, mixing well with hands. Mixture should be firm enough to hold shape. Cover. Let stand 15 minutes to blend flavors. Then shape into flat, oblong patties. Heat peanut oil or clarified butter in a large skillet until moderately hot. Add patties. Turn down heat. Cook uncovered until brown on both sides (about 5 or 10 minutes on each side).

Serves 6. (For a more economical dish, use leftover meats; make your own combination. Grind all meats before using.)

RITA E. KAPUSTY
SHANDAKEN, NEW YORK

Griddles
(Hamburg, Germany)

This recipe is from a Mr. Fahrenholz, whose grandparents lived in Eddlesen near Bremen, Germany, and came to America in 1850, bringing treasured family recipes along. They have no idea how the name originated but they do know they had better have some on hand when their son comes for a weekend, as he has been known to never eat less than twenty at a sitting.

1½ pounds beef, in chunk
½   pound pork, in chunk
1   18-ounce box oatmeal
    salt
1   tablespoon allspice

Boil beef and pork together until tender. Remove from broth, cool meat, then grind together with small blade. Add ground meat and oatmeal to the broth (about 1 quart should remain). Cook until broth is absorbed, stirring most of the time. When thick as mush, set aside and stir in allspice. Pour into pan, cool, slice like mush, and fry in oil. Serves 8 to 10.

Dave's note: Very good, very different dish. Mix the flour with a little cold water before adding to the other ingredients. Actually griddles won't pour into the pan, but they'll push easily.

MRS. O. M. HAMILTON
MIDDLETOWN, OHIO

Beef en Croute

1   4-pound eye round roast
2   tablespoons flour
2   teaspoons mixed salad herbs
2   teaspoons salt
2   teaspoons paprika
1   package refrigerated crescent rolls
4   tablespoons butter, melted

Trim fat from roast. Mix flour and seasonings together and pat well into meat. Place meat on a rack in a shallow baking pan. Do not cover pan or add any water. Roast at 325° for 1 hour. Remove roast from oven; keep warm until ready to add pastry blanket. Remove crescent rolls from package; unroll dough and separate into triangles. Place 3 triangles on each side of roast; fold up over roast and overlap at top. Place remaining 2 triangles at either end; fold up over top. Brush entirely with melted butter. Bake at 375° for 15 minutes, or until crust is richly golden. Place roast on heated platter. Carve through pastry covering into ½-inch-thick slices. Serves 8.

Dave's note: Easy Wellington.

JUDY BARNES
ANDOVER, MASSACHUSETTS

Julia's Leftover Sunday Roast

We discovered this recipe in 1950 while in Europe. Julia owned a very small hotel and bistro in Sampigny, France. The kitchen was much like one you'd expect to find in the 1920s —large wood stove with a water tank to provide hot water, the sink a shallow soapstone slab that drained into the street, and a trap door that led to a wine cellar with a dirt floor. The wine cellar was also used to store perishables as there was no refrigerator.

4 potatoes
   bacon fat, oil, or butter
   leftover roast beef
½ cup red wine
   seasoning to taste (garlic, parsley, leek, and oregano are suggested)
   Gruyère cheese, grated
   Parmesan cheese, grated

Cut potatoes in half lengthwise and scoop a large oval out of each half, leaving about a ½-inch edge all around. Brush with bacon fat, oil, or butter. Partially bake potato shells and boil potato that was scooped out, then mash and season. Grind or chop cooked meat, add mashed potato, red wine, and seasonings and mix well. Fill partially baked potato shells with meat mixture, return to oven, and continue to bake at 350° until edge of shell is golden brown and potato cooked. Top with grated cheese, half Gruyere and half Parmesan.

Note: You may use fresh ground beef, adding a few chopped chicken livers if available, but omitting the mashed potato. Naturally you will have to bake longer than the above, but first you have to bake the potato partially. Serves 4.

Dave's note: A good lesson in elevating a pot roast.

MISS C. QUINT BUXTON
HAMPTON, NEW HAMPSHIRE

Steak Cosmopolitan

I'm sorry there is no big story behind the recipe. Wish I could say it came over on the *Mayflower* with my ancestors, but no such luck. The recipe came from my daughter about five years ago when she was a new bride. She invited her family over for dinner, and this was the dish she served. I think it's a scrumptious meal. So that's how I got a hold of it and we have it often. It looks like a complicated recipe, but it's not. Reading through the recipe just once, before starting, will show you that it can be made in about one-half hour.

1 pound round steak, thinly sliced in 1-inch strips
3 tablespoons oil
1 cup onions, sliced
2 cups carrots, sliced diagonally
⅓ cup red wine
1¾ cups beef broth
1 small can mushrooms
1½ teaspoons salt
¼ teaspoon garlic powder
¼ teaspoon pepper
1 tablespoon Worcestershire sauce
2 cups celery, sliced diagonally
2 tablespoons cornstarch
¼ cup water

Saute steak in oil until brown. Add onions and cook 2 minutes longer. Stir in carrots, wine, broth, mushrooms with liquid, and seasonings. Bring to a boil. Reduce heat, cover, and simmer for 10 minutes. Add celery and continue cooking 10 minutes more. Dissolve cornstarch in ½ cup water. Stir into meat mixture. Cook, stirring constantly, until thickened. Serve over rice. Serves 2 to 4.

Dave's note: Keep vegetables crunchy. Reduce salt to ½ teaspoon, as there's already salt in broth and Worcestershire sauce.

MRS. REUBEN KERTSCHER
SAUKVILLE, MICHIGAN

Moussaka Souffle

2 pounds eggplant
1 pound ground beef
1 cup onion, chopped
2 tablespoons butter or margarine
1½ teaspoons salt
　 pepper
1 tablespoon parsley
⅛ teaspoon nutmeg
½ cup tomato sauce
½ cup water
2 cups soft bread crumbs
6 eggs, separated
½ cup cheese, grated

Pare and dice eggplant. Soak in a bowl of cold water while preparing meat. Rinse and drain well. Meanwhile, brown ground beef and onion in butter or margarine. Season with salt and pepper. Add eggplant cubes and stir over moderate heat to brown slightly. Add parsley, nutmeg, tomato sauce, and water. Simmer until eggplant is soft, stirring occasionally. Remove from heat and stir in 1½ cups bread crumbs. Mix well.

Combine well-beaten egg yolks with eggplant mixture. Fold in beaten egg whites, blending thoroughly. Pour into a 2-quart deep baking dish. Combine remaining bread crumbs with grated cheese and sprinkle over top. Bake at 350° for 45 minutes, or until firm and golden. Serve warm. Serves 6 to 8.

Note: Substitute 2 pounds zucchini, sliced, for eggplant.

STELLA TSAPATSARIS
LOWELL, MASSACHUSETTS

Eye of the Round Rancho

This recipe has been used by family and friends for at least ten years, and it still remains one of their favorites.

½ cup olive oil
½ cup red wine or wine vinegar
2 tablespoons bottled steak sauce
½ onion, sliced
1 clove garlic, crushed
1 teaspoon thyme
½ teaspoon salt
¼ teaspoon pepper
3 to 4 pound eye of round

Marinate roast for several hours or overnight. To make marinade, combine all ingredients except roast, and then add the meat.

Broil roast, using marinade as basting sauce. Baste often. Any leftover marinade may be warmed and served to pour over meat. Slice meat diagonally into thin strips. Serves 4 to 6.

Dave's note: Great for barbecue.

DAVID WARREN
WORCESTER, MASSACHUSETTS

Southern Baked Beef with Cheese

I received this recipe in Arizona when I was visiting my daughter and one of her neighbors gave it to me. She said that when she was a youngster, they had a maid who used to make them this dish. The maid told her it was in their family for years. You can also add a few olives to it. We do enjoy this dish for a change. This is also a different way to use hamburg.

1   onion
2   tablespoons oil
1   pound ground beef
1   cup rice
    salt, pepper, and paprika
    several olives
2   cups tomato juice
1½ cups cheese, grated

In a skillet fry onion in oil, toss in hamburg and uncooked rice, until brown. Season with salt, pepper, and paprika. Add olives, then add enough tomato juice and a bit of water to make a soupy mixture.

Transfer mixture to a casserole dish, cover tightly, and cook for 1 hour at 350°. Uncover and sprinkle with grated cheese. Continue baking for 10 more minutes, or until cheese melts through. Serves 6. Enjoy with vegetable or salad.

Dave's note: A cheapy, but who'll know it?

KAY HAMILTON
DANVERS, MASSACHUSETTS

Carpet Bag Steak

I came over here in 1946 as a G.I. bride from a town called Veoril Somerset in England. All I can remember is my dear old mum, who died in 1977 at the age of 83, saying, "Let's make Dad a bag steak, so he can have lots of strength to ride his bike to work and climb the telephone poles."

Oysters have the best reputation for flavor digestibility and are given to invalids. Oyster season is from September to April.

1   4-pound piece of top round or
    tenderloin, pocketed for stuffing

Stuffing:

12 to 18 oysters
¼   pound mushrooms, chopped
1   tablespoon parsley, chopped
3   tablespoons butter
6   ounces white bread crumbs
1   egg, beaten
¼   teaspoon lemon rind
    seasonings to taste

Heat butter and toss in oysters and mushrooms. Cook for 5 minutes, then transfer to a bowl and mix in parsley, bread crumbs, lemon rind, and seasonings. Stir in egg. Press mixture into the pocket in steak and sew or skewer edges together. Roast at 325° for 2 hours. Serve with roast potatoes and pumpkin.

Dave's note: You must put in oysters or it's no go.

EILEEN DICKSON
STOUGHTON, MASSACHUSETTS

Beef 87

Beef Burgundy with Rice

5 medium onions, thinly sliced
2 tablespoons bacon drippings or shortening
2 pounds boneless beef chuck, cut in 1½-inch cubes
2 tablespoons flour
   salt, pepper, thyme, and marjoram
½ cup beef bouillon
1 cup dry red wine
½ pound mushrooms, sliced

In a heavy skillet, cook onions in bacon drippings until brown. Remove onions. Add beef and more bacon drippings, if necessary. Brown beef cubes well on each side. Sprinkle beef with flour and seasonings. Stir in bouillon and wine. Simmer very slowly for 2½ to 3 hours, or until meat is tender. If necessary, add more bouillon and wine (1 part bouillon to 2 parts wine) to keep meat barely covered with liquid. Return onions to pan and add mushrooms. Cook for 30 more minutes, adding liquid if necessary. Adjust seasonings to taste. Serve over rice. Serves 2 to 4.

MARY A. LUKIS
WALPOLE, MASSACHUSETTS

Beef and Mushroom Roll

1 pound ground beef
1 teaspoon salt
1 2½-ounce can mushroom bits and pieces, with liquid
1 small onion, minced
¼ cup sweet pickle, chopped
¼ teaspoon pepper
2 sprigs parsley, chopped
¼ teaspoon dry mustard
2 tablespoons flour
   biscuit dough
1 10¾-ounce can beef gravy

Biscuit Dough:

2 cups flour
2 teaspoons baking powder
½ teaspoon poultry seasoning
1 teaspoon salt
¼ cup shortening
¾ cup plus 1 tablespoon milk

Cook beef, stirring with a fork until it is no longer red. Add all ingredients except the last three. Simmer for 10 minutes, then pour off most of fat. Blend in flour, add ⅓ cup water, and cook until thickened, stirring constantly. Cool while preparing biscuit dough.

Make biscuit dough by sifting flour with baking powder, poultry seasoning, and salt. Cut in shortening. Add milk. Mix only to moisten.

Roll dough into a 12 x 9-inch rectangle. Spread beef mixture on dough to within ½ inch of edges. Moisten edges with water. Roll like a jelly roll and pinch edges together. Put roll in a greased shallow pan and brush with milk. Slit top with knife in 4 places to allow inside to bake and steam to escape. Bake at 425° for about 30 minutes. Cut into slices and serve with heated gravy. Serves 6 to 8.

Dave's note: This is good cold too.

MAUREEN RAINHO
SOMERVILLE, MASSACHUSETTS

Corned Beef Brine

4 quarts cold water
½ ounce saltpeter
1 tablespoon whole mixed spices
4 cloves garlic, crushed or sliced
(optional)
6 pounds chuck beef
2 cups coarse salt
1 tablespoon brown sugar
12 bay leaves

Combine all ingredients but beef and boil for 5 minutes. Pour over chuck which has been placed in a crock. Put a weight on meat to keep it under the brine. Store in a cool place, covered with a cloth, for 2 weeks.

Tongue may be made the same way. When ready to use, soak in cold water for 15 minutes and pour off water.

IZZETT CHAPIN
ATHOL, MASSACHUSETTS

Yankee Cheddar Steak

1 pound round steak, ½-inch thick
¼ cup flour
1 teaspoon salt
¼ teaspoon pepper
oil
1 medium onion, thinly sliced
1 8-ounce can tomato sauce
1 teaspoon garlic powder
1 4-ounce package shredded
sharp cheddar cheese

Cut steak into serving-size pieces. Combine flour, salt, and pepper and pound into steak. Brown in oil. Place meat in a shallow baking dish or pan. Cover with onion slices, tomato sauce, and garlic powder. Bake at 350° for 40 minutes. Sprinkle with cheese and return to oven until cheese is melted. Serves 4.

FLORENCE WALKER
CHELMSFORD, MASSACHUSETTS

100 Per Cent Nature Dinner

½ cup onion, chopped
2 tablespoons oil
½ pound green beans
2 cloves garlic, minced
½ teaspoon oregano
1 to 1½ pounds flank steak
½ cup cold water
8 to 10 small new potatoes
1 teaspoon hot pepper sauce
1 teaspoon salt
1 bay leaf
2 tomatoes

Sauté onions in oil, then add everything else except tomatoes. Put those in 30 minutes before meat is done. Cook at 275° to 300° for 1½ hours. Garnish with bread crumbs. I cook this in electric fry pan, covered. Serves 3 to 4.

MRS. L. L. HUTCHINSON
LUNENBURG, MASSACHUSETTS

Sarah Jane's Pot Roast

It's a never-fail treat any day...and the next day, cold...for a sandwich or heated in its gravy. Recipe is varied only slightly from the way it was made on P.E.I., Canada, about one hundred years ago. It was my grandmother's, my mother's, and now my specialty on Cape Cod.

It was a Sunday (after-church) treat that had been cooked on Saturday and heated up with vegetables right from the garden (especially yellow turnips).

4 pounds round steak, 2 inches thick
2 teaspoons salt
1 teaspoon allspice
½ teaspoon pepper
3 tablespoons oil
2 medium onions, sliced
3 anchovy fillets
2 bay leaves
2 tablespoons vinegar
1 tablespoon dark corn syrup
¾ cup water
  flour to thicken
¼ cup cream, sour or other (optional)

Sprinkle steak with salt, allspice, and pepper. Brown well in oil. Add onions, anchovy fillets, bay leaves, vinegar, dark corn syrup, and ½ cup water. Simmer, covered, for about 2 hours or until "fork-done." Then mix ¼ cup water with enough flour to thicken and add slowly to boiling liquid. Extra nice if you stir in about ¼ cup cream (sour cream if you wish) and bring just to a boil. Serves 6 to 8.

Dave's note: My best to Sarah Jane—she gave us hers.

HELEN E. PROUTY
DENNIS, MASSACHUSETTS

Pastel de Carne
(Meat Pie)

Pastel de Carne means meat pie in Spanish. I remember my grandmother using this recipe, so I would think it has been in my family for at least fifty years or so. I come from Colombia, South America.

1 pound ground beef
1 pound ground pork
1 onion, chopped
1 8-ounce can mushrooms
  salt and pepper
  oregano
  oil
2 pounds pastry dough (enough for 2 crusts)
1 16-ounce can stewed tomatoes, drained
½ pound Provolone cheese, coarsely grated
1 8-ounce can mushroom soup

Place beef, pork, onions, mushrooms, salt, pepper, and oregano in a skillet and sauté until meat and onions have browned. Pour off grease, drain meat, and set aside. Grease a 16 x 12-inch baking pan with oil and line with half of dough. Spread meat mixture evenly over dough and add tomatoes, cheese, spices, and mushroom soup. Cover with rest of dough, seal edges with a little water, and cut an opening in the middle for steam to escape. Bake at 450° for 15 minutes. Reduce heat to 400° and bake for another 30 minutes, or until crust is golden brown. Serve while warm. Makes 8 servings.

Dave's note: Try a flaky pie crust dough. Brush with a little milk or egg yolk beaten with a little water.

MRS. MARIA T. ROURKE
LOWELL, MASSACHUSETTS

Flank Steak

I was brought up in the Depression. So my brothers started making home brew (as we called beer then). My mother devised this recipe, which my seven brothers and sisters enjoyed.

1 flank steak, 1-inch thick
⅔ cup beer
⅓ cup vegetable oil
    salt, pepper, and garlic powder to taste

Punch holes in steak with a fork. Marinate steak 3 hours or overnight in beer vegetable oil, salt, pepper, and garlic powder. Pat dry with a towel before broiling for 5 minutes on each side. Cut thin across the grain. Serve on French bread. Top with fried onions. Mix sour cream with 1 tablespoon horseradish for topping, if desired. Serves 3.

ALICE McDONALD
MILWAUKEE, WISCONSIN

Flemish Beef in Beer

1 tablespoon flour
¾ pound round steak, cut in 1-inch cubes
1 tablespoon butter
1 tablespoon vegetable oil
2 medium onions, sliced
2 cloves garlic, minced
¼ cup canned beef broth, diluted with ¼ cup water
2 tablespoons parsley, chopped
2 tablespoons red wine vinegar
1 teaspoon dark brown sugar
1 bay leaf
⅛ teaspoon pepper
1 teaspoon salt
1 cup beer
¼ teaspoon dried thyme leaves
2 small potatoes, peeled and quartered
3 medium carrots, scraped and sliced into 1-inch slices

Dredge meat with flour. Heat butter and oil in a 10-inch skillet over moderate heat. Place meat in skillet and brown it on all sides. Remove meat from skillet. Add onion and garlic to skillet and cook over medium heat until lightly browned. Add beef broth and cook over high heat, stirring to loosen bits in bottom of skillet. Add parsley, vinegar, sugar, bay leaf, salt, pepper, beer, and thyme. Stir to blend. Return meat to skillet. Cover and simmer over low heat for 1¼ hours. Add potatoes and carrots. Simmer, covered, for 45 minutes, or until meat is done. Serves 2 to 3.

Dave's note: There are so many uses for beer in the kitchen (in soup mixes, etc.), and this is a good one. It's a lot like German Rouladen without the pickle.

MRS. MICHAEL LORKIEWICZ
DUDLEY, MASSACHUSETTS

Filet Mignon Sicilian

3 pounds filet mignon
6 strips bacon
2 onions, sliced
   salt and pepper to taste
¼ pound butter
¾ cup sherry

Slice filet 1½ inches thick. Heat a skillet; brown bacon slightly. Add onion and brown for 2 minutes. Remove bacon and onion. In the same pan, brown filet over high flame for about 5 minutes on each side. Lower the flame and continue frying 5 minutes more. Add salt and pepper. Melt butter and pour over filet. Add sherry. Simmer for 2 minutes. Serves 6.

Dave's note: Pour off some of that bacon fat. Bacon and beer make a nice combination.

KATHY KRIKORIAN
HAVERHILL, MASSACHUSETTS

Kima

My mother, Mrs. Claire Wetherell, unfortunately died last January. She was very enthusiastic about your cookbook, and I know she'd be delighted to receive a copy, even posthumously. As for the recipe itself, Kima is originally a dish from India, where ground lamb instead of ground beef is used.

My mother learned this recipe from one of her mother's friends.

1 large onion
3 tablespoons butter
1 pound ground beef
2 tomatoes, peeled and diced
1 teaspoon curry powder
1 teaspoon salt
1 teaspoon paprika
½ teaspoon chili powder
½ teaspoon garlic salt
1 10-ounce package frozen peas, blanched

Sauté onion in butter for 5 minutes. Add ground beef and tomatoes, and cook slowly for 15 minutes. Add curry powder, salt, paprika, chili powder, and garlic salt. Cover and simmer for 30 minutes. Just before serving, add peas. Good with crusty rolls, or corn chips, and a fruit salad.

MARK A. WETHERELL
ATTLEBORO, MASSACHUSETTS

Boat

This recipe was passed on to me by a very dear friend, Mrs. Olga Cavanaugh, who in turn received it from her mother, Mrs. Magdalini Costa, an immigrant to the U.S. from Albania. She learned how to read by herself, and from her smattering of English and Albanian came up with this dish. It's called "Boat" probably because it's filled with Vienna bread and somewhat resembles a boat.

1 Vienna bread, unsliced
2 tablespoons butter or margarine
1 large onion, chopped
1 cup shredded lettuce
1 large tomato, chopped
1 pound hamburger
½ teaspoon salt
¼ teaspoon pepper
  oregano to taste

Refrigerate bread for few hours to make it easier to handle. Then slice off top and scoop out the inside. Set both aside. Melt butter in a frying pan and sauté onion until soft. Add lettuce and tomato, and cook for a few minutes. Add hamburger and cook until brown. Add seasonings, cover and simmer for 5 minutes. Add to hamburger mixture scooped-out bread that has been cut into bite-size pieces and season again to taste. Bread will absorb all the pan drippings; if mixture appears dry, add more melted butter. Pack mixture into Vienna bread shell and place top back on loaf. Place loaf on a baking pan and cover with aluminum foil. Bake at 400° for 20 to 25 minutes. To serve, cut into thick slices and accompany entree with a crisp, tossed salad. Yum, Yum, Yum!!

Dave's note: Two good additions are two tablespoons chopped parsley —add with seasonings—and sliced mushrooms. This savory meat mixture in a crusty, warm bread should be a big hit with kids.

WILMA SWIRBLISS
SOUTHBRIDGE, MASSACHUSETTS

Polynesian Beef Stew

1 medium green pepper, chopped
1 small onion, chopped
1 tablespoon butter
1 tablespoon cornstarch
1 tablespoon water
1 1½-pound can beef stew
1 13½-ounce can pineapple chunks
  drained
¼ teaspoon ginger
1 tablespoon sugar
1 tablespoon vinegar
1 teaspoon soy sauce
¼ teaspoon salt
1 3-ounce can chow mein noodles

Sauté green pepper and onion in butter until tender but not soft. Mix cornstarch with water and add with remaining ingredients, except noodles, to vegetables. Simmer and stir gently until thickened. Serve with noodles. Serves approximately 4.

Dave's note: I usually don't care for fruit and meat cooked together, but this is very peppy and without the pineapple it misses.

RUTH W. FODREY
ELIZABETH CITY, NORTH CAROLINA

Strange as it may seem, ham to me is only a nibbling food: a couple of slices quickly slipped out of an open refrigerator or a ham and cheese sandwich with some fried eggs to snack on. For some reason, ham does not conjure up any interesting and/or imaginative ideas when I'm cooking. I'll admit that if you leave out the proscuitto in a **cordon bleu** dish you won't have a **cordon bleu** dish. But, by itself? If I am invited to dinner and am told ham is the main dish, I suddenly remember an appointment I have to keep in a slot machine parlor downtown. However, if you're preparing a leftover ham recipe, invite me over. I'll bring the beer (I usually bring wine, but I don't think any wine goes with ham).

If you're in agreement, read on. Here are some interesting ways to get rid of ham doldrums. -- Dave

Ham

Ham Sauce

1½ cups apple jelly
1½ cups orange marmalade
1   bottle horseradish
1   6-ounce jar prepared mustard

Mix all ingredients together in an electric mixer. Keep sauce in glass jars in the refrigerator. Delicious with hot or cold ham.

Dave's note: Nice sweet-and-sour combination.

**MRS. LIDA CAMPBELL
ELSIE, MICHIGAN**

Ham Loaves
with Mustard Sauce

My recipe is an original recipe of my mother's, the late Elsie M. Jeffrey. In the mid-1930s, she wrote a cookbook and sent it to a publisher. They liked it but wanted the book enlarged. She never bothered to do it. This was one of her recipes. I still have most of the manuscript.

When I was a kid, we never knew what we were going to have for dinner. My mother was always trying out a new recipe from peanut butter soup (which didn't make the book) to Ham Loaves (which did).

1½ cups cornflakes, crushed
½   cup milk combined with 1 egg
2½ cups leftover ham, ground
2   teaspoons brown sugar
¼   teaspoon ground cloves
1   teaspoon butter, melted

Place 1 cup crushed cornflakes in egg and milk mixture and allow crumbs to soften. Add meat and seasonings and mix. Make 5 small loaves. Roll each in the remaining ½ cup cornflakes to which the melted butter should have been mixed. Bake at 325° for 35 minutes. Serve with mustard sauce.

Mustard Sauce:

2   teaspoons dry mustard
1   egg, beaten
½   cup brown sugar
½   cup vinegar
1   teaspoon flour

Cook all ingredients in a double boiler until thick, stirring constantly. Cool and thin with a little cream or milk. Serve separately to go over ham loaves. Serves 4.

Dave's note: Loaves have nice texture; sauce is very good. A little chopped parsley on top would be nice.

**MRS. BARBARA YOUNG
WAYLAND, MASSACHUSETTS**

Ham-Tomato Toast

2 tablespoons onion, chopped
2 tablespoons green pepper, chopped
4 tablespoons butter
3 cups stewed tomatoes
1 cup ham, chopped
2 eggs, slightly beaten
   toast

Sauté onion and green pepper in butter until tender. Add tomatoes and simmer for 10 minutes. Add ham and eggs. Cook until egg has thickened mixture, and pour over slices of crisp toast. Serves 4.

Dave's note: I would suggest 4 eggs instead of 2, and a good variation would be to add sliced mushrooms to the onions and peppers and some freshly grated Parmesan cheese.

RUTH BEEMAN
QUINCY, MASSACHUSETTS

Ham Loaf

2/3 pound ham, ground
1 1/3 pounds pork, ground
1 1/2 cups graham cracker crumbs
1 teaspoon salt
1/4 teaspoon pepper
2 eggs, beaten
1 cup milk
1/2 cup brown sugar
1 teaspoon prepared yellow mustard
2 teaspoons vinegar

Combine meats, cracker crumbs, seasonings, eggs, and milk in a bowl. Mix thoroughly. Form into a loaf and bake in a loaf pan at 325° for 1 1/2 hours. Meanwhile combine brown sugar mustard, and vinegar and mix well. After 1 hour of baking, spoon sauce over ham loaf, and bake for 1/2 hour more. Remove from oven and allow pan to stand on cooling rack for 5 minutes for easy slicing. Serves 6.

Dave's note: Drain grease before adding sauce. The addition of pork and the sweet-and-sour topping gives a great flavor.

MRS. HAZEL M. TITUS
SHARON, PENNSYLVANIA

Ham Vilma

This recipe came from a friend several years ago. Although the sauce ingredients are a bit strange, it's easy to prepare and is always a hit with company.

12 thin slices boiled ham
1 pint all-purpose cream
1 6-ounce can tomato paste
1/2 cup dry sherry
2/3 teaspoon pepper

Roll ham in tight cylinders and put in one layer in a baking dish. Whip cream, then add tomato paste, sherry, and pepper. Mix well and pour over ham. Bake at 350° for 25 to 30 minutes. Serve over rice. Serves 4 to 6.

Dave's note: Garnish with chopped parsley. If cream breaks down, whisk vigorously. Smooth and rich.

MS. PRISCILLA E. McKAY
GLOUCESTER, MASSACHUSETTS

Green Beans and Ham

A good dish for leftover ham. Is sure sparkles up those frozen or bland canned green beans.

2 packages frozen french style green beans
¼ cup butter or margarine
¼ cup flour
1 cup milk
1 cup cheddar cheese, grated
½ teaspoon nutmeg
  salt and pepper to taste
1 cup ham, diced

Cook green beans according to package directions and drain. Set aside. Melt butter and blend in flour. Add milk slowly, stirring until thickened. Add cheese and seasonings, stirring until melted. Mix in green beans. Top with ham and simmer, covered, for 20 minutes. Serve with a salad and french bread. Serves 4.

Dave's note: If sauce is too thick, add more bean liquid. This can also be baked at 375° for 20 minutes.

MARIAN BARBETT
LAWRENCE, MASSACHUSETTS

Brussels Sprouts with Ham Casserole

My daughter, Dr. Virginia M. Oversby, a scientist at the Australian National University in Canberra, Australia, gave me this recipe when I last visited her in 1977.

2 cups brussels sprouts
2 cups cold water
1 teaspoon salt
1 cup cooked ham, diced
  tomato slices, ¼ inch thick
2 tablespoons Parmesan cheese, grated
2 tablespoons bread crumbs

White Sauce:

1 cup milk
3 tablespoons butter
4 tablespoons flour
⅛ teaspoon nutmeg

Cook brussels sprouts in water, adding salt. Drain, reserving liquid. Put cooked sprouts in a greased casserole dish. Scatter ham over sprouts.

For white sauce, melt butter in a saucepan and add flour, stirring until smooth. Slowly add milk and 1 cup of reserved liquid from brussels sprouts. Add nutmeg.

Pour white sauce over ham. Top with ¼-inch tomato slices. Sprinkle with blend of Parmesan cheese and bread crumbs. Dot with butter. Bake 20 minutes at 375°. Serves 4.

Dave's note: For an especially attractive presentation, place the ingredients in four individual casserole dishes.

MRS. RAYMOND A. McCONN
SHREWSBURY, MASSACHUSETTS

Ham Chablis

3 ham steaks, ¾ inch thick
½ cup butter
⅓ cup flour
1 cup chablis
¼ cup brandy
2 egg yolks
1 cup heavy cream
1 cup mushrooms, drained
1 cup (4 ounces) St. Paulin cheese, shredded
1 tablespoon lemon juice
 salt and pepper

Sauté ham steaks in ¼ cup butter until lightly browned. Keep warm. In a saucepan, melt the other ¼ cup butter. Add mushrooms. Stir in flour, chablis, and brandy over a simmer, stirring constantly, for 5 minutes. Then in a bowl, mix egg yolks, cream, and cheese. Season to taste with salt and pepper. Add to brandy mixture. Place ham steaks on a platter and spoon the sauce evenly over them. Serve garnished with peas. Should serve 6.

Dave's note: St. Paulin cheese is similar to Port Salut. Dish has a wine taste.

PEG BIANCHI
FRAMINGHAM, MASSACHUSETTS

French-Fried Ham

This recipe, from my ninety-nine-year-old mother, originated in Philadelphia about seventy years ago. Through the years, my children have brought their families home for Mom's ham. Now, each Christmas day finds everyone traditionally at Grandma's for dinner.

My family has grown to twenty-five, the ham to twenty pounds, and my love for doing it all, immeasurable.

4 slices ham

Coating:

2 cups bread crumbs
½ teaspoon oregano
1 teaspoon baking powder
2 tablespoons Parmesan cheese, grated
2 eggs, slightly beaten with 2 tablespoons water

Mix coating dry ingredients well. Cut ham into serving sections. Dip each piece in egg, then in bread crumbs, and again in egg and crumbs. Let dry for an hour or so. Deep fry in hot fat until golden brown and drain on paper towels. Enjoy! Serves up to 8—about 8 sticks per ham slice, 4 sticks per person.

Dave's note: If ham is salty, soak in milk for an hour. Bite-sized strips would make a great hors d'oeuvre.

CLAIRE SINGER
LEBANON, PENNSYLVANIA

Schnitz und Knepp

Schnitz und Knepp is a very old Pennsylvania Dutch dish really used by the Amish and others. Of course, today one would call them dumplings.

1 quart dried apples
3 pounds ham
2 tablespoons brown sugar

Wash dried apples and cover with water to soak overnight. In the morning, put ham in a large pot, cover with water, and cook for 2½ hours. Then add apples and sugar; cook for another ½ hour.

Knepp:

2 cups flour
4 teaspoons baking powder
 salt and pepper
3 tablespoons oil or butter
1 beaten egg
 enough milk to make moist, stiff batter

Combine all ingredients, then drop by spoonful into hot liquid. Cover kettle tightly. Cook for 15 minutes in pot with ham. Serve on a large platter. Serves 6.

Dave's note: A little heavier than dumplings but a really nice taste.

EMILY LIBHART
MARIETTA, PENNSYLVANIA

Ham Steak à la Rosie

This recipe has been in our family for about fifty years. It came from my Aunt Rose from Vermont.

1 center-cut ham steak, about 1-inch thick
 softened butter
¼ cup peanut butter
¼ cup seedless raisins, finely ground
3 or 4 cloves
½ cup bread crumbs
1 cup milk

Rub ham steak on both sides with softened butter and place in a baking pan. Cream together peanut butter and raisins and spread over steak. Stud steak with a few cloves and sprinkle with bread crumbs over all. Pour milk in pan and bake at 400° for 15 minutes, basting at 4-minute intervals. Serves 2 to 4.

Dave's note: A great combination, especially with crunchy peanut butter.

MARION CASSIDY
EAST BRAINTREE, MASSACHUSETTS

Mom's Famous Chopped Ham

I have been making chopped ham for well over forty years. And to put it on paper and make a recipe of it was a riot. I'm of the old school—a bunch of this and that and no measuring involved, only hands. No one, only my close family, ever knew it was made of Spam. I ground it for wakes and weddings and any other get-together where sandwiches were served. In fact, friends would rather have chopped ham than cake. People have offered to buy a ham if I will prepare them a bowl of chopped ham. Little did they know the contents.

1 can Spam
3 stalks celery
1 medium onion
1 green pepper
4 tablespoons mayonnaise
¼ teaspoon black pepper

Put Spam, celery, onion, and green pepper through a meat grinder. Add mayonnaise and pepper and mix well. Serve in sandwiches or finger rolls. Delicious! Serves 2 to 4. Double or triple for parties or family gatherings.

Dave's note: Don't turn your nose up at the Spam. This recipe is flavorful.

MRS. PAULINE McKEE
WEST LYNN, MASSACHUSETTS

Hula Ham

1   slice ham, ½ inch thick
6   slices canned pineapple
12 pieces canned sweet potato
2   tablespoons butter
1¼ cups pineapple juice

Put ham slice on the bottom of an ovenproof casserole dish. Overlap slices of pineapple on top of ham. Tuck pieces of sweet potato in and around pineapple and ham. Dot everything with butter and pour in juice. Cover and bake 40 minutes at 350°. Ten minutes before it is done, remove cover and let contents brown but do not let dry out. Serves 4.

Dave's note: When you have only time to open cans, this is a good recipe. The juice does sweeten the ham. One flavor complements another.

ELEANOR WILSON
BOOTHBAY, MAINE

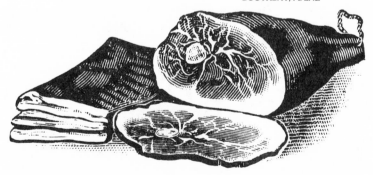

A *couple of years ago at a ski chalet in Vermont, I was asked to prepare a New Year's Day dinner. When I remarked that it would probably be a turkey, another guest, who had been born and raised in Pennsylvania Dutch country, quickly remonstrated (don't get to use that word too often), "Poultry roots backward, pigs root forward. Which is the way to look on New Year's Day?"*

I roasted a fresh ham. It was delicious, but if I remember correctly, I had a lousy year.

It's a constant source of amazement to me the numerous and weird fallacies that people have about pork.

"It's hard to digest."

"It always dries out in the cooking."

"It's plebeian—you can't do anything fancy with it."

"It actually has no real flavor."

Bunk! While it is true that undercooked pork can do quite a job on your digestive system, pork done correctly can be stomached far more easily than that steak you relish. Nor does pork dry out by itself—you let it happen. As for a crown roast of pork with the fancy top and filled with a succulent stuffing—it's a definite ooher and aaher. And if it's flavor you're looking for, follow these recipes.
—Dave

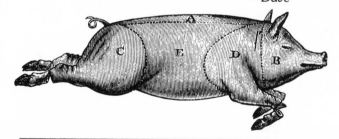

Pork

Pork Pie

2 pounds ground pork
2 pounds ground beef
  water
1 medium onion, chopped
  salt and pepper to taste
4 medium potatoes, cooked and
  mashed
1 teaspoon cloves
1 teaspoon cinnamon
3 two-crust 9-inch pie crusts

Line 3 9-inch pie plates with dough. Cook meat, being sure to cook pork thoroughly. Add enough water to cover. Add onion, salt, and pepper. Cook for at least 45 minutes. Add potatoes and spices and mix. Divide among 3 pie plates and top each with pie crust. Bake at 400° for about 30 to 35 minutes, or until well done. Serves 6 to 8.

Dave's note: This is quite easy to make and freezes up very handily.

NORMA H. DAY
PROVIDENCE, RHODE ISLAND

Seven-Layer Dinner

I could give you a fancy story about the recipe, but then that wouldn't be a true story. We are interested in one-dish meals because we have a card club and like to have meals that can either be prepared ahead or don't take up a lot of time.

4 or 5 potatoes, sliced
4 onions, sliced
3 or 4 carrots, sliced
¼ cup rice
1 can peas, with juice
5 or 6 pork loin chops
1 can tomato soup, diluted

Place potatoes in a 9-inch casserole dish in a layer (about 2 inches deep). Add a layer of onions and a layer of carrots. Sprinkle with rice. Add peas. Add layer of pork chops. Pour tomato soup over the top. Bake at 350° for 2 hours. Keep cover on for the first 1½ hours, and take cover off for the last ½ hour. Serves 4.

GERALDINE FUHRMAN
HANOVER, PENNSYLVANIA

Pork Pie Tourtières

  pastry for 2 2-crust pies
1 pound ground pork
1 pound ground beef
1 small onion, chopped
1 clove garlic
1 teaspoon cloves
1 teaspoon cinnamon
1 teaspoon salt
¼ teaspoon pepper
½ cup boiling water
  cream

Combine meats, onion, garlic, and spices in a large cast-iron or other heavy frying pan. Add boiling water and cook slowly, stirring constantly, until the meat loses its pink color. Spread the mixture into 2 uncooked pie shells and top with pie dough. Seal edges and prick crust. Brush top crust with cream. Bake at 450° for ½ hour. Serve piping hot, or keep in refrigerator until ready to reheat. These pies aquire more flavor when reheated. Serves 4.

Dave's note: Learn how to pronounce tourtières with a true French accent. You'll really impress your guests.

MRS. JESSICA ZABOKOFF
HANOVER, MASSACHUSETTS

Calavacita

The following recipe was handed down to me from my mother. It's an authentic home-cooked Mexican recipe. There is no question that both Spanish and Mexican-Indian influences served to create this dish. The beauty of it is that it is fast and simple to make, and of course, dee-lishous.

1½ pounds pork cutlets
    vegetable or olive oil
3   medium zucchini
1½ cups crushed tomatoes
    salt and pepper to taste
1   heaping teaspoon ground cumin
    seed
2   cloves garlic, crushed and minced
1   10½-ounce can whole kernel corn

Brown pork in a large frying pan with just enough vegetable or olive oil to cover bottom of pan. Then remove cutlets from pan. Add zucchini cut in 1-inch cubes, and cook until tender (approximately 5 to 10 minutes). Add tomatoes and spices, cooking slowly for 20 minutes. Add pork and corn, and cook slowly for another 10 minutes, or until pork cutlets are tender. Serves 4.

Dave's note: Add less cumin seed if you wish to save your taste buds. Cumin can be very spicy, so be careful.

GLORIA VALDEZ FERRINI
BELMONT, MASSACHUSETTS

Saucy Pork Chops

This is an old Macon, Georgia, recipe given to me by my boss' wife's mother, thirty years ago.

4   pork shoulder steaks
2   tablespoons fat
1   cup brown rice
1½ cups water
1   1-pound can tomatoes
1   green pepper, finely chopped
½   cup onion, finely chopped
2   garlic cloves, finely chopped
2   teaspoons salt
½   teaspoon pepper

Brown chops thoroughly in hot fat in a skillet. Remove steaks and sauté washed rice for about 5 minutes until delicately brown, stirring constantly. Add water, vegetables, and seasonings. Place steaks on top. Cover and cook over low heat for 35 to 45 minutes. Serves 4 people or 2 gluttons.

HAZEL FOLEY McCANN
WORCESTER, MASSACHUSETTS

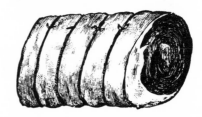

Tahitian Pork

3 tablespoons cornstarch
2 tablespoons soy sauce
2 pounds lean pork, cubed
1 tablespoon vegetable oil
1 20-ounce can pineapple chunks
⅓ cup vinegar
¼ cup brown sugar, firmly packed
1 teaspoon garlic salt
½ head cabbage, finely shredded, or
    fresh pineapple shell

Combine 2 tablespoons cornstarch and soy sauce. Toss with meat until all pieces are coated. Brown meat in hot oil; drain. Drain pineapple, reserving syrup. Place meat in a saucepan and add syrup, vinegar, brown sugar, and garlic salt. Bring to a boil; reduce heat and simmer, covered, for 45 minutes. Dissolve 1 tablespoon cornstarch in water and add to meat. Cook, stirring constantly, until sauce is thickened and translucent. Add pineapple and heat mixture until warm. Serve on bed of shredded cabbage or in a fresh pineapple shell. Serves 4.

Dave's note: Chunks of pork, floating in a thick, tangy sauce and presented in a pineapple shell, make this a festive meal. Terrific taste.

JESSICA ZABOKOFF
HANOVER, MASSACHUSETTS

Breaded Pork Chops

The breaded pork chop idea came about in my family as a result of being tired of tasting chops that were too tough. After some experimentation, we came up with this delicious method, which makes them turn out very tender. No more shoe leather.

6 thin pork chops
    salt and pepper
    Italian bread crumbs
1 egg, beaten
2 tablespoons water

Sprinkle pork chops with salt and pepper. Roll in Italian bread crumbs. Dip in slightly beaten egg, which has been seasoned and diluted with 2 tablespoons water. Roll in the crumbs again. Brown in skillet on both sides Set aside and make gravy.

Gravy:

2 tablespoons butter
½ clove garlic, crushed
2 tablespoons flour
1 cup canned bouillon (or 2 bouillon
    cubes dissolved in 1 cup water)
    salt, pepper, dill, oregano, and basil
    to taste
    sherry

Melt butter in a skillet. Add garlic and sauté lightly. Stir in flour until blended. Stir in bouillon. Permit gravy to reach the boiling point, stirring constantly. Season lightly with salt, pepper, dill, basil, oregano, and sherry. Place cooked chops in gravy. Cover and simmer slowly for 1 hour. Serves 6.

Dave's note: It is important to cook these thin chops slowly so that they do not get overcooked and dried out.

SUSAN CAMPBELL BONNETT
HINSDALE, NEW HAMPSHIRE

Cantonese Pork Chops

This pork chop has been around for some time. My children and grandchildren like their pork chops dressed up. They are real gourmet cooks. All chefs, no busboys.

6   pork chops
    butter or oil
1   8-ounce bottle sweet-and-sour sauce
1   14-ounce can pineapple chunks, drained
½   pound snow peas
¼   cup water chestnuts, sliced
1   medium tomato, cut in wedges

Brown meat in butter or oil; add sweet-and-sour sauce. Cover and simmer until meat is tender (amount of cooking time depends upon thickness of pork chops). Add pineapple, snow peas, and water chestnuts. Cover and simmer until vegetables are tender though still crisp. Add tomato and heat. Arrange meat, fruit, and vegetables on a serving platter. Thicken sauce with cornstarch if desired. Serves 6.

Dave's note: Served on a bed of rice, this makes a colorful dish.

HAZEL W. BALDWIN
ABERDEEN, MARYLAND

Pork Chop and Rice Casserole

This is one of my favorite casseroles. The rice has such a good flavor that my husband and I always take second helpings. I usually get thinnish rib pork chops, counting on two per person, or even three if the chops are very thin.

4   to 6 thin rib pork chops
    garlic powder
    salt
    pepper
    oregano
1   tablespoon bacon fat
2   teaspoons beef bouillon grains or 2 bouillon cubes
2   cups hot water
1   cup converted rice

Preheat oven to 325°. Sprinkle garlic powder, salt, pepper, and oregano on both sides of chops. Brown chops in a skillet in bacon fat. Mix bouillon grains (or cubes) in hot water. Pour into the skillet when chops are browned, and immediately put entire contents of pan into a casserole dish. Add rice. The measure of bouillon to rice should always be 2 to 1. Cover and bake for 1 hour. If water boils away, add more water as necessary. Serves 4.

Dave's note: This has a great flavor and is an easy way to prepare a complete meal in one. All that is needed is a vegetable and perhaps a salad.

MRS. EDNA CRAIG
BYESVILLE, OHIO

A Danish West Indian Dish

This dish may have originated in the West Indies by the Danish settlers, but that's just a guess. I wish I knew more about it.

2 pounds lean pork, cut in 1-inch cubes
seasoned flour
2 tablespoons butter
2 onions, chopped
1 green pepper, chopped
pepper
2 cups water
salt
1 tablespoon curry powder

Dredge pork cubes in seasoned flour and brown in butter in a skillet. Add chopped onions and pepper, and let simmer for 5 minutes. Add water, salt, and curry powder and let simmer, covered, for about 1½ hours. Serves 4 to 6.

To serve, form a ring of fluffy mashed potatoes on a warm platter with the meat in the center.

Dave's note: This dish has a very subtle Middle-Eastern flair to it.

HAZEL WINE
CHARLOTTESVILLE, VIRGINIA

Baked Pork Chops Supreme

oil
5 or 6 thick pork chops
1 can tomato soup, undiluted
2 large onions, shredded
1 green pepper, cut in 1-inch strips
¼ teaspoon basil
½ teaspoon salt
1 large can stewed tomatoes
1 medium can mushrooms

2 stalks celery, cut in 1-inch pieces
dash garlic powder
3 bay leaves
¼ teaspoon pepper

Preheat oven to 325°. Cover the bottom of a skillet with a thin coating of oil. Over low to medium heat, brown pork chops for 12 to 15 minutes on each side. Remove from the skillet and drain on paper towels. Place in 2 3-quart casserole dishes and add all other ingredients. Bake uncovered for approximately 1½ hours, until chops are very soft. Test with fork. If sauce gets too thick while baking, add additional diluted tomato soup to cover chops. This will keep sauce a medium-to-thick consistency. May be served from casserole dish. Serves 4 to 6.

Dave's note: This is a flavorful and complete dish.

MAY T. MURPHY
ROCKLAND, MASSACHUSETTS

Barbecue Pork with Rice

½ cup celery, diced
1 large onion, diced
½ pound cooked pork, cubed
2 tablespoons butter or margarine
1 can mushrooms, drained (reserve liquid)
½ cup chili sauce
1 teaspoon prepared mustard
dash hot pepper sauce
2 cups instant rice

Brown celery, onions, and pork in butter or margarine. Add enough water to mushroom liquid to make 2 cups liquid. Add liquid to pork mixture; then add other ingredients. Bring to a boil; then simmer 5 minutes. Fluff with a fork and serve. Serves 2.

Dave's note: You'd be surprised what a little mustard can do for pork!

BETTY LATIMER
FREDERICKSBURG, VIRGINIA

Aunt Louisa's German Hot Potato Allsaise-Louraine Salad with Pork Chops

Grandmother's German confuses me sometimes, but she spells Alsace-Lorraine this way. Louisa Catherine Neas was "Grandmother" to us children but Aunt Louisa to everybody else and the only one of her family born in Boston (in 1847) in a house torn down to start the building of Boston City Hospital. The family had left Alsace for Le Havre in 1840 and sailed from there bound for New York, but a thunderstorm smashed the mast, and they were lucky to reach Boston.

I have never seen a recipe like this one *anywhere* else. There are plenty of German salads around but never one where hot potatoes are put on crisp lettuce and pork juices are the hot dressing. It's not hard to make, and it's a great family meal.

1 small head crisp lettuce
4 to 6 pork chops, about 1 inch thick
½ to ¾ cup vinegar
6 medium potatoes
2 medium or 1 large onion, peeled
   and sliced thinly into rings
   salt and pepper to taste
½ to ¾ cup milk

Tear lettuce into bite-sized pieces and put in a large, chilled bowl. Put into the refrigerator until ready for use. Snip excess fat off chops, then cut fat into very small pieces. Put these bits of fat into a large skillet. Add 2 tablespoons of water and place over heat. As fat is rendered, pour it off, so that bits will brown. When brown, remove bits and set aside. Pour all the grease out of pan and reserve. Put pork chops in pan and cover, after adding a little water to the pan so that chops steam through on both sides. Cook for approximately 10 minutes. To be sure they're ready, cut chops down beside bone: They must be steamed thoroughly so that no red juice is visible. Pour off juices and add to reserved fat. Uncover the pan and brown chops on both sides. (This method cooks chops through yet doesn't dry them out.) When chops are browned, remove them to a warm platter and place in oven. Loosen any pieces stuck to pan and add reserved fat to oils in pan. Add vinegar and bring to a boil. Turn burner off and reheat dressing when ready.

To make the salad, check the potatoes: if they're old, peel them; if new, leave washed skins on. Boil potatoes in salted water until they break easily with a fork. Then place hot potatoes on top of lettuce and break with a fork into bite-size pieces. Lay onion rings over potatoes. Sprinkle with salt and pepper. Bring juices in pan to a boil. Pour milk over salad. (It helps to make the juices stick together instead of sinking to the bottom.) Then pour the boiling juices from the pan over the salad, and sprinkle with bits of pork fat. Toss salad. Take pork chops out of oven and eat. Serves 4. Keep the family waiting but not the meal.

NICHOLAS J. MATHER
EAST PEPPERELL, MASSACHUSETTS

Pork Chops in Apple Sauce

4 lean pork chops
¼ pound butter, melted
½ cup onions, diced
3 pieces toast, diced
3 apples, diced and unpeeled
1 16-ounce jar applesauce
  dash nutmeg
3 pinches pepper
½ cup apple juice or dry sherry

Preheat oven to 400°. Place chops in a roasting pan and cover with melted butter. Add onions, toast, apples, applesauce, nutmeg, pepper, and wine. Bake for ½ hour. Reduce temperature to 300° and bake for ½ hour more. Serves 4. Note: Chops may be browned first if desired.

Dave's note: If you wish to prepare this dish way before the baking time, it can be frozen with no difficulty.

MRS. JOSEPH W. LUKIS
WALPOLE, MASSACHUSETTS

Rouladen mit Sausage with Beer Sauce

½ pound sausage meat
2 tablespoons onions, chopped
¼ cup dry bread crumbs
2 pounds beef, cut into 8 thin slices
  salt and pepper
8 slices bacon
2 tablespoons butter
6 small white onions, halved
¼ cup flour
2 cans beer
2 cubes beef bouillon
1 tablespoon button mushrooms, stemmed
2 tablespoons parsley, chopped

Combine sausage, onions, and crumbs. Blend well. Pound beef slices until very thin. Sprinkle beef with salt and pepper, and divide sausage meat equally between beef slices. Roll up each sausage together with the beef slice. Then wrap a bacon slice around each roll. Fasten with skewers. Brown rolls in butter in a Dutch oven. Add small white onions and brown. Meanwhile mix flour and ½ cup beer. Pour mixture over meat and add remaining beer. Add beef bouillon and stir to blend. Cover and simmer over low heat for 1½ hours, or until beef is tender. Add mushrooms and parsley and simmer for another 15 minutes. To serve, remove meat rolls to a platter lined with hot cooked noodles. Skim excess fat from top of gravy. Spoon gravy over meat rolls. Serves 8.

For convenience, this entree can be prepared ahead and frozen in foil. Allow two hours at 350° to heat. If completely thawed, allow 45 minutes.

DAVE

Herbed Pork Terrine

1   pound lean pork, ground
½   pound veal, ground
4   ounces pork fat, ground
¾   cup onion, chopped
2   cloves garlic, minced
3   tablespoons butter
1½   cups fresh spinach, washed and
     chopped
3   tablespoons brandy
1   egg, beaten
1   teaspoon basil
1   teaspoon rosemary
1   teaspoon thyme
1½   teaspoons salt
½   teaspoon fennel seeds, crushed
¼   teaspoon freshly ground black
     pepper
½   to ¾ pound bacon
3   hard-boiled eggs

Mix pork, veal, and pork fat together thoroughly. Sauté onion and garlic in butter over medium heat for several minutes. Add spinach and cook an additional minute. Add to meats and mix well. Stir in brandy, beaten egg, and seasonings. Line loaf pan with bacon width-wise, leaving ends to wrap over top. Pour in ½ the meat mixture. Arrange hard-boiled eggs in a row down the center. Add remaining meat mixture. Cover with the bacon. Rap sharply on counter to dispel air holes. Cover with aluminum foil. Set pan in roasting pan filled with boiling water to reach halfway up side of pan. Bake at 350° for 90 minutes. Remove and let cool for 15 minutes. Pour off excess fat. Cover with foil and refrigerate overnight. Serves 2 to 4.

DAVE

Corned Fresh Shoulder

My mother used this recipe for years, and she just passed away three years ago at the age of ninety.

1   fresh shoulder
     coarse salt (amount depends on
     size of crock)
     water
1   raw potato
1   cup brown sugar
¼   cup vinegar
     small red peppers (optional)
1   clove garlic
1   small pickling pepper

In a crock, or equivalent, place shoulder and cover with water to determine quantity. Remove shoulder and place potato in water. Add coarse salt to water until potato floats. When potato floats, remove it and add brown sugar, vinegar, garlic, and pepper. Return shoulder to the mixture with a small saucer underneath shoulder and a very clean washed stone on top to keep meat under water. Cure for 4 to 7 days. Cook as for boiled dinner.

Dave's note: Very good brine. And the raw potato really does work. Important: Have the meat sit for 4 to 7 days in a cool place; beware of spoilage on hot summer days.

PEARL FOULIS
TAUNTON, MASSACHUSETTS

So many good cooks sing the praises of veal, who am I to do otherwise? After all, what other meat has such a distinctive flavor, yet manages with ease to take on different taste when prepared in some exotic recipe? There's no doubt in my mind of the versatility of veal—but only when the veal is done just right. Tenderizing, coating (if necessary), frying, garnishing are steps that have to be done perfectly in order to end up with something superlative.

My own greatest veal experience began with a charcoal broiled veal steak I had one summer's night years ago at a Cape Cod restaurant. My eyes became glazed. I was light-headed yet determined to return for more of the same, if I could negotiate a loan. By the time I got the loot together, the restaurant was out of business.

If you can scrape up the cash or get a co-signer, here are some nice ideas.
--Dave

Veal

Veal a la Ricci

This is a great dish to cook ahead. The cutlets can be cooked several days before serving. And the whole thing takes a minimal amount of preparation time. It is a lovely dish, and I am often asked for the recipe.

2 eggs, beaten
4 veal cutlets
1 cup bread crumbs
¼ cup olive oil
1 can condensed golden mushroom soup
½ cup sherry
1 can mushroom caps, drained
1 cup muenster cheese, grated
lemon slices

Dip veal cutlets into an egg batter, then into a seasoned bread crumb mixture. Sauté cutlets in olive oil until browned. Place cutlets in a shallow baking dish. Cover with undiluted mushroom soup. In a small frying pan, sauté mushrooms. Add sherry and let the sherry cook for 3 to 5 minutes. Pour sautéed mushrooms and sherry over cutlets and sprinkle cheese over top. Garnish with thin lemon slices. Cover with foil and bake 30 minutes at 350°. Serves 4.

Dave's note: An ideal dish for the busy person who likes to entertain and lives alone. Great for company — or eat them by yourself, one by one.

EILEEN RICCI
STOUGHTON, MASSACHUSETTS

Veal That's Real

2 pounds veal, thinly sliced
1 package onion sauce mix
¼ pound butter or margarine
½ cup water
¼ cup dry white wine
½ teaspoon salt
1 teaspoon parsley, chopped
1 teaspoon lemon juice
1 or 2 small cans mushrooms

Cut veal into strips. Place veal and sauce mix in a paper bag and shake well. Brown veal in butter; add water, wine, and salt. Simmer for 10 minutes. Stir in lemon juice, parsley, and mushrooms. Serves 6.

Dave's note: Two tablespoons of fresh, chopped parsley will make this even better.

MS. RUTH J. ALEXANDER
WORCESTER, MASSACHUSETTS

Veal Casserole

1½ to 2 pounds veal, cut in thin 1-inch cubes
½ cup seasoned flour
egg wash (1 egg, 1 tablespoon oil, ¼ cup milk, ½ teaspoon each salt and pepper)
fine bread crumbs
Parmesan cheese, grated (optional)
2 tablespoons oil
2 cups spaghetti sauce and/or tomato sauce

Dip veal in flour, then egg wash, and then bread crumbs. Put veal in an electric frying pan at about 350° and brown on both sides in oil. After thoroughly browned, pour spaghetti sauce and/or tomato sauce over all and simmer an hour or longer over low heat until ready to serve. More sauce can be added if necessary. Pour a little Parmesan cheese over meat while cooking if desired. A small can of mushrooms may be added. Very good served with rice. Serves 6.

Dave's note: I'd add a little chopped parsley and oregano to this.

NELLIE DOUGLASS

Veal Cutlets à la Marsala

1½ pounds veal cutlets, ⅜ inch thick
1 teaspoon salt
½ teaspoon freshly ground black pepper
½ cup flour
2 tablespoons butter
3 tablespoons olive oil
½ cup marsala wine
¼ cup chicken stock
2 cups mushrooms, thickly sliced
2 tablespoons butter

Combine all ingredients, except stock. Cover and simmer for 15 minutes, basting now and then. Transfer the

veal to a heated platter. Add stock to the sauce and boil briskly, stirring constantly. When reduced to syrup, remove from heat and pour over veal. Serve immediately. Serves 4.

Dave's note: Absolutely delicious.

DOT ALEXANDER
TOPSFIELD, MASSACHUSETTS

Veal Bread

2 pounds veal
4 tablespoons flour
½ cup shortening
1 medium onion, chopped
1 cup canned tomatoes
1½ cups water
1 medium green pepper, chopped
1 sprig thyme
1 bay leaf
1 tablespoon parsley

Cut veal in pieces and fry in shortening. Remove meat and make a gravy by stirring in flour. Add onion and tomatoes and simmer for a few minutes. Then add meat and all other ingredients. Cook until meat is tender or about 1½ hours. You might have to add a little water from time to time. Serve over rice. Serves 4.

Dave's note: Nice combination of flavors.

MARGARET SMITH
ELIOT, MAINE

Veal Francoise

One day I started out making Veal Parmigiana because I had a frozen veal roast and wanted to use it up. I found to my surprise that the veal was so tender and tasty that I felt the Parmigiana cheese would mask the flavor and decided to take a recipe and change it to suit my purposes. I slice the veal roast while it's still partially frozen. It's easier to slice thinner.

1½ pound veal roast (partly frozen is easier to slice)
1½ to 2 tablespoons butter
1 medium onion, sliced
½ pound mushrooms, sliced
1 tablespoon parsley, chopped
1 tablespoon flour
1 egg
3 tablespoons water
¼ cup white wine
¾ cup sour cream
½ teaspoon salt
⅛ teaspoon freshly ground pepper

Slice veal thinly and then pound with a tenderizing hammer. Dip each slice first in egg beaten with a little water, then in flour, then back in egg mixture, and then in bread crumbs. Brown the cutlets in butter and remove to an ovenproof dish. Add onion and mushrooms to skillet, stir, and sauté lightly. Remove the skillet from the heat, and slowly stir in remaining ingredients. Pour the sauce over the meat. Cover and bake at 250° for 1 hour, or until done. Serves 4.

Dave's note: Sneak a little extra butter in.

FRANCES M. RICHARDSON
SOUTH EASTON, MASSACHUSETTS

Veal Deluxe

Several years ago, my husband and I were traveling through the South. We were invited to the house of a southern lady, a gourmet cook, who served this to us for dinner. I asked her to share her recipe with me, hence the following.

8 boneless veal cutlets, pounded thin
⅔ cup dry sherry
2 tablespoons olive oil
4 tablespoons margarine
¾ cup mushrooms, sliced
1 ¾-ounce envelope brown gravy mix

Marinate veal in sherry for 2 hours. Pour off sherry and reserve. Pat meat dry with towels and brown in oil and 2 tablespoons margarine. Set aside. In remaining margarine, saute mushrooms. Place gravy mix in a bowl; add reserved sherry and enough water to make 1 cup liquid, and stir into gravy mix. Combine mushrooms and veal. Pour gravy over meat, cover, and simmer meat for 30 to 45 minutes, until veal is tender. Serves 6 to 8.

HELEN TARUTZ
WEST NEWTON, MASSACHUSETTS

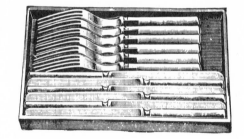

Layered Meat
and Mushroom Loaf

2 cups soft bread crumbs
½ cup milk
½ cup mushroom liquid
1 egg
2 tablespoons parsley, finely chopped
2 tablespoons green pepper, finely chopped
1 teaspoon onion, finely chopped
½ teaspoon poultry seasoning
¼ teaspoon pepper
¾ teaspoon salt
1 pound veal
1 4-ounce can mushrooms, sliced and drained
1 1-pound ham
½ teaspoon red vegetable color (optional)

Mix together bread crumbs, milk, and mushroom liquid. Beat lightly and add egg. Then add parsley, green pepper, and onion, together with poultry seasoning and salt and pepper.

Grind veal and add mushrooms to it. Separately, grind the ham. Add vegetable color, if desired.

Divide the bread mixture into two parts; add ½ to ham and ½ to veal. Mix each one thoroughly. Pack veal mixture into a greased loaf pan, 5½ x 9½ inches. Pack ham mixture firmly on top of the veal. Bake at 350° for 1 hour. Serve hot or cold. Serves 6 to 8.

Dave's note: Be sure to pack meat firmly. Rap pan several times to eliminate air holes.

E. THOMAS
SOLON, OHIO

Veal Paprika

I have had this recipe over twenty-five years. Originally a good friend of Hungarian descent gave the recipe to me and assisted with the first preparation. Much to my family's delight, I then prepared veal for every Sunday dinner. Later when they referred to all Sundays as "Poppy-kosh" day, I decided it was time to vary the menu. However, veal paprika is still a great favorite, whenever veal prices fit into the budget.

4 tablespoons shortening or butter
1 clove garlic, halved
1 egg
1 tablespoon water
1½ teaspoons salt
1½ pounds veal, cut in 2-inch cubes
⅔ cup fine bread crumbs
½ cup water
1 cup sour cream
1 tablespoon paprika

Heat shortening, fry garlic, and remove. Beat egg and add 1 tablespoon water and salt. Dip veal into egg mixture and then into crumbs. Add veal to a skillet and brown well. Add the ½ cup water and simmer over low heat for 1 hour. Add sour cream; do *not* stir. Add paprika, cover, and cook 15 minutes longer. Serve over noodles. Serves 4.

Dave's note: Might need some more water.

HELEN CRAM
TOEDO, OHIO

Veal Roll
with Mushroom Sauce

8 slices white bread
2 tablespoons butter or margarine
1 small onion, minced
3 teaspoons celery, chopped
¼ teaspoon thyme
   salt and pepper
   water
2 pounds veal cutlet, cut ½ inch thick
3 tablespoons seasoned flour
3 tablespoons shortening
1 10½-ounce can condensed
   mushroom soup
½ cup milk

Shred bread with a fork, discarding crusts. Melt butter or margarine in a skillet, add onion and celery, and cook until tender. Combine with bread crumbs, thyme, salt, and pepper to taste. Moisten with a little water. Lay veal out flat, sprinkle with a little salt and pepper, and spread with stuffing. Roll veal up and secure with toothpicks. Dredge with flour and brown on all sides in hot fat. Dilute soup with milk and pour over veal. Cover and cook over medium heat for 45 minutes or until tender. Serves 6.

Dave's note: Add ¾ cup white wine and ¾ cup water with a little flour (enough to thicken) and simmer until thick, instead of 1½ cups of water.

BEA FERRO

The lamb dishes for this section were really fun to make. They all had different qualities about them.

Lamb is truly an overlooked and misunderstood meat. Bring lamb out on the table where it belongs rather than hiding it away. It suffers from the same problem that turkey does — lamb is generally eaten only in February as turkey is generally eaten only in November.

The flavors that were evidenced in this section warrant lamb as a commodity in your household at least once a month. If, of course, you win at poker.

One last thought. If you eat overcooked lamb, it's a lot like eating a cold bruised peach — good, but it could be better. Think pink! — Dave

Lamb

Lamb Cacciatore

2½ pounds lamb shoulder, cubed
2 tablespoons olive oil (or vegetable oil)
¾ teaspoon salt
   pinch pepper
½ teaspoon rosemary
1 tablespoon flour
1 clove garlic, minced
½ cup wine vinegar
1½ cups water or stock
   parsley, minced

Trim fat from meat and wash meat. Dry with paper towel. Brown in hot oil. Season with salt, pepper, and herbs. Sprinkle with flour and continue to brown. Add garlic, wine vinegar, and stock, stirring to scrape brown crumbs from bottom of pan. Lower heat and cover pan. Let simmer gently until lamb is tender and gravy has thickened slightly, about 45 minutes to 1 hour. Add more water as necessary to keep a light gravy around meat as it cooks. Serve topped with parsley. Serves 6 to 8.

Dave's note: That rich brown sauce makes this a winner.

RUTH RINALDI
PROVIDENCE, RHODE ISLAND

Kibbi

This is a Lebanese recipe and has been popular in my grandmother's family since I was a little girl.

2 cups lean lamb or beef, put through grinder
1 onion
1 cup bulgur wheat, washed and drained
1 teaspoon salt
½ teaspoon freshly ground pepper
   allspice and cinnamon (optional)
½ cup pine nuts or walnuts

Grind meat and onion together twice. Add drained wheat and spices and grind again. Pat half of the mixture into a baking pan, making a layer about ½ inch thick. Sprinkle with pine nuts or walnuts, then pat another layer of meat mixture on top. Keep hands wet to prevent mixture from sticking. Cut in diamonds. Spread with butter and bake at 425° for 20 or 30 minutes. Check halfway for doneness. Make as patties and fry like hamburgs, if desired, instead of baking. Serves 4.

Dave's note: If you've never used bulgur wheat before, consider it a permanent addition to your kitchen staples. It can be bought at most health food stores, if you can't find it at your local supermarket. The addition of allspice and cinnamon gives an extra dimension to the flavor of the lamb.

MRS. ADELE CHETTLEBURGH
WINGHAM, ONTARIO, CANADA

Baklava Stuffed with Lamb

2 pounds lamb, coarsely ground
4 tablespoons butter
¼ cup pine nuts
  salt
  pepper
1 medium onion, chopped
⅔ cup plain yogurt
  juice of 1 lemon
  baklava dough (phylo)
  rendered butter

In a frying pan, brown ground lamb, butter, pine nuts, salt, pepper, and onion. Let cool, then add yogurt and lemon juice. Mix well. Thaw baklava dough (available at most supermarkets). Cut dough in thirds, spread with heated rendered butter. Drop 1 tablespoons of meat onto dough and roll like a cigar, keeping ends tucked in. Place on baking sheet. Brush each with rendered butter. Bake at 350° for approximately 30 minutes, or until golden brown. Serves 4 to 6.

Dave's note: Spread phylo dough lavishly or at least generously with butter.

PEG BIANCHI
FRAMINGHAM, MASSACHUSETTS

Baked Lamb and Cabbage Norwegian

I got this recipe out of a newspaper about thirty-five years ago. I've made it for my family many times. It was one of our favorites. There was a little write-up in the paper about how this recipe was introduced at Fort Leonard Wood, Missouri, during the war. The enlisted men thought they did not like lamb. But after all excess fat was removed and the lamb was cooked the Norwegian way, they liked it.

3 pounds cabbage, sliced 1 inch thick
½ tablespoon flour
½ teaspoon salt
⅛ teaspoon pepper
½ teaspoon caraway seeds
5 pounds lamb shoulder

In a roasting pan put a layer of cabbage. Mix flour, salt, pepper, and use ⅓ of this mixture to dust lamb. Remove excess fat from lamb and cut into serving pieces. Cover cabbage layer with a layer of lamb. Dust again with flour, salt, pepper and caraway. Top with cabbage and a final layer of lamb, adding the last ⅓ of dusting mixture. Pour in boiling water to cover and bake at 375° for 2 hours. Serves 8 to 10.

FRANCES LEARY
WALTHAM, MASSACHUSETTS

Wine-Barbecued Lamb Chops

I found this recipe in my mother's handwritten recipes. We still use it.

½ cup salad oil
½ cup red wine
2 tablespoons onion, grated
1 garlic clove, slashed
1½ teaspoons salt
1 **teaspoon MSG (optional)**
   few drops hot pepper sauce
6 thick lamb chops

Make marinade by combining all ingredients except lamb chops in a bowl, mixing well. Pour over lamb chops in a shallow pan. Cover and store several hours (or overnight) in the refrigerator, turning chops occasionally. When ready to cook, remove chops from marinade, drain, and cook in preheated broiler 7 to 10 minutes on each side. Baste frequently with remaining marinade. Serves 6.

LESTER SHEPARD
WEST BRIDGEWATER, MASSACHUSETTS

Roast Lamb

1 5½-pound leg of lamb
1 teaspoon salt
½ teaspoon ginger
½ teaspoon thyme
½ teaspoon marjoram
1 clove garlic, minced
½ teaspoon pepper
1 bay leaf, crushed
½ teaspoon sage
1 tablespoon olive oil or salad oil

Wipe lamb with a damp cloth, then cut gashes ¼ inch long randomly over top and bottom surfaces of lamb. Combine all remaining ingredients except oil and rub mixture into meat, filling all the gashes completely. Coat lamb with oil. Roast it at 500° for 15 minutes, then reduce heat to 350° for remaining time. Serves 8 to 10.

Dave's note: Remaining time with lamb really varies. I like it pink in the middle.

"OLGIE"
ARLINGTON HEIGHTS, MASSACHUSETTS

Boiled Lamb with Dill Sauce
(Swedish)

This is an excellent recipe and has been successful in literally dozens of "amateur kitchens" for those of us who fancy ourselves "gourmets." It was a favorite of mine, growing up with Swedish parents, but was considered a most ordinary meal in the days of inexpensive food (some cuts of lamb as low as 10¢ a pound), Now, at prices far over $1.00 a pound, I have served it at dinner parties and have never heard of anyone disliking it.

2 pounds lamb shoulder, boned
1 quart boiling water
1 bay leaf
   dill sprigs
5 whole allspice
2 teaspoons salt
8 peppercorns

Dill sauce:

2 tablespoons butter or margarine
2 tablespoons flour
2 cups lamb stock

2 tablespoons chopped dill or dried dill weed
1 tablespoon white vinegar
2 teaspoons sugar
¼ **teaspoon salt**
2 egg yolks, beaten

Place meat in a saucepan and add boiling water. Bring to boil and skim surface until clear. Add all other ingredients (except dill sauce ingredients). Cover and simmer until meat is tender, about 1½ hours. Save stock for use in sauce. Slice meat and arrange slices on hot serving platter. Garnish with dill. Serve with dill sauce and small new or red boiled potatoes.

To make dill sauce, melt butter or margarine and blend in flour. Gradually stir in hot stock. Cook slowly, stirring until smooth and thick. Remove from heat and stir in dill, vinegar, sugar, and salt. Quickly stir in egg yolks and serve immediately. Serves 4 to 6.

Serve with aquavit (schnapps) and pilsner (if you dare); otherwise, a nice chablis goes well!. Note: veal may be substituted for lamb.

Dave's note: If you get nervous adding the egg yolks to the stock, don't. It merely cooks the egg yolks quickly and adds another color and taste to the dish.

BARBARA CARLSON
WESTON, MASSACHUSETTS

Super Lamb Shanks

Delicious with mashed potatoes or noodles. You can even substitute shoulder chops for lamb shanks.

4 meaty lamb shanks
1 large clove garlic
½ lemon
1 cup flour
1 teaspoon salt
½ teaspoon freshly ground pepper
½ cup salad oil
1 can condensed beef consommé, undiluted
1 cup water
½ cup vermouth
1 medium yellow onion, chopped
4 carrots, sliced in chunks
4 stalks celery, sliced in chunks

Rub lamb with garlic, make a few slashes in the lamb shanks, and then rub with lemon. Let stand for 10 minutes. Combine flour, salt, and pepper in a bag and shake to coat shanks one at a time. *Save flour.* Brown shanks in hot oil in a large, heavy skillet, then remove meat from pan. Add to pan 4 tablespoons flour and stir with a fork or wire whisk to brown. Add consomme, water, and vermouth, stirring and cooking until slightly thickened. Add onion.

Place shanks in a single layer in a baking dish and pour consomme mixture over them. Bake at 325°, uncovered, for 1½ hours, basting once in a while and adding more water if necessary. Turn shanks, add carrots and celery, and continue baking for 1 more hour. Serves 4.

Dave's note: You may want to remove the pan from heat while adding flour so you won't smell burning. Really lovely gravy.

ANNE R. JACOBSEN
SARANAC LAKE, NEW YORK

Syrian Green Beans with Lamb

(Lubey be-lahm)

1 pound lamb (forequarter)
2 medium onions, chopped
2 pounds green beans
1 cup tomato juice

Cut meat into 1-inch cubes and cook in a little water with onions until gold- en. Halve beans, add them to the meat mixture, and season to taste. Continue cooking, stirring often. When beans are tender, add tomato juice. Boil for another 10 minutes. Serve with boiled rice. Serves 6.

Dave's note: Add a little rosemary and a dash of salt and pepper.

JO MAURIN
LIVONIA, MICHIGAN

How many of us, I wonder, recoil, I mean really shudder, at the memories of that horrid phrase, "Eat your liver!"? So much antipathy is built up during our childhood for this much maligned viand that it carries right through our adult years. What a shame. Forget the low prices of liver, kidneys, hearts, and so forth. Forget their many health-giving qualities. When cooked right and with a little help from other tasty friends, these variety meats are delicious.

Recently, while conducting a cooking demonstration on the Queen Elizabeth II, *I decided to try an experiment. Now keep in mind that you can find something to eat twenty-four hours a day on this Queen of the Cunard Line. Can you imagine—folks getting back into line just to savor another German liver dumpling? I even used liver in several different (and disguised) ways and I didn't tell a single passenger just what I was cooking.*

Read on for more ways to add variety meats to your meals. —Dave

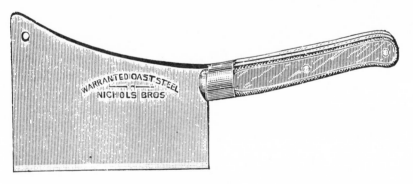

Variety Meats

Gizzard or Gizzardless Stew

2 tablespoons shortening
1 medium onion, diced
½ teaspoon salt
½ teaspoon black pepper
½ teaspoon paprika
½ to ¾ pound chicken gizzards, clean
  and chopped (for gizzardless stew,
  substitute beef or veal)
1 small can tomato paste
½ green pepper, chopped
1 small can whole mushrooms, pieces
  and stems

In a large skillet, melt shortening. Add onion, salt, pepper, and paprika. Cook until onions soften. Add gizzards and brown. Then add tomato paste and 3 cans of water. Add green pepper and mushrooms. Simmer gizzards for 2 to 3 hours, until tender. Serves 2 to 4.

Dave's note: Different and inexpensive. Has a strong tomato taste, which could be improved with a little chopped parsley, dried basil, or oregano.

R. J. (BOB) KAKOCZKI
WHITE CLOUD, MICHIGAN

Liver Patties

1 pound liver, beef or calves'
½ pound fresh pork
1 onion
2 potatoes
1 egg
1 tablespoon flour
4 tablespoons oil (for sautéing)

Put liver, pork, onion, and potatoes through food grinder. Add egg and flour. Form into patties and fry in hot oil. Delicious! (You can substitute bacon for the fresh pork.) Yields about 12 patties.

Dave's note: The mixture tends to be rather moist. You could add a bit more flour. Savory.

MRS. ALBIN GAHN
CHEBOYGAN, MICHIGAN

Baby Beef Liver, Sicilian Style

I must tell you from the beginning. We arrived in Newburyport in 1920. In 1923 we bought a house with a store attached. We eventually turned the store into a deli, where I could cook things and sell them. This liver recipe made a hit. My friends say that the liver tastes more like steak when cooked this way.

1 pound baby beef liver, freshly sliced
  wheat germ
3 tablespoons oil
1 large onion, sliced
2 cloves garlic
3 green peppers, sliced
  salt, pepper, and oregano
½ cup wine vinegar

Wash and dry liver and cut in serving pieces. Heat oil in a frying pan. Dip liver in wheat germ, then brown both sides quickly in hot oil. Remove liver from pan. Fry onion, garlic, and peppers in the same pan. When cooked, return liver to pan with vegetables. Add seasonings and vinegar, cover tightly, and continue to cook for about 5 more minutes. Serve with salad and Italian bread. Serves 4.

Dave's note: Good strong flavor.

MRS. JENNIE SANTORO
NEWBURYPORT, MASSACHUSETTS

Chopped Liver, Hungarian Style

I wish I had called this recipe "Lever-postej," pronounced "lever post I," which is the Danish name for it. My husband's mother brought the recipe with her (in her head) when she came to this country as a young woman from Denmark. As she was a person who could never tell you how she made a thing—she would always say "a little of this, a few of that"—it was hard for me to get specific measurements. But a few years ago, we attended an open house at a class reunion where this delightful appetizer was served. It looked and tasted exactly like Mumsie's, and the hostess kindly gave me the recipe. She had been a Hungarian refugee of World War II, and it was her mother's before her.

1 onion, chopped
3 tablespoons chicken fat or oil
½ pound chicken livers
1 egg, hard-boiled
   salt, pepper, paprika to taste
   prepared mustard

Fry onion in chicken fat or oil. Add the chicken livers, which should be very fresh, and fry until done. Grind in a meat grinder or blender with egg. Add salt, pepper, and paprika to taste. Add mustard to obtain the right consistency and taste. You may add additional chicken fat. Do not freeze or keep liver too long, even in refrigerator. Serve on crackers as an hors d'oeuvre. Yields about 1 cup.

Dave's note: Smooth and fairly rich.

MRS. AXEL C. HANSEN
SOUTH PORTLAND, MAINE

Baked Liver and Onions

¼ cup flour
1½ pounds liver, baby beef or calves'
½ cup fat
3 medium onions, sliced
¼ teaspoon paprika
½ cup water
1 teaspoon salt
1 cup sour cream

Rub flour into liver and brown in hot fat on both sides. Put liver into a shallow baking dish. Brown onions in fat and spread over liver. Mix remaining fat with remaining ingredients and pour mixture over meat. Cover dish with aluminum foil and cook at 300° for about 1½ hours, until meat is tender. Serves 6.

Dave's note: If overcooked, the sauce dries out and liver becomes too mealy. If sauce separates in cooking, whisk while adding a little milk or cream.

DICK BLACK
ARLINGTON, MASSACHUSETTS

Broiled Tripe

This is my husband's favorite recipe. When I was a bride forty-three years ago, my husband was forever telling me about the delicious tripe his mother made for him on cold winter mornings. He described it, but not having a recipe, I made it many times and he wouldn't eat it. I just stopped trying to improve it and actually stopped making it. Let him stick to bacon and eggs and oatmeal like any other Irishman, I thought. Then I found this recipe.

½ pound fresh honeycomb tripe per
  person
  salt and pepper
1½ tablespoons flour
  olive oil (enough for dipping)
¼ cup bread crumbs

Mustard Sauce:

1 tablespoon onion, minced
1 tablespoon butter
2 tablespoons vinegar
2 teaspoons dry English mustard
1 cup brown gravy

Always pick out what is known as pocket tripe. Cut tripe in 4 x 6-inch pieces. Dry pieces well. Season with salt and pepper. Sprinkle with flour, dip in olive oil, and sprinkle generously with fine bread crumbs. Broil slowly about 3½ inches from heat source, preferably over charcoal, for 2 or 3 minutes on a side, or until crumbs are browned. Serve with mustard sauce, which should be made as follows:

Sauté onion in butter. Add vinegar and boil for 2 minutes. Moisten mustard with a little water, stir in gravy, and add gravy mixture to vinegar and onion. Boil for 5 minutes and strain through a sieve. Serve hot.

Dave's note: I'm not a tripe lover, but this wasn't too bad.

MRS. JOHN RYAN
WATERTOWN, MASSACHUSETTS

Sweet Tongue with Vegetables

This recipe has been in my family for more than half a century. My mom was considered the best cook around and always had many friends and relatives over for meals. You never had to ask them twice — before you knew it they were ringing our bell. My mom had ten children and also took in a boy without a home. That was my mom, bless her soul!

3 to 4 pounds beef tongue
2 green peppers ⎫
2 onions   ⎬ diced
2 stalks celery ⎭
¼ pound mushrooms
8 carrots, scraped
3 or 4 potatoes, peeled and cubed
2 or 3 bay leaves

Preheat oven to 475°. Put tongue in a roasting pan and cook, uncovered, for 30 minutes. Then add green peppers, onions, celery, mushrooms, carrots, and potatoes. Reduce heat to 350°. Add a few bay leaves to the vegetables in pan. Cover and put back in oven. After 1½ to 2 hours, peel skin off tongue. Cover and continue cooking for 1 more hour. Serves 4 to 6.

Dave's note: Believe it or not, I had never eaten tongue before, but our testing staff snuck it by me. It was too late to tell anybody I didn't like tongue because I was on my fifth piece. By the way, it's pretty good cold, too.

FLORENCE CHANSKY
BEVERLY, MASSACHUSETTS

Grandma's Steak and Kidney Pie

2 pounds chuck stew beef, cut into 1-inch cubes
1 pound beef kidneys, cut into ½-inch pieces
½ cup flour
1 teaspoon salt
¼ teaspoon pepper
2 bay leaves
1 to 2 cups beef stock (or water)
2 tablespoons parsley, chopped
½ cup onion, finely chopped (optional)

Suet Crust:

½ pound suet, chopped
1 pound flour
1 teaspoon salt
¼ teaspoon pepper

To make suet crust, put flour into mixing bowl with a little salt and pepper. Then add chopped suet. Mix with cold water until mixture has the consistency to be rolled.

Line a deep meat pie dish with suet crust. Flour meat and season with salt and pepper. Fill dish with meat and soup stock (or enough water to cover meat). Then cover dish with remaining pastry (be sure that there are no places where gravy can work through). Put a pudding cloth or heavy cheesecloth over the top and tie a little below the rim; then pin the four corners together on top so that you can lift out easily.

Boil 2½ to 3 hours according to size. Don't draw the pudding cloth too tight over the pudding. Serves 8 to 10.

Dave's note: For something special and nicely English, use ½ pound fresh oysters instead of the kidneys.

MRS. HESTER I. BILLINGS
NEEDHAM HEIGHTS, MASSACHUSETTS

Tripe, California Style

6 pounds honeycomb tripe, well washed
lightly salted water
4 cups chili sauce
1 8-ounce can tomato sauce
2 teaspoons oregano
1 onion, finely chopped
1 clove garlic, finely chopped
2 tablespoons oil

Place tripe in a large pot and cover with lightly salted water. Bring to a boil, cover, and simmer until tender (about 1 hour). Remove tripe from water, reserving 2 cups of liquid. Cut tripe into strips or small pieces. Combine chili sauce, tomato sauce, and oregano in a 4-quart pot. Saute onion and garlic in oil. Add to sauce and boil for 2 minutes. Add the tripe and reserved liquid and cook slowly for 30 minutes. Serves 10 to 12.

Dave's note: Tripe served this way is very tender. It's a nice dish and inexpensive. For a less vinegary taste, use plain water instead of the reserved liquid in the last 30 minutes of cooking.

MRS. MICHAEL CONDARDO
MARLBORO, MASSACHUSETTS

Rice Casserole with Chicken Livers

1 can mushrooms
½ pound chicken livers
1 cup rice
3 onions, finely chopped
  oil
  salt and pepper
2 or 3 dashes soy sauce

Drain mushrooms, reserving liquid. Chop mushrooms and livers into tiny pieces. Boil rice, substituting mushroom liquid for part of water, and drain.

Sauté onions in oil, adding salt and pepper to taste. When onions are browned, add liver, mushrooms, and soy sauce. Saute thoroughly. Add cooked rice and mix thoroughly, browning entire mixture. Pour into a greased casserole dish and bake at 350° for about 1 hour. Tastes like wild rice! Serves 6.

Dave's note: Goes great with roast chicken, but be careful: after 60 minutes, it tastes like mush.

ANN BALFOUR
WESTBURY, NEW YORK

German Liver Dumplings

2 slices bread
1 cup milk
1 pound liver
¼ stick butter
1 medium onion, finely chopped
2 sprigs parsley
  salt and pepper
½ cup (or more) flour

Soak bread in milk for 5 minutes. Wring out. Place in food processor with liver, butter, onion, parsley, salt and pepper, and enough flour to form into balls approximately ½ inch in diameter. Drop with a teaspoon into hot beef broth and simmer for 30 minutes.

DAVE

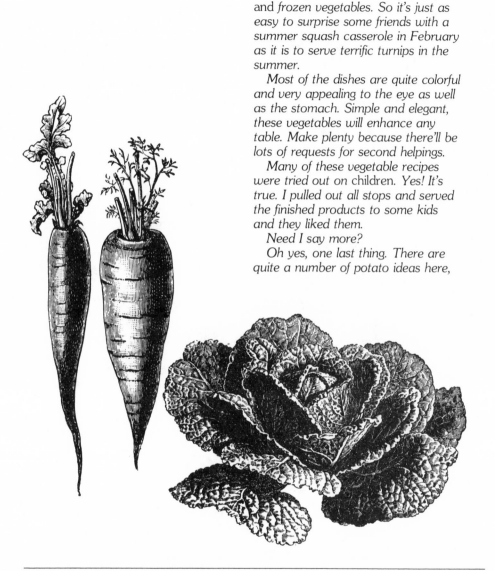

Although summer is the height of most people's vegetable experience, the following recipes offer extremely clever ways to make use of both fresh and *frozen vegetables.* So it's just as easy to surprise some friends with a summer squash casserole in February as it is to serve terrific turnips in the summer.

Most of the dishes are quite colorful and very appealing to the eye as well as the stomach. Simple and elegant, these vegetables will enhance any table. Make plenty because there'll be lots of requests for second helpings.

Many of these vegetable recipes were tried out on children. Yes! It's true. I pulled out all stops and served the finished products to some kids and they liked them.

Need I say more?

Oh yes, one last thing. There are quite a number of potato ideas here,

Vegetables

because so many good ones were sent in. Besides, I really like spuds. Two years ago, I stopped at a small pub in a tiny village above Galway for lunch. I was returning to Ashford Castle, which is really beautiful. Sidling up to the bar, I ordered some sandwiches and lager for my wife and myself, and also some french fries (Joan loves potatoes). The lady behind the bar told us she was boiling some spuds in their jackets for her own family's lunch. Would we like some? We almost jumped over the bar. After we finished three apiece, I asked for the check. Don't know what made me look at it but when I did, it was apparent the potatoes were not on it. I told this pretty-eyed woman about the mistake and choked back a tear when she said, "Sir, anybody who would stay at such a fine place as Ashford Castle and belly up to my bar for spuds doesn't pay for them . . . not a penny."

Gee, I loved Ireland. —Dave

Alfalfa Sprouts

These sprouts are a good source of fresh vegetables in winter and are rich in vitamin E. They can be used in sandwiches, salads, and tossed into baked goods. And they are a lot less expensive than buying them all sprouted. You can do the same thing with mung beans and other seeds and beans. (You can buy alfalfa seeds in health food stores and cooperative stores.)

$\frac{1}{8}$ cup alfalfa seeds

Put alfalfa seeds in a quart mayonnaise jar and fill the jar with water. Let stand overnight. In the morning cover jar with a nylon net with an elastic band (to hold it on over the top of the jar) and pour out the water. Rinse seeds and pour water out again (leaving nylon net over the top at all times). Lay the jar with the sprouts on its side and put it in a cupboard or other dark place.

Rinse once more during the day and again at night, laying the jar back on its side and returning it to the cupboard. Continue the same process for about 3 days. The jar should be full of sprouts by then. Bring the jar of sprouts out into the light and leave until the ends turn green (this isn't necessary but adds another dimension when the sunlight activates chlorophyll in the sprout).

Dave's note: Smoked turkey, sprouts, and a little Russian dressing on light caraway rye is a hummer of a sandwich delight.

BETTY LAMPLOUGH
PEAKS ISLAND, MAINE

Roasted Herb Barley

Don't know where I got this but, whether you make it on top of the stove or in the oven…it's a winner! Served it with roast beef one night and had more requests for second helpings of this than for beef.

1 large onion, minced
½ stick butter
½ pound fresh mushrooms, sliced
1 cup pearl barley
1 teaspoon salt
3 cups chicken broth
1 teaspoon thyme
½ teaspoon marjoram
½ teaspoon rosemary
¼ teaspoon sage
¼ teaspoon summer savory

In a large ovenproof pan, cook onion in butter for 3 to 5 minutes or until soft. Add mushrooms and cook for 3 minutes. Stir in pearl barley, salt, thyme, marjoram, crushed rosemary, sage, and summer savory. Saute over moderately high heat, stirring for 3 minutes to coat barley. Add hot chicken broth and bring to a boil. Bake covered for 55 minutes in oven preheated to 350°. Serves 2.

DAVE

Red Kidney Bean Loaf

The recipe was given to my mother around 1920 by an aunt who lived in the Boston area. She was a city gal who was quite thrilled to visit us as we lived on a small farm. She made the Bean Loaf for us and we liked it as we were all cheese lovers.

We have always called it Red Kidney Bean Loaf. We made it in a loaf form as we slice it and serve it hot. Sliced cold and served with a tossed salad or a cold slice as a sandwich are also good. We sometimes mix horseradish with sour cream to spread on it when eating it cold.

2 15-ounce cans red kidney beans, drained (reserve liquid)
1 medium onion
¼ pound medium-sharp cheese (do not use mild or extra-sharp)
8 salted crackers

Put all ingredients except liquid through a food grinder. Or mash beans with a fork, mince onions, crumble crackers very fine, and either grate or cut cheese very fine. Mix until well blended. Add pepper to taste, but do *not* add salt as there is enough salt in the cheese and crackers. Add 2 or 3 tablespoons of the bean liquid—just enough to make it moist but not wet.

Put into a lightly greased loaf pan or a small casserole dish. Cover and bake at 350° for 30 minutes; uncover and bake 15 or 20 minutes longer to brown a little on top.

Let sit about 15 minutes before serving. Serves 6 to 8, depending on how well you like it.

Dave's note: A hearty dish, of which a little goes a long way. Two dashes of Worcestershire and one dash of hot pepper sauce will sharpen that heavy bean taste.

OLIVE MAHAN
NILES, OHIO

Vermont Baked Beans

Early in my homemaking days I found this recipe in an old cookbook which had been my mother's, *The Barre Hospital Cookbook,* which was compiled around 1913 or 1914. I recognized the fact that this would yield the light brown, fairly dry and flavorsome beans I had eaten as a child. No one wanted beans swimming in molasses after eating these. The original recipe called for sugar but I substituted syrup many years ago and think it is an improvement.

These beans provided the protein of many a Saturday night supper and were accompanied by hot rolls and cabbage salad, which was never called cole slaw. After I began to use an electric bean baker, I cheated a bit and darkened the beans to an appetizing shade with bottled gravy extract. I find that it doesn't alter the flavor so that I can detect it.

1 pound pea or navy beans
1 medium onion, peeled
½ cup sugar (or ¼ cup maple syrup and ¼ cup sugar)
1 teaspoon salt
1 teaspoon powdered ginger
¼ pound salt pork, cut into strips or cubes

Pick over and wash beans and soak them overnight. Next morning, parboil beans until barely tender and place in a beanpot. Bury onion in bottom of pot. Add sugar, salt, and ginger. Put salt pork on top of beans, add boiling water to barely cover. Cover pot and bake for 6 to 8 hours, adding more water as needed. Remove cover from pot for the last ½ hour of cooking so that pork may brown.

For additional taste, I sometimes add burgundy during the last few hours of cooking. Serves 6 to 8.

Dave's note: These beans make a great cold sandwich, especially with a little mayonnaise.

HELEN R. WIOT
QUINCY, MASSACHUSETTS

Green Beans in Lemon Honey

2 tablespoons butter
2 to 3 tablespoons honey
1 teaspoon vinegar
½ teaspoon salt
½ lemon, thinly sliced
1 unpared apple, cored and diced
1 medium onion, chopped
1 teaspoon cornstarch
1 tablespoon water
2 cups green beans, cooked

Mix together butter, honey, vinegar, salt, and lemon slices. Bring to a boil, stirring constantly for 5 minutes. Stir in apple and onion to cook until apple is tender. Mix together cornstarch and water and add to liquid. Bring to a boil and cook gently for 3 minutes. Add beans and heat. Canned beans can be used. Serves 4.

Dave's note: Lemon is nicely contrasted with the honey. This recipe also works well with other vegetables.

UNA GARDNER
NORTH EASTON, MASSACHUSETTS

Baked Baby Lima Beans

This is an old Pennsylvania Dutch recipe, given to my wife over twenty years ago by Mrs. Hassick, the wife of a *Philadelphia Bulletin* editor. It is so tasty and easy to make.

1 pound dried baby lima beans
2 sticks butter
¾ cup brown sugar
1 tablespoon dry mustard
2 teaspoons salt
1 tablespoon molasses
1 cup sour cream

Soak beans overnight. Drain, cover with water and 1 teaspoon salt, and cook for 30 minutes. Drain and rinse with hot water and put into casserole dish. Dab with cubes of butter. Mix brown sugar, mustard, and remaining salt and sprinkle over beans. Stir in molasses and gently pour sour cream over this mixture. Bake at 350° for 1 hour. Serves 4 to 6.

Dave's note: Try this one on a lima bean hater.

JOHN D. FRECHETTE
VERO BEACH, FLORIDA

Broccoli with Wine

This is one of my mother's recipes which I took with me as a bride from northern California to Athens, Georgia, and to my husband's first position (Instructor in Physics, University of Georgia).

1   bunch broccoli
¼   cup olive oil
2   cloves garlic
4   shallots, minced
     salt and freshly ground pepper
1½ cups dry white wine

Wash broccoli, drain, and dry between paper towels. Trim and cut into small florets. Peel thick stems and slice lengthwise. Set aside. Heat olive oil in a large frying pan. Add garlic cloves and shallots and cook until lightly browned. Remove and discard garlic cloves. Add prepared broccoli and season with salt and pepper. Cook over medium heat, stirring constantly, for 3 or 4 minutes. Turn heat to low and add wine. Stir to mix. Cover and simmer for 5 to 10 minutes. Stir occasionally with a wooden fork, taking care not to break the pieces. Transfer from pan to a serving dish with tongs. Serves 2 to 4.

LUCILLE POOL BECKERLY
COHASSET, MASSACHUSETTS

Tricia Pain's Australian Cabbage

This was sent to me by a Freeport, Maine, girl who went to Australia to teach, brought her Australian back to Maine to get married, and returned to Jandowae, Australia, to live.

1 small cabbage, finely shredded
1 medium onion, chopped
1 carrot, grated
1 teaspoon powdered ginger
3 tablespoons margarine
½ cup water

Combine all ingredients in a saucepan. Simmer until tender. Serves 4.

Dave's note: We thought the use of ginger unusual. It adds a very nice flavor.

ROSALIND L. WEATHERBEE
NEEDHAM, MASSACHUSETTS

Carrot Ring with Green Beans

This is a recipe that my mother made for company, especially during the early summer months when we were thinning the carrots in our garden and picking off the green beans that had matured early.

The recipe has been one of my standbys, especially for buffet dinners. It has always been a favorite.

2 tablespoons onion, choppped
2 tablespoons green pepper, chopped
2 tablespoons butter
1 cup soft bread crumbs
2 cups cooked carrots, mashed
2 eggs, separated
1 cup thick white sauce
1 teaspoon baking powder
  seasoned green beans, whole, french-cut, or sliced

Sauté onions and pepper in 1 tablespoon butter. When soft, add enough bread crumbs to absorb whatever butter is left. Add to carrots, then add unbeaten egg yolks and white sauce. Mix well. Beat egg whites; when frothy, add baking powder and beat until stiff. Fold into carrot mixture.

Sauté about ½ cup bread crumbs in 1 tablespoon butter. Lightly butter a ring mold. Sprinkle mold with slightly browned bread crumbs. Pour carrot mixture into mold on top of bread crumbs and bake at 300° for 75 minutes. Just before carrot mixture is ready to leave oven, prepare green beans as you desire. Unmold carrot mixture on serving plate and fill center with green beans. Serves 10 generously.

MARY TRACY
ALEXANDRIA, VIRGINIA

Copper Pennies

I first had this in a restaurant outside of Williamsburg, Virginia, when I visited there in April 1976. On our route home, we visited with friends in Earlysville, Virginia, and Copper Pennies appeared again at dinner one night! We liked it so much. The homemade was even more savory. I was so pleased to be given a copy of the recipe.

2   pounds carrots, sliced and cooked
½ cup salad oil
¼ cup vinegar
1   can tomato juice
¾ cup sugar
1   teaspoon prepared mustard
1   teaspoon Worcestershire sauce
1   green pepper, sliced
1   onion, sliced and separated into
    rings

Mix all ingredients. Refrigerate at least 12 hours before serving in a covered bowl. Serves 8 to 10.

Dave's note: More of a summer dish with cold meats. Very colorful. However, I would reduce the sugar and increase the salt. It retains the flavor longer.

GERTRUDE F. PALMER
HAMPTON, NEW HAMPSHIRE

Curried Celery

I cannot remember where I found the recipe for Curried Celery. All I know is that it is delicious and my family wants me to serve it when I invite them for roast lamb, which is not too often today when a leg of lamb for ten of us costs over twenty dollars. I sometimes use this with chicken, but it is best with lamb.

3   cups celery, diagonally cut
1   cup chicken stock
½ cup onions, sliced
½ cup butter
½ teaspoon salt
1½ teaspoons curry powder

Cook celery in chicken stock until tender but still crisp. Drain. Sauté onions in butter until tender. Add curry powder and salt; cook for 2 minutes. Add drained celery and cook for another 3 or 4 minutes. Serves 4 to 6.

MARGARET BRADY
MEDFORD, MASSACHUSETTS

Scalloped Corn and Peppers

This recipe has been in the family for over fifty-odd years. It came from a cooking school I attended, Nickerson House in Rhode Island. I had to learn to cook as I was about to get married. Boy, would I look great not to be able to cook?

2   tablespoons butter
4   tablespoons green peppers, chopped
2   tablespoons onion, chopped
2   tablespoons flour
2   eggs
1   teaspoon salt
1   teaspoon prepared mustard
1   cup milk
2   cups corn, cooked
⅔   cup bread crumbs

Melt butter and add peppers and onion. Cook slowly for 5 minutes. Add flour, salt, and milk. Blend and cook. Add corn, eggs, and mustard. Turn mixture into well-buttered dish. Sprinkle with crumbs, dot with butter. Bake at 325° for about 15 minutes. Serves 4 to 6.

MRS. CORINNE GAGNON
EAST PROVIDENCE, RHODE ISLAND

Gibson's Stuffed Cucumber Delight

This recipe is about seventy years old and is from a Methodist family that came from Milford, New Hampshire. I guess they didn't have much to do in those days except experiment with their cooking. Whoever would think to create a recipe for stuffed cucumbers these days? I wouldn't.

4   cucumbers, peeled and seeded
3   tablespoons sherry or other wine
½   teaspoon msg (optional)
3   tablespoons soy sauce
1   teaspoon cornstarch
2   tablespoons sugar
2   tablespoons scallions, chopped
½   teaspoon ginger powder
½   pound ground pork
2   tablespoons oil
½   cup chicken broth
     dash salt

Halve cucumbers lengthwise. Then stuff cucumbers with a mixture of 1 tablespoon sherry or other wine, msg (optional), 2 tablespoons soy sauce, cornstarch, 1 teaspoon sugar, scallions, ginger powder, and pork. Brown stuffed cucumbers in oil for 2 to 3 minutes. Mix chicken broth, salt, 1 teaspoon sugar, 1 tablespoon soy sauce, and 2 tablespoons sherry or other wine and add to cucumbers. Cover and simmer for 12 to 15 minutes. Serves 4.

Dave's note: Scoop cuke out with a baller and drain on paper towels for about ten minutes. Very attractive and good strong flavor. Delicious with a roast.

MARY PAGLIARINI
PEABODY, MASSACHUSETTS

Eggplant with Tomato Sauce

This eggplant recipe has been a favorite in our family for over thirty years and is so simple to make.

1 large eggplant
1 small onion, peeled and diced
1 small can tomato paste
1 teaspoon basil
1 teaspoon oregano
  salt to taste
  Parmesan cheese, grated

Peel and dice eggplant. Set aside. Saute onion in small amount of oil until onion is transparent. Dilute tomato paste with sufficient water to make a sauce of medium thickness. Pour over sauteed onion, add seasoning, and simmer for a minute or two. Cook on top of stove, adding water if necessary to achieve desired consistency. Cooking time is relatively short, since eggplant cooks quickly. Sample for tenderness and "doneness." When done, combine the sauce with the eggplant.

Transfer to a serving dish and sprinkle with Parmesan cheese. Serves 6.

R. H. DUGUID
BEL AIR, MARYLAND

Eggplant Puff Puffs

1 medium eggplant
1 egg, beaten
¾ teaspoon garlic salt
¼ cup flour
¾ cup sharp cheddar cheese, grated
¾ cup bread crumbs
2 teaspoons lemon juice
  olive oil

Peel and cut eggplant into cubes. Place cubes in a saucepan with enough water to cover, then cover saucepan. Boil until tender for about 10 minutes, or steam them. Drain and mash. Add all other ingredients except oil to the pulp. Chill 1 hour. Form mix into bite-size pieces. Roll each into flour and cook in oil until crisp and brown. Drain on paper towels.

May be made ahead of time and frozen. When ready to serve, place under broiler or in a 400° oven for 10 minutes. Yields 50 puffs.

Dave's note: Be sure to remove skin before mashing eggplant. The cheddar cheese gives it a great taste, but if you're a sissy, try muenster or some mild swiss.

POLLY POWELL
YORK BEACH, MAINE

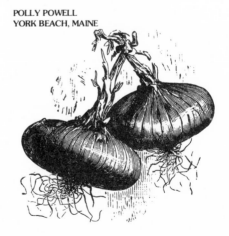

Lentils and Rice with Tomatoes

Here's a recipe that's unbeatable.

1 cup dry lentils
3 cups water
1 bay leaf
3 sprigs parsley
1 medium onion, chopped
3 tablespoons margarine or oil
1 cup rice, cooked
¼ teaspoon mace or nutmeg
1 teaspoon salt
   dash pepper
1 cup canned tomatoes

Sort and wash lentils; soak in water overnight. The next morning, add bay leaf, parsley, and salt to the lentils and water. Cook until lentils are tender, approximately 1 hour. Meanwhile, brown onion in margarine or oil in a frying pan. Add to it all other ingredients and bake at 350° for 15 minutes. Remove bay leaf and cooked parsley before serving. Serves 3 or 4.

Dave's note: Nice on a cold, crisp day. Very filling.

CAROL YAKISH
PITTSBURGH, PENNSYLVANIA

Deviled Lettuce

This recipe was concocted because of my husband's diet. For years I had been mixing no-cal salads for him. One day I did a reverse—made him a high-caloric one.

1 8-ounce package cream cheese
1 can deviled ham
¼ cup green pepper, chopped
1 tablespoon onion, chopped
½ cup salad dressing
1 cup celery, diced
2 tablespoons pimiento, chopped
1 head lettuce, hollowed out

Mix all ingredients except lettuce well. Stuff mixture in lettuce, wrap in foil, and chill overnight. Serve cut in wedges. Serves 4 to 6.

Dave's note: Garnish with pimiento and pepper strips. Try a dash of hot pepper sauce for some extra zap.

MAYBELLE WOOLSTRUM BROWN
NORTH RIDGEVILLE, OHIO

Baked Mushrooms and Bleu Cheese

This is a great brunch dish with lots of crisp bacon or grilled Canadian bacon, and is also a lovely buffet casserole dish served with roast beef.

2 pounds large mushrooms
½ cup heavy cream or yogurt
½ cup bleu cheese, crumbled
1 cup dry bread crumbs
2 tablespoons butter
½ cup sherry
1 teaspoon chives, minced

Remove stems from mushrooms and place a bit of cream and some crumbled bleu cheese in each mushroom cap. Sauté crumbs, butter, and remaining cheese. Place in layers in a buttered casserole dish and add crumbs, saving some crumbs to sprinkle on top of casserole later. Add mushrooms flat side up. Sprinkle with sherry, remaining crumbs, and chives. Cover with remaining cream and bake, covered, at 375° for 25 minutes. Serves 6.

VIRGINIA LEDGER
GEORGETOWN, MASSACHUSETTS

Scalloped Mushrooms with Almonds

We have been market farmers for forty-eight years. Our town doctor would buy lots of parsley and always remind us it's good for the heart.

3 cups small mushrooms
⅓ cup butter
2 cups light cream
4 tablespoons butter
⅓ cup almonds, toasted and chopped
    salt, pepper, parsley, paprika

Sauté mushrooms in butter for about 5 minutes; do not brown. Add cream, bring to a boil, and thicken with flour mixed with a little water. Simmer for several minutes. Add almonds. Season to taste with salt and pepper. Place in a casserole dish and bake at 350° until done. Sprinkle with chopped parsley and paprika before serving. Serves 6 to 8.

Dave's note: Cream and mushrooms are so compatible. The addition of the almonds makes the dish very memorable.

MARIA E. THEODOROS
LITTLETON, MASSACHUSETTS

X-c-lent Mushrooms

X-c-lent Mushrooms get raves whenever served at our table. It's a recipe from a friend who has since moved away. What pleasant memories and conversation it brings to mind every time it is used.

3 4-ounce cans mushrooms, drained
1 tablespoon butter or margarine for sautéing
8 slices bread
½ cup celery, chopped
½ cup onion, chopped
½ cup green pepper, chopped
2 eggs
1½ cups milk
1 can mushroom soup
    cheddar cheese, grated

Sauté mushrooms slightly in butter or margarine. Butter 3 slices bread and cut them into 1-inch cubes. Place bread in a large, greased baking dish. Mix mushrooms with celery, onion, and green pepper. Distribute over cubes. Spread with 3 more slices buttered, cubed bread. Beat eggs and milk together. Pour over bread and mushroom mix. Refrigerate at least 1 hour before cooking. When ready to bake, spread mushroom soup over top. Cover with 2 more slices buttered, cubed bread. Bake 60 to 70 minutes at 350°. Ten minutes before it is done, spread top with cheese. Return to oven for 10 minutes. This is excellent with chicken and molded cranberry salad. Serves 4 to 6.

MRS. MICHAEL T. NICHOLSON
MALDEN, MASSACHUSETTS

Fabulous Fried Onion Rings

If you make these fabulous onion rings, keep them hidden in the oven until serving time, or there won't be any left to serve.

1½ cups flour
1½ cups beer, active or flat, cold or at
    room temperature
3   very large yellow onions
3   to 4 cups shortening

Combine flour and beer in a large bowl and blend thoroughly using a whisk. Cover the bowl and allow the batter to sit at room temperature for no less than 3 hours. Twenty minutes before batter is ready, preheat oven to 200°. Cut onions into ¼-inch thick rings, removing the papery peeling carefully so that the outside onion layer is not cut. Separate rings and set aside. On top of the stove melt shortening in a 10-inch skillet. Heat to 375°. With metal tongs, dip a few of the rings into the batter. Then carefully drop them into the hot fat. Fry rings, turning them once or twice, until a delicate golden color. Then remove to a paper-lined (with paper toweling layers or brown paper) jelly-roll pan and place on shelf of preheated oven. Repeat until all rings are fried.

This batter holds up very well, and can be fried and kept warm in the oven for several hours. Serves 2 to 4.

Dave's note: Beer batter is good for deep-frying many things.

JUDY BARTLETT
NORTH SMITHFIELD, RHODE ISLAND

Surprise Parsnip Balls

A lot of people eat only meat and potatoes, hot dogs, hamburgers and potato chips, etc. If you mention anything out of the ordinary like parsnips, tongue, stuffed beef hearts, garlic, dandelions or artichokes, you get an amazed look. Blah, they say.

My husband, who didn't relish boiled parsnips, went crazy over the parsnip balls. They can be used as a hot hors d'oeuvre or side dish at any meal.

4   or 5 parsnips
2   tablespoons butter
2   tablespoons cream
1   egg, beaten
    salt and pepper to taste
¼   pound cheddar cheese, cubed

Boil parsnips until tender, drain, peel, and mash. Mix with butter, cream, egg, salt, and pepper. Cool. Cut cheddar cheese into ½ x ½-inch cubes. Shape the parsnip mixture into balls. Push 1 cube of cheese into the center of each ball and reshape to cover cheese. Dip into egg mixture, then into crumbs. Fry in deep fat until brown. Serves 4 to 6.

MRS. EDWARD P. WILSON
WALTHAM, MASSACHUSETTS

Sweet Pepper Patties

This recipe has come down in our family by word of mouth from my grandmother (who would be 140 years old today). It is very, very good served with any kind of meat.

1 medium pepper per serving
1 large onion per serving
1 egg, beaten
  dash pepper
  dash salt
½ cup fine cracker crumbs
  vegetable oil

Remove seeds from peppers and put peppers through a food chopper with onion, or chop very fine. Cook for 8 to 10 minutes in a little water. Strain pepper-onion mixture, add egg, pepper, salt to it. Add enough cracker crumbs to bind mixture. Form 4 patties. Fry slowly in a small amount of vegetable oil. Using 1 red pepper makes this mixture colorful.

Dave's note: I loved them. I preferred the taste without cooking them at all in water beforehand.

EDITH P. BARDIN
PUTNAM, CONNECTICUT

Carrot and Sweet Potato
(Tzimmes)

This is an ethnic Jewish dish from Eastern Europe. The Yiddish word *tsimes* literally means a crazy mixed-up affair.

1 pound sweet potatoes (or 1 large can), peeled and shredded
½ cup pitted prunes, chopped
4 to 5 large carrots, peeled and grated
1 cup water
2 tablespoons butter or margarine
1 teaspoon lemon juice
1 teaspoon salt
½ cup honey

In a large saucepan over medium heat, mix all ingredients except honey. Reduce heat to low after mixture reaches a boil. Simmer until potatoes are tender. Mash slightly and add honey, stirring well. Serves 6 to 8 as a side dish or vegetable.

Dave's note: If you're using canned sweet potatoes, add them after the other ingredients have simmered awhile. Otherwise they get too soft.

ANN BALFOUR
WESTBURY, NEW YORK

Cottage Potatoes

This recipe came all the way from Sao Paulo, Brazil, over ten years ago. My Toledo friend carried in this dish to a "Gourmet Tasting Luncheon" at the Community Church. Cottage Potatoes was instantly popular, We often recall how it took a move to South America for me to get this recipe, which originated in Toledo.

10 large white potatoes
½ pound American cheese, cubed
½ cup butter or margarine, melted
1 onion, diced
1 green pepper, diced
2 slices of bread, cubed
  salt
  pepper
½ cup milk
1 cup corn flakes, crushed

Cook white potatoes with skins until firm but tender; peel and dice when cool. Mix into potatoes all other ingredients except milk and corn flakes and put into a long buttered pan or a casserole dish. Pour milk over top and cover with corn flakes. Bake for 45 minutes to 1 hour at 325°. Serves 12 to 14 (and maybe a few more).

Dave's note: If you'd like a stronger taste, use a sharper cheese. I think it would be better to saute the diced onions and pepper in a little butter first —then you'd only need to bake about 30 minutes. I think you could use 8 potatoes and still serve 12 to 14.

HELEN CRAM
TOLEDO, OHIO

Donegal Pie

This recipe has been in our family for over one hundred years. It was one of my grandmother's special ones, and when my mother came from Ireland seventy-five years ago, she brought it to America with her. After her death in 1962, I neglected to make it. However, on a recent trip to Ireland, we were again served Donegal Pie, and it brought back precious memories. This pie is a favorite for Sunday supper in Ireland.

2 hard-boiled eggs, sliced
4 slices bacon, fried and sliced
6 potatoes, cooked and mashed with
  a little butter and milk
  salt and pepper
1 pastry crust

Butter a deep pie plate. Line it with half of the hot, freshly mashed potatoes, pressing down evenly with a fork. Cover with sliced hard-boiled eggs. Fry bacon and dice, reserving drippings. Then cover potato mixture with a layer of bacon. Pour the rendered bacon fat over the contents of the pie plate. Top with remaining mashed potatoes. Cover with a pastry crust. Slit with a knife in several places. Brush with milk. Bake at 325° or until pastry is well browned. Serve hot. Serves 6 to 8.

Dave's note: If you'd add some smoked sausage (cooked first) to this, you'd have a one-dish meal. Cooked sliced onions and grated cheese layered over the potatoes would make an interesting variation.

MARGARET A. MITCHELL
LOWELL, MASSACHUSETTS

Potato Puffs

This recipe has been in my family for over seventy-five years. "When you get to heaven, you will likely view many folks whose presence there will be a shock to you. But keep your thinking quiet, do not even stare, doubtless there will be many folks surprised to see you there."

3 medium potatoes
½ cup boiling water
½ cup butter
½ cup flour
2 **eggs**
1 teaspoon salt
¼ teaspoon pepper
¼ teaspoon nutmeg
   oil or butter for frying

Pare potatoes and cook in boiling, salted water. When done, put through a ricer or coarse sieve. Put water and butter in a saucepan and bring to a boil. Add flour and cook, stirring constantly, until the mixture leaves the sides of the pan. Cool. Add eggs one at a time, beating well after each egg is added. Add potatoes to this mixture, along with salt, pepper, and nutmeg. Season more if necessary. Drop by tablespoonfuls in hot butter and fry 8 to 10 minutes until brown. Drain on a paper towel. Makes 16 puffs.

Dave's note: These don't taste high in calories, but they are. Try a touch of dry mustard to sharpen the flavor. I'd fry them in a little butter and oil, as hot butter burns.

MRS. ELIZABETH M. WESSA
BROCKTON, MASSACHUSETTS

Sweet Potato Pone

When I was eighteen years of age, my father was transferred to New Orleans. The epicurean delights of that city were very intriguing to us. Whenever we visited our newly acquired friends and they served us a dish we were unaccustomed to, we asked for the recipe. Sweet Potato Pone is one of our favorites. We have used it for fifty years and want to share it with you.

1 cup sugar
1 teaspoon salt
½ cup butter, melted
¼ cup milk
1 egg, beaten
¼ teaspoon cinnamon
   pinch nutmeg
   a little white pepper
2 cups raw sweet potato, grated
   rind of orange, grated
   juice of ½ orange

Mix together sugar, salt, butter, milk, egg, cinnamon, and nutmeg. Blend ingredients into sweet potato. Add orange rind and juice. Bake in a shallow pan for about 1 hour at 325°. Serves 4 to 6.

Dave's note: Goes great with broiled hamsteak or a baked ham without the glaze. Start recipe with half the sugar—one cup is a little sweet. Then, to taste, add a little honey or brown sugar.

FLORENCE DORKS
CINCINNATI, OHIO

Sweet Potato Surprise Balls

1 teaspoon baking powder
small marshmallows
2 cups sweet potatoes, mashed and
seasoned with salt, pepper, butter,
and cream
egg, beaten
cracker crumbs
oil

Add baking powder to the sweet potatoes. Form into small balls. In the center of each, put a small marshmallow.
Seal. Roll in beaten egg, then in cracker crumbs. Deep fry. When done,
drain on absorbent towels. Yields
about 24 balls.

*Dave's note: Chopped ham or
cubes of sharp cheddar cheese could
be substituted for the marshmallows.
A great dish for skinny kids. Be sure
the potatoes are well-seasoned, otherwise the flavors won't hold up.*

RUTH BEEMAN
QUINCY, MASSACHUSETTS

Scalloped Potatoes

My recipe for Scalloped Potatoes has
been in my family for many years. My
mother came up with the idea of something different to serve to some special
guests. Each time my family visits me,
it's "will you have scalloped potatoes
and baked ham with it?" Being a good
mother and grandmother, I guess you
know what they had.

4   tablespoons margarine or butter
1   medium onion, chopped
3   tablespoons green pepper,
    chopped
1   tablespoon pimiento, chopped
2½ tablespoons flour
2   cups milk
    salt
    pepper
3   cups potatoes, cooked and cubed
¾   cup sharp cheese, grated

Saute first three ingredients until soft.
Add remainder of ingredients except
shredded cheese. Put in a casserole
dish and cover with cheese. When
ready to use, put in a 350° oven until
heated through and cheese has melted. This is better made the night before and then reheated. Serves 4 to 6.

MRS. DOROTHY O'NEIL
ARLINGTON, MASSACHUSETTS

Hungarian Creamed Potatoes

My mother came from a village that was in Hungary but is now part of Austria. We (seven of us) grew up on Hungarian and German cooking. My sister and I had to learn to cook when we were very young. Most of my cooking is not measured, but we had to use measuring to send this recipe.

¼ cup butter, melted
¼ cup flour
½ cup milk
1 teaspoon salt
¼ teaspoon pepper
2 tablespoons onion, grated
2 tablespoons parsley, chopped
½ cup cheese, grated
4 cups raw potatoes, diced
  paprika

Blend butter, salt, and pepper over low heat; add flour and blend well. Gradually add milk, stirring constantly over low flame, until thick. Add cheese, onions, and parsley. Place potatoes in a buttered casserole dish. Pour sauce over potatoes. Cover and bake 45 minutes at 375° or until well done. Shake paprika lightly over top. Serves 6.

Dave's note: Any flavor of cheese can be used. If you like a sharp flavor, try cheddar. If not, use swiss, gruyère, muenster, or even American cheese for a variety of flavors.

MRS. HELEN GALL
TOLEDO, OHIO

Paprika Potatoes

3   or 4 medium potatoes
2   tablespoons bacon fat
¾   cup onion, chopped
1   tablespoon sweet paprika
1   teaspoon salt
⅛   teaspoon pepper
1¼ cup sour cream
    parsley, chopped

Wash, pare, and cut potatoes into ½-inch cubes; you should have about 2½ cups. Heat bacon fat in a skillet and add onion. Cook until onion is transparent, stirring often. Stir paprika, salt, and pepper into onion mixture. Remove the skillet from heat and blend sour cream into the onion mixture, stirring vigorously. Add potatoes to mixture and mix gently and thoroughly. Cover skillet and cook over *very low* heat for about 30 minutes, or until potatoes are done. Garnish with chopped parsley. Serves 4 to 6.

Dave's note: It is important to cook the potatoes at a low temperature or they will burn.

MARY K. LYNCH
CANTON, OHIO

Onion-Barbecued Potatoes

There is no special family tie to this recipe. I am a recipe nut and this is one of our family's favorites. I find cooking boring if I don't explore different foods and add new recipes all the time.

6 medium potatoes, peeled
1 medium onion, thinly sliced
⅓ cup butter, melted
½ package dry onion soup mix

With a knife, slit each potato in thirds slicing almost to the bottom but not all the way through. Arrange onion slices in slits. Place potatoes on individual squares of foil and brush with melted butter. Sprinkle each with some onion soup mix, dividing it evenly among them. Close foil over potatoes with a double fold to seal. Bake at 350° for 1 hour. Can be cooked outdoors on grill. Serves 6.

Dave's note: What a refreshing way to serve baked potatoes! The flavor is great for those of you who love onions. For a little variety, try some grated cheese. More vitamins if you don't peel the potatoes.

RONNIE LEMIEUX
BOONVILLE, NEW YORK

Potato Baked Stuffed Peppers

4 small green peppers
   bread crumbs
   butter

Stuffing

2 cups potatoes, mashed with a little butter and milk; season with salt and pepper
1 teaspoon onion, grated
¼ teaspoon paprika
¼ cup cream
1 tablespoon butter
½ teaspoon sage
2 egg yolks, beaten
   salt

Preheat oven to 400°. Mix all stuffing ingredients together (makes 2½ cups). Cut peppers in half lengthwise and remove seeds and membrane. Simmer in boiling water for 5 minutes. Drain and put peppers in a shallow baking dish. Fill peppers with potato stuffing. Sprinkle with dry bread crumbs and dot with butter. Bake for 20 minutes, or until tops are lightly browned. May be served with a tomato sauce or even a good mushroom and onion sauce. Serves 4.

Dave's note: For another attractive presentation, leave peppers whole, cut off top, remove seeds and membranes, parboil peppers and tops, and then stuff and bake.

ROSE KRIKORIAN
HAVERHILL, MASSACHUSETTS

Potatoes in Wine

4   strips bacon, diced
1   tablespoon butter
6   small onions
1½ pounds potatoes
1   bay leaf
    salt
    pepper
    dry white wine

Sauté bacon until golden in a pan with butter and onions. Peel potatoes and cut in egg-sized discs. Add to bacon with bay leaf, salt, pepper, and enough dry wine to reach the top of the potatoes. Cook slowly for 1 hour; remove potatoes with onion and bacon and keep warm. Boil the wine sauce and pour over all piping hot. Serve with a good steak. Serves 4.

Dave's note: Nice potato recipes, Rose. What keeps you thin? A little rosemary, while the brew is simmering, will add a lovely flavor.

ROSE KRIKORIAN
HAVERHILL, MASSACHUSETTS

Martinique Potatoes

I have served this to friends and family for a long time. I hope your readers will enjoy it as much as we have. I've been married for fifty-three years and the old boy still likes my cooking. Must have done something right.

4   baked potatoes
1½ tablespoons butter
3   tablespoons milk
1   egg, separated
    salt
    pepper
    nutmeg

Remove skin from potatoes and force through a ricer. Heat potatoes, butter, cream, beaten egg yolk, and seasonings and cook for 3 minutes, stirring constantly. Gradually fold in egg white that has been beaten stiff. Shape mixture between 2 buttered tablespoons. Place on a buttered sheet and bake at 375° until delicately browned. Yields about 24 balls.

Dave's note: Very tasty and a lot less calories if baked instead of fried.

MRS. CORINNE GAGNON
EAST PROVIDENCE, RHODE ISLAND

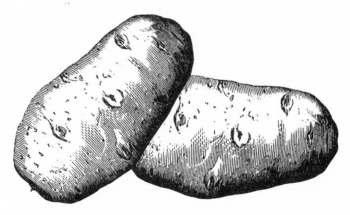

Vegetables 149

Potatoes Boulangère

2 large onions, thinly sliced
2 tablespoons butter
4 large potatoes, sliced in
   1/3-inch thick pieces
1 cup beef bouillon
¼ teaspoon thyme
1 bay leaf
   salt and pepper to taste

Sauté onions in butter for 4 to 5 minutes. Add potatoes. Add bouillon, thyme, bay leaf, salt and pepper to taste. Simmer until tender.

This is a lot like Potatoes Anna, except that it is prepared and served freestyle. Serves 6.

DAVE

Grilled Potatoes with Sauerkraut

There is no special story to my recipe. I just pulled it out of my German file because everyone likes it. It's a real different way to serve potatoes and sauerkraut. It would be good to serve sour cream with herbs and paprika alongside the potatoes.

4 large baking potatoes
   salt
4 teaspoons butter
3½ ounces lean bacon, diced
1 small onion, diced
½ pound sauerkraut
4 slices bacon

Wash potatoes, slice off a cover lengthwise, and hollow out a little more than half. Discard cover piece or save for soup. Put a little salt and 1 teaspoon butter in each potato. Mix diced bacon and onion with sauerkraut and fill the potatoes. Wrap each one in foil and bake at 425° for 1 hour.

Top each with a crisp slice of fried bacon. Serves 4 to 8.

Dave's note: Rinse sauerkraut before using. Drain well. Bring to table with a little chopped parsley. Looks spectacular! Delicious with roast.

HANNELORE TRAMONTOZZI
ARLINGTON, MASSACHUSETTS

German Sauerkraut

My parents brought this recipe with them from Switzerland (German section) eighty years ago, where it had been in the family long before. Sauerkraut is treated this way all over Germanic-speaking countries. My father was a chef. I learned many recipes from him, including Spatzle, Swiss style — delicious. Also Stengeli (a carrot and potato combination much admired).

1 small can sauerkraut
1 large onion, sliced
1 tablespoon bacon fat or oil
1 cup (or less) water
1 apple, peeled and diced
5 juniper berries (optional)

Drain and wash sauerkraut in a colander. Saute onion in bacon fat until soft, not brown. Add apples for last few minutes. Add sauerkraut and water to the pot, stirring occasionally. Garnish with slices of ham, boiled bacon, sausages and frankfurts — constitutes a French (Alsatian) choucroute garni. Usually served with boiled potatoes. Serves 6 with a semi-dollop.

Dave's note: Don't forget the apple. It sweetens the kraut just right.

PROFESSOR A. J. WATZINGER
TENANTS HARBOR, MAINE

Spinach a la Maison Bahr

This is a very favorite recipe that is wonderful frozen and reheated. It's great for cookouts and wonderful for a buffet supper, and a great favorite with men. Since I cook with a dash of this and a dab or two of that, I'll try to translate it for you as best I can.

4 packages frozen, chopped spinach
1 can cream of mushroom soup, undiluted
1 cup mushrooms, sliced
1 small onion, diced
4 to 5 tablespoons sour cream
  several dashes garlic powder
  several dashes nutmeg
  Parmesan cheese, grated
  paprika

Defrost and drain spinach. Place in a large casserole dish with soup, mushrooms, and onion. Mix well. Add sour cream, garlic powder, and nutmeg. Mix well. May add salt and pepper to taste. Cover top with Parmesan cheese and sprinkle on parsley and paprika. Bake at 350° until bubbly. Even more delicious the next day.

If it is to be frozen, place in the freezer uncooked. Do not salt if it is to be frozen for any length of time. Serves 8 to 12, but recipe increases easily to feed an "army"!

Dave's note: Yea, team! A spinach sure-thing for picky eaters.

MRS. VIRGINIA KEARNEY BAHR
BREWSTER, MASSACHUSETTS

Mother Liesinger's Spinach

The name my family gave this was Mother Liesinger's Spinach as it was one of my mother's ways to get spinach into us — iron, you know.

1 package fresh spinach
¼ cup olive oil
4 cloves garlic, minced

Cook spinach. While it is cooking, mix olive oil and garlic. As soon as spinach is cooked and drained, add olive oil–garlic combination. Mix thoroughly. Serves 4.

Remember to cook spinach using only the water that clings to the leaves from rinsing. Do not add extra water.

Dave's note: Yum! The simpler, the better.

MRS. THEODORE R. SLIFIR
BUFFALO, NEW YORK

Spinach Pudding

This is really good and it is pretty. If not mixed too much, the cottage cheese looks like tiny marshmallows.

1   10-ounce package frozen chopped spinach, cooked and drained
⅓ cup Parmesan cheese, grated
2   cups cottage cheese, drained
1   teaspoon salt
2   eggs

Mix all ingredients together until well blended. Pour into a 1-quart casserole dish. Bake at 350° for 30 minutes. Serve with additional Parmesan cheese. Serves 4 to 6.

Dave's note: Add a pinch of nutmeg. This dish goes well with roast lamb or baked ham. By the way, serve it immediately.

MRS. BEN GUNTER, JR.
ACCOMAC, VIRGINIA

Baked Summer Squash Casserole

Sometime in my youth, I detested eating vegetables. Mom decided a casserole camouflage would help me to get some necessary vitamins and it worked —voila! At times I substitute corn bread stuffing for the herb stuffing mix.

2   pounds yellow summer squash, sliced
¼ cup onion, chopped
1   can cream of chicken soup
1   cup sour cream
1   cup carrots, shredded
1   8-ounce package herb stuffing mix
½ cup butter or margarine, melted

In a saucepan, simmer squash in water for 10 minutes. Add onion and cook approximately 5 minutes more, or until tender. Drain. In a separate bowl, combine undiluted soup and sour cream. Stir in carrots. Fold in drained squash and onion. In a separate bowl, mix melted butter and stuffing mix.

Put half of stuffing mix into the bottom of a 12 x 7½ x 2-inch baking dish. Top with vegetables. Sprinkle with remaining stuffing. Bake at 350° for 25 to 30 minutes. Serves 6. Keep refrigerated overnight; any leftover casserole tastes better the next day!

Dave's note: Very filling. Please don't overcook squash.

MRS. JAMES SIMS
HYDE PARK, MASSACHUSETTS

Snappy Tomatoes

This snappy tomato recipe is one I always get compliments on. I fondly remember the woman who passed it along. She had a beautiful, smiling face and lovely white hair, and most of all she was so very kind to children.

This is an old state of Maine recipe that my family has enjoyed for more than forty years!

2   cups canned tomatoes, not drained
2   tablespoons onions, finely chopped
1   teaspoon salt
½ cup cheese, finely cut
½ cup cracker crumbs
4   tablespoons butter, melted
    dash paprika
1   egg, well beaten

Mix all ingredients thoroughly and pour into a buttered baking dish. Bake at 350° for 25 minutes, or until set. Serve from baking dish. Serves 2 to 4.

Dave's note: We added another egg to set it. Very nice with a poached whitefish.

MARGARET DORNEMANN
NEEDHAM, MASSACHUSETTS

Caramel Tomatoes

All I can tell you is that this was a favorite recipe of Mrs. Herbert Hoover and was a favorite luncheon dish at the White House. So it was said.

6 tomatoes
6 tablespoons butter
12 tablespoons sugar
salt to taste

Select medium tomatoes, not too ripe. Cut off point end and take out a bit of pulp. Fill each tomato with 1 tablespoon butter and 2 tablespoons sugar. Sprinkle with salt to taste. Place tomatoes in a shallow pan and bake at 275° for 45 minutes, or until rendered juice becomes a caramel brown. Place tomatoes on toast squares and pour sauce over them. Serves 6.

HARRIET HUGHES
JAMAICA PLAIN, MASSACHUSETTS

Turnip Fluff

This is an old Finnish recipe passed down by my great-grandmother. It has been in our family for four generations.

1 2-pound turnip
¼ cup water
¼ cup light brown sugar
salt and pepper
1 egg, beaten
butter
¼ cup light cream
2 tablespoons Cream of Wheat cereal

Pare and cube turnip and place in a pressure cooker, with water. Cook 3 to 5 minutes at 15 pounds pressure. (Boil until tender if you do not have a pressure cooker.) Quickly reduce pressure, drain and mash turnip, add seasoning, egg, butter, cream, and Cream of Wheat cereal. Pile lightly into buttered casserole dish and bake at 350° for 40 minutes. Serves 6.

Dave's note: Turnip isn't everybody's favorite, but it will be. Don't tell anyone what the dish is until they taste it. Add a little extra butter.

JANET A. KING
MAYNARD, MASSACHUSETTS

Ratatouille

A luscious vegetable dish served hot or cold. This recipe seems to have been given to my wife by her former boyfriend's mother.

1 cup onion, diced
⅓ cup olive oil
1 can tomatoes
1 medium eggplant
3 tablespoons chicken bouillon or 3 cubes
2 teaspoons oregano
½ teaspoon salt
3 medium zucchini, sliced
1 teaspoon oregano
½ teaspoon sugar
½ teaspoon garlic powder

Sauté onion in oil in a dutch oven until soft. Add all other ingredients. Stir well. Cover and cook over low heat for 35 to 40 minutes, stirring occasionally. Uncover and cook 10 more minutes. Serves 6 to 8.

Dave's note: This is good enough to serve as a light luncheon by itself. You could also sneak in some cooked Italian sausage rounds, or maybe a little kielbasa.

JIM ROBBINS
TITUSVILLE, PENNSYLVANIA

In my, as they say, younger days, rice was served in my house one way only and that was hot, in a cereal bowl, with sugar and milk and cream — if we had money coming in that week. By the way, add raisins (that have been plumped in hot brandy) and you have a whale of a way to start the day. Just don't let the kids get hooked on the raisins.

How I remember my first pasta machine — I was too lazy to use a board and rolling pin. That was the very day I made ravioli by the hundreds, and then spaghetti, macaroni, tortellini. It was a pasta frenzy! Since then, canneloni, gnocchi, lasagna have been churned out. It's better to make pasta on a rainy day than to sit around in front of the t.v. and watch moss grow on your shoes.

I put these recipes in one section because they are fairly interchangeable. When you're putting a meal together, I hope you have a difficult time choosing among them.

I've tasted both starches prepared in at least 100 different ways, I'll bet, and it's amazing that perhaps the best, most acceptable way to prepare them all is simply: HOT, (never overcooked), with lots of butter, pepper and salt. And sometimes, freshly grated cheese.

Try every one of the following. You'll be a better person for it. —Dave

99 LBS. NET WEIGHT
WHOLE BEAN
UNCOATED
TABLE RICE

Pasta and Rice

Hungarian Spaghetti

This originally came from Poland. An aunt of mine had a friend whose mother brought it to America, and she gave it to my aunt, who is now deceased. I've had it about forty years. The nice thing we like about this recipe is it tastes better after the first day it's made. Of course it's delicious when it's first made also.

1 large onion, chopped
1 large green pepper, chopped
1 tablespoon shortening
1 pound ground beef
1 pound American cheese, grated
1 large can tomatoes, drained
1 tablespoon flour
1 pound spaghetti, cooked and
   drained
   garlic, minced (optional)

Sauté onion and pepper in shortening, but do not brown. Add meat, cheese, tomatoes, garlic, and flour. Let simmer until done. Add cooked spaghetti, mix thoroughly, and serve. This is even better the second day after it has been made. Serves 8 to 10.

Dave's note: There's no need to drain the tomatoes. If you do, reserve the liquid in case the mixture starts to dry out.

VINA A. SIPES
WARREN, MICHIGAN

Italian Baked Macaroni

¼ cup olive oil
1 onion, diced
2 cloves garlic, minced
1 large can tomato paste

1 large can peeled, crushed
   tomatoes
3 slices bread, softened in water
1½ pounds ground beef
1 teaspoon salt
½ teaspoon pepper
4 eggs
2 teaspoons Parmesan cheese,
   grated
6 slices provolone cheese
8 Italian sweet sausages
1½ pounds boneless pork
2 tablespoons sugar
1 pound ziti macaroni
1 can mushrooms

Heat oil slowly. Add onion and garlic. Do not brown. Add paste and tomatoes plus 2 paste cans of water and 1 tomato can of water. Bring to boil, stir, then simmer. Make meatballs: soften 3 slices of bread in a little water. Squeeze dry and add to ground beef. Add salt, pepper, 1 egg and 2 teaspoons grated cheese. Mix well. Shape into bite-size meatballs and add to sauce.

Add sausages, pork, mushrooms, 1 teaspoon salt, ¼ teaspoon pepper and 2 tablespoons sugar. Mix well. Simmer for 2 to 2½ hours. When sauce is cooked, cook ziti in boiling water until chewy. Drain. Toss with margarine until melted. Add ½ cup sauce. Mix well. Add layer of pasta. Spoon over generous amounts of sauce. Arrange half of provolone cheese slices over sauce. Beat 3 eggs and pour half over cheese. Repeat pasta, sauce, cheese and eggs, ending with layers of pasta covered with a little sauce and grated Parmesan cheese. Bake at 350° for 25 to 35 minutes. Serves 8 to 10.

CATHERINE A. SANCES
SOUTH BOSTON, MASSACHUSETTS

Spaghetti Sauce

2   14-ounce cans Italian tomatoes
    salt
    pepper
    Italian seasonings
1½ pounds ground beef or pork
2   6-ounce cans tomato paste
6   Italian sweet sausages
6   hot Italian sausages

Put tomatoes in a large pan and add 2 tomato cans of water. Season lightly with several shakes of salt, pepper, and Italian seasonings — that's a mixture of oregano, basil, and parsley. Simmer for 20 to 30 minutes. While tomatoes are cooking, brown beef or pork in a bit of fat. (Any meat could be used — pork country-style ribs or chuck or even sirloin.) Also brown the sausages. When browned, combine meat plus pork fat from the skillet with tomato paste and sausages. Cook for at least 1½ hours uncovered. This recipe can be made in advance, but do not add the meatballs until the day it's served. If meatballs are added the day before, they become soggy.

Dave's note: I don't know how many sauce recipes we received, but it was difficult to pick one. I myself like a simple tomato sauce with no meat at all. I was overruled.

MARIE MULCAHY
WEST MEDFORD, MASSACHUSETTS

Manicotti

4   eggs
1   cup warm water
1   cup flour
    little salt

Beat eggs lightly with fork. Add water. Add flour and salt a little at a time so batter won't lump. Keep stirring until smooth. Drop batter by tablespoonful into a small frying pan (4½ or 5 inches) that has been preheated and oiled once. Shake and twist pan to allow batter to cover bottom of pan completely. Cook for a few seconds on one side only. Peel out and repeat until batter is used up. Stack like pancakes on a plate. Yields about 30. Next make filling.

Filling

5   eggs
2   pounds ricotta cheese
    handful grated cheese
    parsley, chopped
1½ to 2 cups tomato sauce

Beat eggs lightly; add cheeses and parsley. Mix until smooth. Place a spoonful in each pancake. Fold 2 opposite ends over. Arrange seam side down in a baking pan lined with tomato sauce. Pour more sauce over top. Bake for about 20 minutes at 325°. Let stand a few minutes before serving.

JENNIE SANTORO
NEWBURYPORT, MASSACHUSETTS

Pasta and Greens

My mother came from Italy in 1921 and they had pasta and greens there. We love it. It's about eighty years old.

2 cups fresh asparagus stems
1 small onion, chopped
1 large carrot, diced
3 tablespoons olive oil
½ cup elbow macaroni
    salt
    pepper
    Parmesan cheese, grated

Cut green asparagus stems into 1-inch cubes to measure about 2 cups. In a large skillet, combine carrot and olive oil with asparagus and slowly simmer until vegetables are *al dente* (slightly hard). In a separate pot, cook elbow macaroni until tender but firm. When done, drain macaroni and add to vegetable mixture. Season with salt and pepper to taste. Before serving, top with cheese. Serves 2 to 4.

Dave's note: Lots of chopped Italian parsley added with the cheese will make it taste even better.

LUCY R. MITCHELL
WALTHAM, MASSACHUSETTS

Fettuccine a la Romana

Today, pasta is one of America's most popular dishes. When I cook it, my children want it hot and dressed with butter and cheese (as my mother would do for us when we were their age). Most often I would add an egg and other ingredients which would make it a more colorful and nourishing meal.

Adding a little meat and vegetables to any pasta makes a delicious protein-rich meal with little fuss. It could be called "Mama Nina's Gourmet Pasta."

1   16-ounce package thin egg noodles
½   cup butter, melted
1   cup Parmesan cheese, grated
½   cup whipping cream
1   10-ounce package frozen peas, cooked
2½ cups ham, finely shredded
      salt to taste
      pepper to taste

Cook noodles *al dente* according to package directions; drain. Combine melted butter with remaining ingredients; mix well. Pour sauce over hot noodles and toss lightly. Serves 6 to 8.

Dave's note: This is such a basic dish, but made right it's one of the best. It's a watch-dish: don't go away and leave it.

MRS. NINA PILLA
WALTHAM, MASSACHUSETTS

Asparagus with Linguine

The Italian title would be "Sparagi con Linguini." As far as I can remember (and I'm sixty-seven), this dish has been in the family since they came from Sicily. It was one of my mother's favorite one course meals when meat was hard to come by. Of course, asparagus was about a dime for a large bunch.

As kids, we always griped when we knew we were going to have a meatless supper, but today I enjoy it so much.

1 pound fresh asparagus
¼ cup olive oil
   salt to taste
   pepper to taste
1½ cups water
2 cloves garlic, minced
½ cup Romano cheese, grated
4 tablespoons butter
¾ pound linguine
½ cup fine bread crumbs, browned in oil

Wash asparagus and break off into 2- or 3-inch pieces, discarding tough end. Blot with paper towel and saute in oil for about 5 minutes. Add salt, pepper, and water, and bring to a boil. Simmer for 5 minutes. Add garlic, cheese, and butter. Slowly simmer 5 more minutes. Meantime, cook linguine according to package directions and drain. Spoon asparagus with some broth into individual dishes in which portions of pasta should first be placed. Spoon lightly browned crumbs over asparagus and pasta. Extra cheese may be added. Exact amounts are not important. Serves 6.

Dave's note: We added a little lemon juice to the sauce. Delicious.

SARAH L. PITTS
ROCKLAND, MASSACHUSETTS

Lazy Man's Pierogi

I am of Polish descent and as you know, Polish people are lovers of cabbage. The reason it's called Lazy Man's Pierogi is that once your cabbage and bows or egg noodles are cooked, you just mix all together, not like the old-fashioned way of preparing this dish by making the turnovers, boiling, etc.

1 large head cabbage
1 medium onion
2 sticks margarine
1 teaspoon salt
½ teaspoon pepper (or a little less)
1 pound noodle bows or shells

Finely grate cabbage and onion. Melt 1 stick margarine in a frying pan; add cabbage, onion, salt, and pepper. Sauté until cabbage and onions are soft and light brown. Boil noodles according to directions on box. Drain and add to them cabbage and onion mixture Cube 1 stick margarine over mixture and mix well. Serve hot with a side dish of cottage cheese or a glass of buttermilk. This is even better heated the second day — the flavor improves. Serves 6 to 8.

Dave's note: You might try adding some caraway seeds in the final mixture. If you don't, make sure that you do the next day when you reheat the pierogi in a skillet with a little butter. Oh, boy!

GENEVIEVE CAISSE
PELHAM, NEW HAMPSHIRE

Spanish Noodles

6 slices bacon
1 medium onion, chopped
1 medium green pepper, chopped
1 pound ground beef
1 28-ounce can tomatoes in puree
1½ cups water
2 teaspoons salt
½ teaspoon oregano
   few red pepper flakes
   dash black pepper, freshly ground
6 ounces (about 3 cups) medium
   egg noodles

Cut bacon in 1-inch pieces. In a dutch oven, fry until brown and crisp. Remove and set aside. Sauté onion, green pepper, and ground beef in bacon drippings until beef is browned. Skim off fat. Add tomatoes, water, and seasonings. Cover and simmer for 10 minutes, then bring mixture to a full boil. Add noodles a few at a time so that mixture continues to boil. Reduce heat, cover, and simmer 10 minutes longer. Serves 4.

Dave's note: A nice, hearty dish. If you don't have the pepper flakes, use a few dashes of hot pepper sauce.

MRS. L. L. HUTCHINSON
LUNENBURG, MASSACHUSETTS

Essex Spaghetti with Clam Sauce

¼ pound butter
⅓ cup olive oil
3 cloves garlic, minced
1¼ teaspoons basil
½ cup Parmesan cheese, grated
3 tablespoons parsley, chopped
½ teaspoon oregano
1 teaspoon pepper, coarsely ground
½ teaspoon salt
2 small cans minced clams
1 pound linguine or vermicelli

Melt butter and oil in a pan. Add all other ingredients except pasta and heat thoroughly. Cook pasta following the directions on the package, then combine pasta with clam mixture and stir. Serves 4 to 6.

Dave's note: It's worth the trouble to buy fresh hardshell clams at a seafood store. If you've never shucked them before, ask the proprietor to show you how. If you do it wrong, you'll end up with a sledgehammer.

ALICE ERKKILA
GLOUCESTER, MASSACHUSETTS

Stuffed Shells

1 quart spaghetti sauce
1 pound ground beef
1 pint ricotta cheese
    dash garlic salt, salt, and pepper
¼ cup water
1 package large shells, cooked *al dente*
    Parmesan cheese to taste
    oregano (optional)

Line a lasagna pan with aluminum foil. Pour half of the sauce into the pan. Mix ground beef with ricotta, garlic salt, salt, and pepper. Use to stuff cooked shells and place in pan. Pour remaining sauce over shells, then pour water over shells. Shake Parmesan cheese over shells and a little oregano if desired. Cover pan tightly with foil and bake for 1½ hours at 350°. Serves 4 to 6.

Dave's note: Make sure the shells are not overcooked. Overcooking any pasta ruins it.

MRS. ALICE THOMAS
ROSLINDALE, MASSACHUSETTS

Homemade Noodles

I was taught this recipe when I worked in Walpole, Massachusetts in 1935. An Italian lady used to give my employer these noodles.

4 cups flour
1 teaspoon salt
4 eggs
1 tablespoon oil

Combine flour and salt in a mound on a board. Depress the middle slightly, and into the center, drop eggs and oil. With your fingers, slowly draw in the flour until well mixed and the dough is formed. (Can also be mixed in a bowl, if preferred.) Knead dough until smooth and elastic (about 15 minutes). Cover; set aside for 30 minutes. Then divide dough into 4 parts. Roll each part on floured board to paper thinness. Place on a floured towel; dry for 30 minutes. Then roll up each sheet tightly, like a jelly roll, and cut ½-inch-wide noodles. With your fingers under the cut noodles, lift and shake them loosely back onto the towel and spread evenly to dry for 30 minutes. Drop into boiling salted water and cook until tender. Drain well. Serves 4 to 6.

Dave's note: Your own noodles are so far superior to store-bought. I'll never forget the first time I made them: I put up string clotheslines over which I hung the noodles to dry. It looked like a pasta no-man's-land for 24 hours. And it really wasn't necessary.

BETTY UNDERWOOD
FITCHBURG, MASSACHUSETTS

Leone's Quick, Tasty Lasagna

2 pounds ground beef
1 48-ounce jar meatless tomato sauce
1 pound curly lasagna
2 tablespoons oil
2 tablespoons salt
1 48-ounce container whole-milk
ricotta cheese or large-curd cottage
cheese
3 eggs
18 ounces whole milk mozzarella
cheese, shredded
pepper

Brown meat in a large skillet. Add sauce and let simmer for 45 minutes. Cook lasagna according to package directions, adding oil and salt to water when it comes to a boil. Mix ricotta cheese and eggs lightly in a bowl. Pour a light covering of sauce on bottom of a 9 x 13-inch pan to prevent lasagna from sticking. Spread a layer of lasagna over sauce, add meat and sauce combination over the lasagna, then ricotta. Then add a sprinkling of mozzarella. Sprinkle lightly with pepper. Repeat this layering process.

Bake lasagna in a preheated oven at 350° to 375° for 40 minutes, or until bubbly. Let stand for 25 minutes before serving so lasagna "jells" together. Pour any leftover sauce over each serving. Serves 9 hearty portions.

Dave's note: Everybody says he or she makes the best lasagna. There are as many recipes as there are people. This one is very quick and will taste just as good as the prepared sauce and cheeses that you use.

SAL LEONE
OLD ORCHARD BEACH, MAINE

Cheese Custard Macaroni

My recipe has been in the family since I was seven years old. I am now seventy-two. Served warm, this macaroni and cheese does not run all over your plate like they serve in eating places. Served cold, it can be cut in a wedge or slice and eaten with a vegetable salad. It is yummy.

1 cup elbow macaroni
1 pint milk
sprinkle of pepper
pinch soda
2 eggs, beaten
¾ cup sharp cheese, grated
pinch salt

Cook macaroni in boiling, salted water until tender. Drain. In a bowl mix all other ingredients. Put macaroni into a baking dish; add the cheese custard. Bake at 325° for 30 minutes, or until set. Serves 2.

Dave's note: This is also great for a late, late snack, such as when you're watching a movie that's so old, Walter Brennan gets the girl.

IRENE M. DE MARTIN
SPRINGFIELD, MASSACHUSETTS

Rice Salad with Bacon

8 slices bacon, cooked and crumbled
3 cups rice, cooked
1 cup green peas, cooked
1 cup celery, thinly sliced
½ cup mayonnaise
¼ cup pimiento, diced
¼ cup chives, minced (or scallion
  tops, thinly sliced)
¼ teaspoon salt
¼ teaspoon pepper
  a little vinegar to sharpen (or lemon
  juice to lighten)

Combine all ingredients and toss. Chill.
Serves 6.

*Dave's note: You might try a vinai-
grette dressing with garlic instead of
the mayonnaise—the taste is a little
sharper and you cut down the calories. Also, this looks pretty good when
served in large, scooped-out tomatoes.*

MRS. MABEL C. BRYANT
COLONIAL BEACH, VIRGINIA

Rose's Super Pilaf

⅔ cup fine noodles, broken into
  small pieces
½ cup pignoli nuts (optional)
¼ cup peanut oil
2 cups long-grain rice
4⅓ cups chicken broth
1 teaspoons salt
¼ teaspoon pepper
¾ tablespoon onion powder
2 tablespoons butter

Brown noodles and pignoli nuts in oil
until golden. Stir constantly, watching
carefully to avoid burning noodles.
Remove from heat, add rice, and mix
to blend. Add hot chicken broth to
rice mixture. Place over medium heat
and add salt, pepper, onion powder,
and butter. Stir, cover, and cook for
20 minutes. Stir once during the first 5
minutes and do not stir again. Cook
until all liquid has been absorbed and
the rice is tender. If not tender at that
point, add ¼ cup more broth; cover
and simmer 10 minutes more. Serves
10 to 12.

*Dave's note: Hope you can afford
the pine nuts, because they add a lot
of flavor. For a little extra color and
flavor, add chopped parsley or finely
chopped scallion tops.*

ROSE PANOSIAN
STONEHAM, MASSACHUSETTS

Hawaiian Rice

This recipe was given to me thirty years ago by a friend I was visiting in Van Nuys, California. I have used it many times for buffet suppers. There is never any left over, and many who claim not to care for rice have come back for seconds.

2 cups long-grain rice
4 cups boiling water
1 teaspoon salt
¼ cup oil
1 green pepper, chopped
1 onion, chopped
1 teaspoon garlic salt (fresh clove, minced, would be better)
½ teaspoon pepper
3 tablespoons soy sauce
1 cup slivered almonds

Delicately toast rice to a light tan in a 400° oven, stirring occasionally in a shallow pan for about 10 minutes, watching carefully all the while. Put the toasted rice into a casserole dish with boiling water and salt. Place in a 350° oven for 30 minutes. While rice bakes, sauté in oil for not more than 5 minutes the green pepper and onion. When rice is cooked, stir in vegetables and garlic salt, pepper, soy sauce, and slivered almonds. Mix well. Taste — add a pinch of sugar if necessary — then return to casserole dish. Reheat when ready to use. Serves about 10. Goes well with any buffet menu.

Dave's note: Nice flavor, nice texture. Make sure the vegetables are crunchy.

MRS. FRANK F. COOK
WAKEFIELD, RHODE ISLAND

Rice Jardin

The addition of a couple of sliced frankfurters and about ½ cup canned tomatoes with juice and you have a tasty one-dish meal.

¼ cup onions, chopped
5 ounces zucchini, thinly sliced
1 tablespoon butter or margarine
⅓ cup whole kernel corn, drained
⅓ cup canned tomatoes, chopped and partially drained
1 cup rice, cooked
½ teaspoon salt
    dash pepper, oregano, and sugar (optional)

Saute onions and zucchini in butter until tender. Add remaining ingredients. Cover and simmer 15 minutes. Delicious. Serves 2 to 4.

Dave's note: This is a very colorful dish. Great for hiding left-over corn-on-the-cob. The second time I made it, I used fresh tomatoes and snuck in some other left-over vegetables. Crafty, eh?

MARIAN BARBETT
LAWRENCE, MASSACHUSETTS

Jag: Cape Verdian Rice

The original recipe also had butternut squash cut in pieces, blanched kale, and hominy (soaked overnight in water, then drained) added on top of the recipe below in layers. This was a complete meal in the Cape Verde Islands. But after awhile it was shortened to the recipe below and served as a side dish with chicken, pork, or beef.

2 tablespoons onion, chopped
2 tablespoons oil
½ bay leaf
1 teaspoon salt
pepper, freshly ground
½ teaspoon paprika
2 cups water
1 can shell beans, washed and drained
1 cup rice

In a 2-quart pot with a tightly fitting cover, sauté onions in oil until tender. Add bay leaf, salt, pepper, paprika, and water. Bring to a boil. Add shell beans and rice. Bring to a boil, stir, and cover. Lower flame to lowest point. Cook for 20 minutes. Remove from heat. Let stand for 10 minutes. Before serving mix well. Serves 6 to 8.

Variations: Substitute butter for oil, 1 cup cooked lima beans for shell beans, and 2 cups chicken broth for water.

Dave's note: Maybe I'm a spicy food fan, but I believe this would taste a bit better with a little lemon juice or some minced fresh garlic or a few dashes of Worcestershire sauce.

JULIETTE SILVA
ROXBURY, MASSACHUSETTS

Rice with Cabbage

This dish was good during the Depression years as it is filling and tasty, if you happen to like both ingredients. I did and do!

½ medium head cabbage, finely chopped
½ cup green peppers, thinly sliced
2 slices bacon, diced
1½ cups rice cooked
½ cup chicken stock (or bouillon cube)
salt and pepper

Cook cabbage, green peppers, and bacon for 30 minutes over low heat. Add rice, chicken stock, and salt and pepper to taste. Simmer for 15 minutes. Serves 4.

Dave's note: Better to hold salt until the end inasmuch as bacon and stock have salt in them. You might stir in a little paprika and, for variation, use grated carrots and some freshly snipped dill instead of green pepper.

MRS. EDWIN H. LOWELL
BATH, MAINE

Wild Rice Dressing

About all I can tell of the origin of this recipe is that it was given to me by a farmer neighbor who now lives in Iowa. It came from her mother.

We use it mainly as a side dish rather than a dressing for fowl, and it goes well with both pork and beef as well as fowl.

1 onion, chopped
1 cup celery, diced
¼ cup butter or margarine
2 cans chicken broth
1 pound pork sausage, fried in small chunks
8 slices wheat bread, toasted and torn in small pieces
1 8-ounce box wild rice, cooked

Sauté onions and celery in butter or margarine until tender. Mix with all other ingredients and place in a greased casserole dish. Bake at 350° about 45 minutes. Serves 6 to 8.

Dave's note: Good strong flavor. Would go well with game or poultry.

JEAN KETTLE
JANESVILLE, WISCONSIN

Spanish Rice

My maternal grandmother, Susan Weeks, gave this recipe to my mother when she was married in June of 1898. It has always been a family favorite. I serve it with a green salad, hot rolls and coffee for a winter's night supper. The following little poem (author unknown) accompanied the original recipe.
"The good old things have passed away in silence and retreat,
We've lots of hifalutin things, but nothing much to eat,
And while I never say a word and always pleasant look,
I've always had dyspepsia since my daughter learned to cook."

1 cup sharp cheese, grated
3 cups rice, cooked
3 large green peppers, chopped
1 large onion, chopped
6 heaping teaspoons chili sauce
1 teaspoon salt
1 teaspoon hot pepper sauce

In a buttered baking dish, combine all ingredients but cheese. Sprinkle cheese on top and bake at 350° for 45 minutes to 1 hour, or until brown. Serves 6 to 8.

Dave's note: You might want to go easy on the hot pepper sauce. One teaspoon gives the rice a great taste— but it is hot. Very flavorful with a thick cheesy crust.

ELSIE WEHLE
LEXINGTON, KENTUCKY

Emerald Fried Rice

This recipe was from a Taiwan cook-book given to a Chinese bridegroom with whom I had the pleasure of working.

1 pound Chinese cabbage, shredded
1 teaspoon salt
4 tablespoons oil
1 egg, beaten
4 tablespoons scallions, chopped
¼ cup ham or roast pork, chopped
¼ teaspoon msg (optional)
4 cups rice (cooked a day before so it won't get mushy)

Sprinkle cabbage with salt and let stand for 10 or 15 minutes. Then squeeze dry and chop up again. Heat 1 tablespoon oil in a frying pan. Pour in egg and make a thin pancake. Re-move egg pancake and dice it in ⅓-inch pieces. Heat 1 tablespoon oil in a pan. Stir-fry cabbage for about a min-ute and remove. Heat another 2 table-spoons of oil in same pan. Fry scallions for 10 seconds. Then add rice and meat and mix well. Reduce heat and stir until rice is thoroughly heated. Add 1 teaspoon salt, msg, cabbage, egg pancake, and ham. Stir well and serve on platter. Serves 6 to 8.

Dave's note: If you choose to add more ham or pork, this becomes a meal in itself. Be very careful with the msg—some people cannot take it.

MARY SKINNER
BRIGHTON, MASSACHUSETTS

Rice with Shrimp Italienne

One of our favorite seafoods is shrimp. I have prepared it in many ways, but my family prefers tomatoes in sauces, so I tried my recipe and it made a big hit with everyone. It is delicious, easy and in this way, it is a hearty first course.

1½ pounds medium shrimp (with shells)
3 cups salted water
¾ cup butter
½ medium onion, sliced
1 carrot, finely diced
1 teaspoon parsley, chopped
⅛ teaspoon thyme (or oregano)
1 bay leaf
2 tablespoons brandy
½ medium onion, minced
1 tablespoon olive oil
1 pound rice
1 cup dry red wine

Shell shrimp. Boil shrimp for 20 minutes in salted water. Drain shrimp, reserv-ing stock. Place ¼ cup butter, onion, shrimp, carrot, parsley, thyme, and bay leaf in a saucepan and sauté until brown. Add brandy and cook until evaporated. In a larger pan, place on-ion, olive oil, and ½ cup butter and saute until lightly browned. Add rice and cook until lightly browned; then add wine. Cook until wine evaporates, then add 2 cups of stock and cook rice until tender (about 20 minutes). Remove from heat, and arrange on platter. Pour shrimp over rice and serve. Serves 6 (one cup of cooked rice per person).

Dave's note: How can you go wrong? It looks good, tastes good, and is rela-tively easy to prepare.

MRS. WILLIAM E. CIPRIANO
CRANSTON, RHODE ISLAND

Tofu and Brown Rice Casserole

1¼ tablespoons butter
4½ teaspoons oil
1½ onions, thinly sliced
1 cup brown rice, cooked
12 to 16 ounces tofus, press liquid out
dash pepper
1 cup milk
½ cup wheat germ
3 ounces mild cheese, grated

Preheat oven to 350°. Heat a large skillet and coat with butter and 2 teaspoons oil. Add onion and saute until lightly browned. Add brown rice, then tofu, and saute each for 2 minutes. Season with pepper. Place tofu and onion mixture in a 1½- to 2-quart casserole dish, coated with remaining oil. Pour in milk; sprinkle with wheat germ and cheese. Bake for 20 minutes, or until cheese is browned.

Dave's note: I make no bones about the fact that I hate bean curd, but — when used in recipes such as this — it does taste pretty good. And when I eat all of that pure protein, I feel like Popeye.

BARBARA CHAMPEON
CAPE ELIZABETH, MAINE

Braised Rice and Onions

½ cup rice, raw
2 cups water, salted
4 tablespoons butter
6 cups yellow onions, thinly sliced
½ teaspoon salt
⅛ teaspoon white pepper
¼ cup whipping cream
¼ cup Swiss cheese, grated
2 tablespoons butter, softened
1 tablespoon parsley, minced

Drop rice in boiling water for exactly 5 minutes, then drain. Melt butter in a 3-quart casserole dish and coat dish well; stir in onions. Add rice, salt, and pepper. Cover and cook for 1 hour at 300°, stirring from time to time. This can be made early and reheated. When ready to serve, reheat, stir in cream, cheese, and butter, and sprinkle with parsley. Very good with fowl, lamb, and small game. Serves 4 to 6.

Dave's note: The onion flavor really makes it. A rich, creamy rice dish.

EBBA WITTKONSKI
GRAND RAPIDS, MICHIGAN

Green Rice Bake

Sorry I do not have much to offer you in the way of anything to do with the recipe. It is old, I truly have no idea where it came from, and I have changed it from basic rice and broccoli to the tasty dish it is today. The rice remains white, and people do expect it to be green! However, that was the original name and I kept it.

2 eggs, beaten
2 cups milk
1 cup sharp cheddar cheese, shredded or chopped
1 package frozen broccoli, partially thawed, drained, and coarsely chopped
1 cup rice, cooked
1 tablespoon onion, minced
1 small can mushrooms (optional; fresh would be better)
1 clove garlic, finely minced
  salt
  pepper
½ to 1 cup unflavored bread crumbs

Combine eggs and milk. Add remaining ingredients except bread crumbs and mix well. Pour into a buttered 2-quart casserole dish. Sprinkle with unflavored bread crumbs. Bake at 325° for 35 to 40 minutes, or until a knife inserted into the center comes out clean. Makes 4 to 6 servings.

Dave's note: Instead of frozen vegetables, this dish offers a great chance to use fresh, seasonal vegetables. So do it.

T. E. BARTON
MILFORD, MASSACHUSETTS

Italian Rice Balls

I learned how to cook very early in life at my father's apron strings. He was born in Italy and brought with him many ways to stretch a food budget. These Italian Rice Balls have a center of melty mozzarella that strings when eaten. So we called them "Suppli al Telefono," or "Telephone Wires."

2 cups rice
4 eggs, separated
½ cup provolone cheese, shredded
8 ounces mozzarella cheese, cut into 24 cubes
1 cup Italian bread crumbs
  vegetable oil
1 package hollandaise sauce mix
  parsley, chopped

Cook rice and drain. Fold in egg yolks and provolone. Shape into 24 balls. Push a cube of mozzarella into center covering completely with rice mixture. Beat egg whites slightly. Gently roll rice balls in egg whites and then in crumbs. Place on a sheet pan and chill thoroughly until firm. Fry balls 2 or 3 at a time in 3 inches of hot oil in a heavy pan. Drain balls and keep warm. Prepare hollandaise sauce following directions on label. Stir in parsley. Arrange rice balls on a platter and spoon sauce over them. Yields 24.

Dave's note: Delicious, and very good without the sauce, too. Just sprinkle with chopped parsley. These aranchini *can be popped into lunchboxes and bags the next day, too.*

RAYE PATRONE
JOHNSTON, RHODE ISLAND

Delicious Rice Kugel

I am happy that you plan to use my recipe, for it truly is delicious.

2   cups rice
1½ teaspoons salt
4½ cups water
6   eggs, separated
½   cup sugar
½   cup raisins
½   cup butter or margarine, melted

Bring rice, salt, and water to a boil. Stir, cover, and simmer for 12 minutes. Remove from heat and let stand 5 minutes. Meanwhile beat egg yolks with sugar until pale yellow. Add to rice together with raisins and butter. Mix well and fold in egg whites, which have been beaten until they hold a peak. Bake in a greased 9 x 13-inch casserole dish for 30 minutes at 350°. Makes about 20 2-inch squares.

Dave's note: Sweet, puffy and light but filling. I'd use a little less sugar and a few more raisins. Jewish people serve this with meat dishes, but I think it's sweet enough to make a great snack.

ROSE BENJAMIN
WORCESTER, MASSACHUSETTS

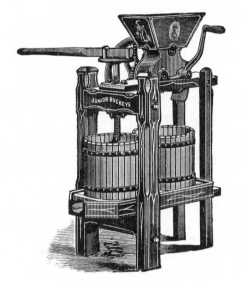

Never in my wildest dreams did I foresee how many winos listen to me at night. I say that in good fun, of course. When the recipes for home-made wine poured in (no pun), I knew that you were my people. Good Lord, I know now, without doubt, that you can make wine out of almost anything. Berries, fruits, flowers, Vegetables (including tomatoes). And I really thought that it wouldn't be too long before somebody sent in a recipe for making wine out of leftover potato salad. It's nice to see that the art of winemaking is being practiced more and more all over America, and why not? I'll quote Mr. Ludwig of Mayhill Vineyards in Goffstown, New Hampshire: "You can order a bottle at an outstanding restaurant, pay through the nose and discover your homemade brew is better. I know some amateur oenologists whose product in blind tests outrank even the best California vintages."

Not only that, but it's fun...it's exciting and if it's done right, you can feel pretty lordly. Making wine is like making love. Some people take the trouble to learn the technique...others don't. —Dave

Beverages

Flower Teas

1 teaspoon dried leaves for each cup
  of tea
1 teaspoon for the pot
  OR
3 teaspoons fresh leaves
  boiling water
  Use dried flowers of camomile, dried
  or fresh leaves and flower buds of
  lavender, dried or fresh leaves of
  geranium, dried or fresh rose petals,
  or dried leaves of sweet goldenrod.

If you are using fresh leaves, bruise
them gently by crushing carefully in a
clean cloth. With boiling water, rinse
to heat the pot. Throw this water out.
Now add the leaves to the warmed
pot and pour boiling water over them.
Let steep for 3 to 5 minutes.

CHRIS ARMSTRONG
NEW YORK, NEW YORK

Glog

The Horse and Mule live thirty years,
and nothing know of wine or beers,
  The Goat and Sheep they also die,
and never taste of scotch or rye,
The Cow drinks water by the ton, and
at eighteen years is mostly done,
  Without the aid of rum or gin, the
Dog at fifteen cashes in,
The Cat in milk and water soaks, and
then in twelve short years it croaks,
  The modest sober bone-dry Hen,
lays eggs for nogs then dies at ten,
All animals are strictly dry, they sinless
live and swiftly die,
  But sinful ginful rum-soaked Men,
survive by three score years and ten,
And some of us — a mighty few, keep
drinking till we're ninety-two.

This is an old English recipe.

1 ounce bitters
¾ cup sugar
1 pint claret
1 pint sherry
½ pint brandy
13 raisins
13 almonds

Mix bitters, sugar, and liquors in a
large pan. Heat until piping hot but
not boiling. For individual servings, put
a raisin and almond in an old-fashioned
glass or punch cup and fill ¾ full. A
spoon in the glass before pouring will
prevent cracking.
  Makes 13 3-ounce servings. May be
served in a coffee pot on a warmer, or
even ladled from a bean pot.

*Dave's note: A definite whoopee
juice. I'll bet that many a dull Christmas party has been turned into a rip-
roarer with this.*

BARBARA JEFFREY YOUNG
COCHITUATE, MASSACHUSETTS

Coffee Carnival

Coffee Carnival was one of Mama's
recipes, and when I was married forty
years ago, it was one of her recipes I
took to my new home. I have no idea
how she got it.
  I served it one night when I had a
committee meeting. My husband laughed
at the quantity I made and said he'd
be eating it all week. With a good dab
of cream on top, it stretched to serve
us all. However, he got just *one* serving instead of his usual *two*.

⅓ cup tapioca
½ cup sugar
¼ teaspoon salt

1½ cups water
⅓ cup raisins
1 cup strong coffee
1 teaspoon vanilla
1 cup whipped cream

In a saucepan combine tapioca, sugar, salt, water, and raisins. Bring to a full boil, stirring constantly. Add coffee and vanilla. Cool, stirring occasionally. When chilled, fold in cream. Serves 8.

Dave's note: You could add some spirits here, if you wanted to. It wouldn't harm anything.

MRS. HENRY P. TILDEN
WEYMOUTH, MASSACHUSETTS

Russian Instant Tea

This makes forty cups and is good to serve when crowds drop in.

2 cups orange concentrate
½ cup instant tea mix
1 envelope lemon-flavored tea
1⅓ cups sugar
½ teaspoon ground cloves
1 teaspoon cinnamon

Mix all ingredients well. Use 1 teaspoon of this dry mixture to 1 cup boiling water for each serving.

MARGIE MELTON
ORANGE, VIRGINIA

Salem College Iced Tea

From Old Salem, a historical Moravian (German) settlement restored in Winston-Salem, North Carolina.

4 sprigs fresh mint
8 to 12 whole cloves
3 quarts water

1 ounce tea
juice of 8 lemons
juice of 6 oranges
1 46-ounce can pineapple juice
1 pound sugar

Add mint and cloves to water and bring to a boil. Simmer for 10 to 15 minutes. Add tea and allow to steep for 10 to 15 minutes. Strain and while hot, add juices and sugar. Stir well to dissolve sugar. Makes 3 quarts.

MRS. THADDEOUS SHORE, JR.
BOONVILLE, NORTH CAROLINA

Tomato Juice Cocktail

This is *the best!*

½ bushel tomatoes, stems removed
1 bunch celery, cut up
celery leaves
3 red peppers, seeds removed
9 onions, peeled
16 sprigs parsley
50 whole cloves
14 bay leaves
2 cups sugar
½ cup salt

Wash the vegetables. Place them together with the other ingredients in a kettle and cook slowly until well cooked. Strain and reheat to a boiling point. Pour in hot jars. Shake before using.

Dave's note: They say that a Bloody Mary without booze is a bloody shame. The cocktail is refreshing as is! Non-drinkers, take heart!

MARIAN L. PIPER
ACTON, MASSACHUSETTS

Dandelion Wine

Many years ago our family doctor used to call on my aged aunt next door. He was white haired and pale and walked slowly as he carried his worn black bag to the door. After prescribing for my aunt, he always came out cheerful with rosy cheeks and seemed real spry as he got into his horse-drawn buggy and trotted away.

A few years later my aunt told me the doctor always had a glass of her dandelion wine, the recipe which had been in her family for one hundred years.

3 quarts dandelion blossoms
4 quarts boiling water
4 pounds granulated sugar
3 lemons, cut in thin slices
4 oranges, cut in thin slices
1 compressed yeast cake

Put blossoms in a jar and pour boiling water over them. Cover and let stand 48 hours. Squeeze blossoms but don't strain them. Add lemons and oranges and sugar. Dissolve yeast cake in a little warm water and add.

This makes about a gallon or so. Put in a 2-gallon jar so it will not run over while fermenting, which takes about 10 days in a warm place.

Stir each morning. When fermenting stops, strain and bottle. Store in a cool place to age.

Dave's note: According to some folks the wine will be better if you pick blossoms while the sun is shining.

ANN RICE JACOBSEN
SARANAC LAKE, NEW YORK

Rice Wine

I believe this came from the old country—Sweden—as it was my mother's from a long time ago! She used to make it in a big clear glass crock, and she could sit my kiddos in the high chair to watch the rice "work." But as they got older, they were told the rice were "bees" that were making honey! The rice would go up and down, and when my father would have a drink, they really thought he was drinking honey.

1 yeast cake
3 gallons lukewarm water
18 cups seedless raisins
2 pounds white rice
5 pounds sugar
1 large orange

Dissolve yeast in a small amount of water. Put in a crock with all other ingredients. Cover with cheesecloth. Put in warm place, stir every day for 3 weeks, then filter into bottles.

HELEN SYVERTSON
WILMINGTON, MASSACHUSETTS

Hot Wine

Excellent for a wine and cheese party.

1 cup port wine
1 bottle burgundy
1 cinnamon stick, broken in pieces
1/4 teaspoon ground cloves
1/4 teaspoon nutmeg
1/4 cup lemon juice
2/3 cup sugar

Combine all ingredients in a saucepan and heat but do not boil. Float lemon slices on top. Serve from a fondue pot or a carafe over a candle.

Dave's note: Virginians don't really appreciate this spicy hot vino as much as I—as a New Englander—do. This wine gives you an excuse to go out and build a snowman.

DONNA MEYER
STERLING, VIRGINIA

Tomato Wine

Most everyone expects this to be red or even pink, but it is a beautiful, clear amber—a lovely way to enjoy your tomatoes all winter.

6 pounds ripe tomatoes
2 cakes yeast
6 pounds sugar
1 pound seedless raisins
1 gallon lukewarm water
1 potato, pared and cubed

Wash and quarter tomatoes, removing stem and blossom ends. Dissolve yeast in 1 cup warm water.

Then mix all ingredients in a large container.

Stir mixture once a day for 14 days. Then strain into several ½-gallon bottles and let set for one week (this will give you a clear wine).

Bottle, being careful not to stir up the settlings from the bottom.

Yields: 1 gallon plus (depending on tomatoes)

MRS. GORDON (ANNE) WALTON
NEWBURYPORT, MASSACHUSETTS

Blackberry Wine

This was given to me by a little old lady called the "Herb Lady" of the Plymouth Antiquarian Society. She is gone now, but her recipes carry on, thanks to her generosity.

6 quarts blackberries
6 cups water
2 cups sugar
1 slice rye toast
1 cake yeast

Boil berries and water gently for 15 minutes. Press out juice, and to each quart of juice add 2 cups sugar. Pour into a large jar. Spread one cake yeast on rye toast and float on top of juice. Keep jar covered for 1 week, then carefully pour off wine into gallon jugs.

Dave's note: Three glasses of this and you'll never make cracks about little old ladies again.

SYLVIA F. COFFIN
PLYMOUTH, MASSACHUSETTS

Deep Red Elderberry Wine

This wine is really wonderful, even after three months. Wish one could buy wine as good.

4 quarts elderberries
4 quarts water
8 cups sugar
1 cup muscat raisins, chopped
1 ounce yeast
1 slice white toast

With scissors, cut away fleshy stalks from elderberries, leaving intact the weblike stems (the little stems add color). Put into an enamel canning kettle with water. Bring to a rolling boil and boil for 30 minutes. Cool and strain through jelly bag. While still lukewarm, add sugar and stir until dissolved. Add raisins. Moisten yeast and spread on toast. Float yeast-side down. Set in a warm place to ferment two weeks (don't touch).

Strain through several thicknesses of cheesecloth into sterilized bottles and cork lightly. When fermentation has definitely ceased, cork bottles tightly and seal with paraffin. Keep one year—if you can!!

Dave's note: My favorite. When it gets robust, it's an excellent wine for making sangria.

GRAMIE RODENHISER

Orange Julius

My husband spent twenty years in the U.S. Navy. We were in Hawaii for three years from 1957 to 1960 (oh, so hard to take!) when he was stationed at N.A.S. Barber's Point. While there, many of us navy wives exchanged recipes. Orange Julius was one of the many I received. It is our favorite refresher in the summertime. It can also be made with frozen pineapple for Pineapple Julius.

1 6-ounce can frozen orange juice concentrate
1 cup milk
1 cup water
1/2 cup sugar (or less)
1 teaspoon vanilla extract
10 to 11 ice cubes

Combine all ingredients and blend on low speed until smooth. Serve immediately. Serves 4.

Dave's note: This is sensational when juniper berry juice is added on a 1 to 5 basis.

DOROTHY B. MCLAUGHLIN
WOBURN, MASSACHUSETTS

Fish House Punch

This recipe is believed to be the authentic Fish House Punch from the famous Fish House Club of Philadelphia. It assures the party host a never-to-be-forgotten occasion.

3/4 pound sugar
juice of 12 lemons
1 quart Jamaica rum
1 quart brandy
2 quarts water
1 glass peach brandy or peach cordial

Dissolve sugar in about a pint of water. When entirely dissolved, add lemon juice. Then add rum, brandy, water and peach brandy or cordial. For dramatic results, allow to stand in the refrigerator for a couple of days. When ready to serve, pour over a large piece of ice in a punch bowl. Any unused punch may be kept in sealed bottles for the following day.

Dave's note: If served at your next party, take away everybody's car keys and get set for a long night. This punch is a lip-loosener.

MARY JENKINS
SCITUATE, MASSACHUSETTS

Percolator Hot Punch

9 cups unsweetened pineapple juice
9 cups cranberry juice
4 1/2 cups water
1 cup brown sugar
4 1/2 teaspoons whole cloves
4 cinnamon sticks, broken up
1/4 teaspoon salt

Put juices, water, and sugar in a coffee percolator and stir. Into coffeepot basket, put cloves, cinnamon, and salt. Plug in pot or set on burner. Allow to percolate for three cycles. Makes 25 to 30 cups.

MRS. LAWRENCE WICHERTS
STERLING, ILLINOIS

Honey Liquor

I am a sixty-eight-year-old, first-generation American, raised in the true Lithuanian fashion. Lithuanian cuisine bespeaks a good, solid, thrifty folk with a long background of agricultural undertaking. This and many other typical recipes of Lithuanian culinary lore were carried to America only in the minds and hands of our mothers in the late 1800s and early 1900s.

Honey Liquor was mainly a Christmas holiday treat and was generally served warm. It was permitted to "wet the lips" of all who gathered for the traditional Christmas feast following midnight Mass, including the very youngest who either stayed awake or was awakened for the traditional family toast.

8 to 10 whole cloves
5 to 6 peppercorns
2 pieces ginger
1 nutmeg, cracked
3 sticks cinnamon
2 cups honey
1 cup water
2 1/2 cups pure grain alcohol

Add spices to honey and water. Boil for about ½ hour, until flavor of spices is fully extracted. Cool. Strain through cloth. Measure. Add equal amount of alcohol. Bottle. Serve warm or cold.

Dave's note: Very smooth.

ALICE B. CRISTOPHER
ROCKY POINT, NEW YORK

Real Old-Fashioned Ginger Beer

This is a fond childhood recipe given to my mother many years ago by an elderly farmer's wife who kept more than busy making root beer, switchel, and this wonderfully zingy thirst quencher for the workers in the hayfields. Visiting the farm as a child, I helped fill the stonecrock bottles with the clamp-type wired china tops and red rubber washers. For this I was given a soup bowl full of homemade strawberry ice cream, which I shared with the family dog. As I remember it, this ginger beer was a country fair prize winner.

1 pound sugar
1 gallon water
1 ounce lemon juice,
   freshly squeezed
1 tablespoon honey
1 ounce ginger root, crushed
1 package yeast OR
   1 compressed yeast cake
1 egg white, beaten

Dissolve sugar in boiling water. Add lemon juice, honey, and ginger. Stir well. When lukewarm, add yeast, which has been dissolved in a little warm water with ½ teaspoon sugar. Allow to cool thoroughly. Add egg white (to clarify). Let stand in a kettle or crock at room temperature covered lightly with a clean cloth for 4 or 5 days. Bottle and cork or cap. Keep in a cool place away from sunlight.

INGRID M. PARIDON
CLIFTONDALE, MASSACHUSETTS

Dave's Fancy Moselle

1 fancy deep burgundy glass
1 (or more, if people are going to ask
   for some) bottle of very cold
   moselle wine
1 container of fruit (peaches,
   strawberries, green seedless
   grapes, cherries, melon if
   it's fresh and very firm)
2 cups Grand Marnier
1 slice lime

Peel and dice fruit into large pieces. Marinate in Grand Marnier for 24 hours. Place fruit in bottom of fancy glass, cover with the Deutsch wein, add a twist of fresh lime and, my dears, that's it. School's out.

By the way, serve the Grand Marnier in a pony after dinner if it's not mysteriously gone by then.

DAVE

Give me some hot cherry pie and a lot of vanilla ice cream, a beautiful girl, and a cool shady tree to sit under in summer, and you can keep the girl and the tree. That's how much I love cherry pie. Then why no recipe of one in this chapter? Simple. Just about everyone already knows how to bake a cherry pie. But praline pumpkin? Kentucky Derby Pie? Old-fashioned white potato?

The week in which these pies were tested was, without a doubt, bad day at Black Rock. My caloric intake nearly tripled. I mean, you can't be fair to someone's labor with just a taste, so needless to say, I went all out. Ate some, snuck some more. I thought I'd be walking around naked for lack of clothes to wear. Didn't scare me, though—I love to hear people laugh.

Cookies, Pies, and Cakes

One suggestion. When you make one of these, don't. Make two.

Cakes, though, are not a big favorite with me. I have been known to turn on to a seven-layer tort if it was handy, but otherwise, I'm a slab-of-pie and cookies-and-milk man myself.

I'm clearly in a minority. Plans are already underway for another book of desserts, or a cookbook for cakes alone. Unbelievable as it might seem, some 2700 cake ideas were sent to me. Although there was some duplication, I dare say I could make a different cake every day for the next three years! I hope you're impressed. I was.

(And as for duplication, perhaps an apology should go to those who sent in one of the following recipes only to find somebody else's name on the bottom of the page. It only means that someone sent theirs in first.)

So troops, here you go. Get that unbleached flour ready and full speed ahead. I'll see you 10,000 calories from now.—DAVE

Colorado Oatmeal Cookies

This recipe is over fifty years old. My mother-in-law baked them regularly for her cookie jar. It was a favorite. A neighbor's daughter sent the recipe home from Denver, Colorado.

1 cup raisins (boil in enough
   water to cover until
   tender and save the
   water)
1 cup sugar
1 cup lard
1 egg beaten
1 teaspoon baking soda
   dissolved in raisin water
1 teaspoon cinnamon
2 to 2 1/2 cups flour, sifted
2 cups rolled oats

Combine together sugar and lard. Add egg, baking soda dissolved in raisin water, cinnamon, flour, rolled oats, and boiled raisins. Drop teaspoonfuls of batter (size of a walnut) onto a well-greased cookie sheet. Bake at 350° for 8 to 12 minutes. Makes about 3 dozen.

Dave's note: Thought it could use 1/4 teaspoon of salt. This is a healthy-tasting cookie—really—it tastes healthy. Should make about 3 dozen cookies, but my kids eat the batter.

ARTHUR E. LEFAVOR
CLINTON, MASSACHUSETTS

Castor Oil Cookies

This is of early 1800 vintage. It is also called "Scooter Cookies." They were palmed off on small children especially. If they ate enough, it was scoot for the outhouse. When they got older and smarter, they wouldn't eat them.

1 cup sugar
1 cup molasses
1 cup milk
1/2 cup castor oil
1/2 teaspoon salt
2 teaspoons ginger
about 6½ cups flour

Mix in enough flour to make dough. (Drop by teaspoon into free-form shapes.) Bake at 400⁰ for 10 minutes. Makes 8 to 9 dozen.

Dave's note: Strange but pleasant-tasting cookie. Chopped nuts would make a nice addition. Sneaky and not too sweet.

MRS. FRANCIS KYLE
TOLEDO, OHIO

Dutch Honey Cookies

When I was in Holland visiting my husband's sister in the Velp, she said they just called these cookies "Honey Cakes." Only she spoke in Dutch most of the time.

1/3 cup cooking oil
1/2 cup unsalted butter, softened
1/3 cup sugar
1 tablespoon orange juice
1 teaspoon baking powder
1/2 teaspoon baking soda
1 3/4 to 2 cups flour

Syrup:
3/4 cup sugar
1/2 cup water
1/3 cup honey
1/3 cup walnuts, finely chopped

In a mixer bowl, beat cooking oil into butter until blended. Beat in sugar. Add orange juice, baking powder, and baking soda. Mix well. Add enough of the flour, a little at a time, to make a medium-soft dough. Shape dough into 2-inch ovals and place on an ungreased baking sheet. Bake at 350° for 20 to 25 minutes, or until cookies are golden. Cool on a wire rack.

Meanwhile, in a saucepan combine sugar, water, and honey. Boil gently, uncovered, for 5 minutes. Dip cooled cookies into the warm syrup. Sprinkle with nuts and dry on a wire rack. Store in a loosely covered container. Makes 2 to 3 dozen.

Dave's note: Delicious, buttery, rich and quite special.

MRS. H.H. VAN WINKELEIN
WEST ROXBURY, MASSACHUSETTS

Whistlin' Acres Hermits

Forty years ago, when I was a bride and made cookies for the first time, my husband said, "I wish you could make a good chewy hermit cookie." So for over twenty years, I tried every recipe I could. I finally found this one by trial and error. To date, I've made thousands. I named the Hermits "Whistlin' Acres" after our small farm to differentiate my recipe from other recipes.

1 1/2 cups shortening
  2 cups sugar
  3 eggs
  1/2 cup light molasses
4 1/2 cups flour
  1/2 teaspoon salt
  2 teaspoons cinnamon
1 1/2 teaspoons ground cloves
  4 teaspoons baking soda
  1 cup raisins

Mix all ingredients together. Wet hands and roll dough like a sausage until it is 1 inch in diameter. Place on an ungreased cookie sheet. To sugar the top, dip the bottom of a glass in water, then in sugar, and touch lightly onto dough. Bake for 8 to 10 minutes at 375°. Important: Remove pastries from oven when yellow cracks appear and brown on top. Don't overcook or they won't be chewy. Cool and cut. Yields about 30 cookies.

Dave's note: We needed to bake them longer than 10 minutes. Very nice taste.

LOIS BERNIER
WEST BRIDGEWATER, MASSACHUSETTS

Potato Chip Cookies

  1 cup brown sugar, firmly packed
  1 cup white sugar
  1 cup butter or margarine
  2 eggs
2 1/2 cups flour, sifted
  1 teaspoon baking soda
  1 6-ounce package
    butterscotch bits
  2 cups potato chips,
    finely crushed

Cream together sugars and butter or margarine. Add eggs and beat well. Add flour and baking soda, then butterscotch bits and crushed potato chips. Drop by teaspoonfuls onto a greased cookie sheet. Bake for 10 to 12 minutes at 375°. Makes 5 dozen.

Dave's note: Butterscotch may be a bit overpowering for some of you. You might try chocolate bits.

JENNIE H. MATTHES
SUDBURY, MASSACHUSETTS

Cheesecake Cookies

1/3 cup brown sugar, packed
1/2 cup walnuts, finely chopped
  1 cup flour
1/3 cup butter or margarine, melted
  8 ounces cream cheese, softened
1/4 cup white sugar
  1 egg
  3 tablespoons lemon juice
  3 teaspoons vanilla

Mix brown sugar, walnuts, and flour. Then stir in butter and mix until crumbly. Reserve 1 cup. Press remainder in a greased 9 x 9-inch pan and bake at 350° for 10 to 12 minutes. Meanwhile, heat cream cheese with sugar. Beat in egg and add lemon juice and vanilla. Blend thoroughly. Pour on top of baked crust, top with remaining crumbs. Bake for 25 minutes at 350°. Cool and chill.

Dave's note: Can be cut into any shape. Very decorative as well as good tasting. The smaller you cut them, the more cookies you'll get.

JENNIE H. MATTHES
SUDBURY, MASSACHUSETTS

Bake While You Sleep

This recipe was a lifesaver when the children were small. I would whip up a batch each evening and would have enough cookies not only for my girls, but also for all the neighborhood kiddies who seemed to congregate at our home. Could it have been the cookies that drew them here?

  2 egg whites
    pinch salt
1/4 teaspoon cream of tartar
2/3 cup sugar
  1 cup chocolate bits
  1 teaspoon vanilla

Beat egg whites, salt, and cream of tartar until stiff. Then gradually add sugar and beat. Mix in chocolate bits and vanilla. Drop by teaspoonfuls onto a cookie sheet lined with foil. Place in a preheated 350° oven. Turn off heat. DO NOT OPEN THE OVEN DOOR for at least 8 hours. These cookies are very sweet. If you wish, the sugar could be decreased to 1/3 cup. Yields about 2 dozen.

Dave's note: These cookies are real winners. They taste great and they look pretty, too.

MRS. EDNA M. WOLFRAM
SOUTH DEERFIELD, MASSACHUSETTS

Cookies, Pies, and Cakes 183

Grammy's Cookies

In 1954, when we lived in Connecticut (Wethersfield) a friend's mom who was in her late seventies gave me this recipe which she used in her early years of marriage. It is the most versatile recipe I have ever used. You can do so much with it—and it is so easy to make.

    3 sticks margarine
    2 eggs
    1/2 cup milk
       maple, almond, or coconut
       flavoring
    5 cups flour
    2 cups sugar
    2 teaspoons salt
    3 teaspoons baking powder
    2 teaspoons nutmeg (optional)

Melt margarine in a saucepan. Let cool, then add eggs mixed with milk. Add any flavoring you wish according to taste. In a separate bowl, mix flour, sugar, salt, baking powder, and nutmeg. Mix well. Add to it the liquid shortening and mix well. Form batter into rolls, about 2 inches in diameter, which can be frozen and baked as you need them. Bake at 350° for 10 to 12 minutes. Makes about 72 cookies.

Dave's note: The batter definitely needs flavoring. It's a basic recipe to which you add your imagination.

RUTH PETERSON
STAUNTON, VIRGINIA

Lebkuchen
(Spice Bars)

This recipe came from a German war bride back when my daughter Kathy baby-sat for her about twelve years ago. Her husband was stationed in Germany after World War II. His girl back in the states wanted him to bring her back a cuckoo clock. He went into a clock store and struck up a converstion with a sales-girl there who invited him to her home for dinner. The Lebkuchen was served for dessert. Two months later, he married the German girl!

    2 eggs
    1 cup light brown sugar,
       firmly packed
    3/4 cup flour
    1/4 teaspoon salt
    1/2 teaspoon baking powder
    1/8 teaspoon ground cloves
    1/4 teaspoon cinnamon
    2 tablespoons salad oil
    1/4 cup nuts, finely chopped

Beat eggs until slightly foamy. Add sugar and mix well. Sift dry ingredients together and add to egg mixture. Blend well. Add oil, then nuts, and blend. Spread into a greased 8-inch square pan and bake at 350° oven for 35 minutes. May be lightly frosted with a butter frosting and sprinkled with grated nuts. Cut when cool. Yields 18 to 24 cookies.

Dave's note: A little ground ginger is good to sharpen up those spices, and we also tried drizzling on it a thick syrup made from confectioners' sugar, water and lemon juice.

MARGARET WARSAW
BRAINTREE, MASSACHUSETTS

Rolled Oatmeal Cookies

The original recipe came from my grandmother who died at the age of eighty-one in 1914. Although I was a small child at the time of her death, I remember her with love. Her parents came from Germany, so I'm sure the recipe is of German origin. I have never seen another recipe for *rolled* oatmeal cookies.

My mother made these frequently. When I started baking she would say, "Always roll them as thin as possible, they're better that way."

> 2 cups dark brown sugar
> 3/4 cups butter
> 1 teaspoon baking soda
> 1/2 cup hot water
> 2 3/4 cups flour, sifted
> 2 cups quick cooking oatmeal

With a mixer, beat together sugar and butter. Dissolve baking soda in hot water. Beat together the flour and oatmeal. Then add this to the sugar-butter mixture, alternating with the baking soda and water. Refrigerate for 2 hours or overnight. Afterward, roll dough as thin as possible and bake at 350° on a lightly greased cookie sheet for 5 or 6 minutes. Makes 8 to 9 dozen cookies.

Dave's note: We made logs, about 3 inches in diameter, which we refrigerated and then sliced thinly before baking. It's a very sweet cookie

MRS. M.P. GATCHEL
MIDDLETOWN, PENNSYLVANIA

Puffed Riceballs

I got this recipe from my mother who died at the age of 77 in 1947 (and I am presently 82). So you see, this recipe has been in the family a great many years.

My mother used to form these riceballs into the shape of pine cones, rolling them in her buttered hands to do this. However, finding they disappear like "dew before the sun," I have never done this. Rather, I have pressed them down in a jelly roll pan, and cut them into oblongs or squares—it's much easier and takes less time!

> 1 cup molasses
> 2 teaspoons vinegar
> 1/2 cup sugar
> 1 9-ounce package puffed rice
>   (all but 4 cups)
> 2 teaspoons butter
> 1/2 teaspoon baking soda
> 1/2 teaspoon salt

Boil together molasses, vinegar, and sugar over medium-low heat—(molasses burns easily—watch it carefully) while puffed rice is crisping at 275° in a shallow pan. When syrup boils, turn heat to low and boil slowly for 20 minutes. Then, remove from heat, add butter, baking soda, salt, and puffed rice. Mix thoroughly. Form into balls or pine-cone shapes. Place on waxed paper or press down into a greased, shallow pan. Cut into square or oblong shapes.

Dave's note: A couple of suggestions are in order: Because this recipe would yield about 160 1-inch
(Continued)

balls, I'd suggest you cut the amounts in half, using one-half cup of molasses to 6 or 7 cups puffed rice. You could use popcorn and form into larger balls.

RUTH M. BOTT
BEVERLY, MASSACHUSETTS

Whoopie Pie

I gave the recipe to a friend after her children were grown and married. When they came to visit, they wanted to know why she never made these while they were still at home. Another friend made them for five boys. The youngest, who was six, came home one day and told his mother that he sold his whoopie pie for twenty-five cents. At times, he'd come home from school and say his whoopie pie was stolen.

2 1/2 cups flour
1 cup sugar
1 1/2 teaspoons baking soda
1/2 teaspoon salt
2 teaspoons cream of tartar
1/2 cup shortening
1 cup milk
2 eggs
1 teaspoon vanilla
1 cup cocoa

Sift together dry ingredients. Add rest of ingredients and beat for 2 minutes. Drop by teaspoonfuls onto a greased baking sheet. Bake at 350° for 8 to 10 minutes.

Whoopie Pie Filling:

1 cup milk
4 tablespoons flour
3/4 cup shortening
1 cup confectioners' sugar
1 teaspoon vanilla

Mix cold milk with flour, then cook milk until thick. Cool until cold. Beat shortening until creamy. Add cool flour and milk mixture and beat well. Slowly add confectioners' sugar and vanilla. Fill pies.

Dave's note: It would be a lot easier to make an indentation in the "pie" and fill it with marshmallow fluff. Very good for bribing children.

CATHERINE ROBY
HUDSON, NEW HAMPSHIRE

Peanut Butter Pie

4 ounces cream cheese
1 cup confectioners' sugar
1/2 cup milk
1/2 pint heavy cream, whipped
1/2 cup peanut butter (smooth or crunchy)
1 graham cracker pie crust

Beat cream cheese until soft. Add sugar and peanut butter. Beat well. Gradually add milk and blend well. Carefully fold in whipped cream. Pour into a graham cracker pie crust that has been baked for 5 or 6 minutes. Freeze until firm. Wrap in plastic food wrap and put back in freezer. Let stand at room temperature for about 5 minutes before serving.

Dave's note: This is a snap to make. Tastes great: I made the mistake of leaving half a piece on a plate in my office, unattended, for about 3 minutes. It went south.

PEG BIANCHI
FRAMINGHAM, MASSACHUSETTS

Praline Pumpkin Pie

This recipe has not been in the family for long. Actually, my sister brought this pie over to my house one Thanksgiving. It was a big hit and I asked her for the recipe. She gave it to me and told me that she had clipped it out of a newspaper. Maybe someday our children and grandchildren will be making it.

Crust:

 1 cup granulated sugar
1/4 cup water
 1 cup slivered almonds, toasted
 3 tablespoons butter, softened.

To make crust, combine sugar and water in a saucepan and bring to a boil. Boil for 4 minutes, without stirring, until golden brown. Remove from heat and stir in almonds. Pour mixture onto a greased baking sheet and let cool completely. Then pulverize mixture in a blender to powder it. Mix 1¼ cups of this praline powder crust with butter. Press into a 9-inch pie pan. Reserve remaining crust mixture.

Filling:

 1 envelope unflavored gelatin
1/2 cup brown sugar, firmly packed
1/2 teaspoon salt
3/4 teaspoon nutmeg
 1 teaspoon cinnamon
1/4 teaspoon ginger
 1 14-to-16 ounce can pumpkin
 2 eggs, separated
1/2 cup milk
1/4 cup sugar
 praline powder
 1 cup whipping cream

Combine gelatin, brown sugar, salt, cinnamon, nutmeg, and ginger in a saucepan. Beat egg yolks and stir into gelatin mixture. Continue stirring over very low heat until gelatin dissolves and mixture thickens slightly (approximately 5 minutes). Remove from heat and blend in pumpkin. Chill, stirring occasionally, until mixture mounds slightly when dropped from spoon.

Beat egg whites to a soft peak. Gradually add granulated sugar and beat to a stiff peak. Fold into pumpkin mixture and fold in remaining praline powder. Whip cream and fold into mixture. Spoon into the pie shell and chill until set.

Dave's note: This one takes a little doing—but it's well worth it. We increased the cinnamon to 2 teaspoons. Definitely not a pie for dieters.

LEONA M. MONTVILLE
BELLINGHAM, MASSACHUSETTS

Chocolate Meringue Pie

This pie is one that I've been making for thirty years. Small servings are in order as it is quite rich. It's easy to make.

2 egg whites
1/2 cup sugar
1/8 teaspoon cream of tartar
    approximately 1/2 cup
    walnuts, chopped
1 6-ounce package chocolate
    morsels
3 tablespoons hot water
2 tablespoons sugar
1 teaspoon vanilla
1/2 pint heavy cream

For the meringue pie crust, beat egg whites with sugar and cream of tartar until very stiff. Shape with a spoon into a buttered 9-inch pie plate and sprinkle walnuts over surface. Bake at 275° to 300° until light brown and hard. Cool.

For the filling, melt chocolate morsels with hot water and sugar. Add vanilla and cool. Fold in heavy cream, whipped. Fill the cooled pie shell and chill overnight in the refrigerator.

Dave's note: Very different, and very good.

BARBARA HARGHT
SCITUATE, MASSACHUSETTS

Kentucky Derby Pie

This pie is very rich; a little goes a long way!

pastry for 9-inch pie shell
2 eggs
1/2 cup dark brown sugar, packed
1/2 cup sugar
1/2 cup flour, sifted
1/2 cup butter, melted
2 tablespoons bourbon whiskey
1 6-ounce package chocolate
    chips, melted
1 cup nuts, coarsely chopped
1/2 cup heavy cream, whipped
    and sweetened

Line a 9-inch pan with pastry and flute edges. Preheat oven to 350°. In a medium bowl, beat eggs with electric mixer until foamy. Gradually add sugars and flour. Beat until smooth. Add butter, beating until blended. Stir in whiskey, chocolate, and nuts. Pour into prepared pie shell. Bake for about 35 minutes, until surface is golden brown and a knife inserted 1-inch from edge comes out clean. Cool completely. Serve with whipped cream.

Dave's note: I hate to play favorites, but the odds are that this is a winner. I'm embarrassed to admit it, but I ate half the pie.

LILLIAN HOLTON
JEFFERSONVILLE, INDIANA

White Potato Pie

This recipe is an old Sussex County favorite.

1 1/4 cups potatoes, cooked
       and mashed
1 1/2 cups milk
    2 teaspoons cornstarch
    1 teaspoon vanilla
    1 teaspoon salt
  2/3 cup sugar
    2 eggs, beaten
    1 pie shell, unbaked
       nutmeg

Mix mashed potatoes and milk together and put through a sieve, and add remaining ingredients. Pour into unbaked pie shell and sprinkle with nutmeg. Bake at 450° for 20 minutes. Reduce heat to 350° and continue baking for 25 minutes more.

Dave's note: Like many of the really old recipes, this was a little sweet for my taste. But if you like custard-type pies, give it a whirl

ELIZABETH C. DONOVAN
MILFORD, DELAWARE

Cranberry Surprise Pie

A pie that makes its own "crust." Unusual to make, delicious to taste!

    2 cups fresh cranberries
1 1/2 cups sugar
  1/2 cup walnuts or pecans,
       chopped
    2 eggs
    1 cup flour
  1/2 cup butter or margarine, melted
  1/4 cup shortening, melted

Grease well a 10-inch pie plate. Spread cranberries over bottom of plate. Sprinkle with ½ cup sugar and nuts. Beat eggs well, adding 1 cup sugar gradually, beating until thoroughly mixed. Add flour, butter, and shortening to egg/sugar mixture. Beat well. Bake at 325° for 60 minutes, or until crust is golden brown. Serve either warm or cold with generous scoops of vanilla ice cream

Dave's note: Works as well with blueberries as with cranberries. Luscious.

CAROLINE M. WARD
PLYMOUTH, MASSACHUSETTS

Irish Coffee Pie

2 1/2 cups cold milk
    1 tablespoon Irish whiskey
    1 package vanilla-flavored instant
       pudding and pie filling
    2 teaspoons instant coffee
    1 baked 9-inch pie shell

Pour milk and whiskey into a deep bowl. Add pie filling and mix; add instant coffee. Beat slowly with a rotary beater or at lowest speed of an electric mixer for 1 minute. Pour at once into pie shell. Chill for 3 hours. Garnish with prepared whipped topping, if desired.

Dave's note: This is a beauty— especially when you're in a hurry. And remember: Irish Whiskey.

DORA E. HANSON
BROCKTON, MASSACHUSETTS

Pavlova

The recipe for Pavlova was given to me five years ago by a lady who was teaching with me in Houston, Texas. It's an Australian recipe, which she brought to the United States when she moved here from Down Under. Though the recipe calls for passion fruit, crushed pineapple may be substituted.

3 egg whites
6 ounces sugar
  pinch of salt
  few drops white vinegar
  whipped cream
  passion fruit or 1 medium-size
  can of crushed pineapple

Beat together egg whites, sugar, and salt. Add vinegar and beat again. On a flat tray or a cookie sheet, cut waxed paper to fit, then wet paper under tap and shake off drops. Place on cookie sheet. Spread mixture onto sheet. Pre-heat oven to 400° for 2 minutes and then turn oven down to 250°. Place sheet in the oven on the middle or top rack. Cook for about 1 hour and 20 minutes, until batter turns a pale fawn color. Remove from oven and turn sheet upside down. Peel off waxed paper carefully and allow pastry to cool. The middle of the Pavlova will sink. Into this depression, pour the filling, which is made as follows:

Fold passion fruit or pineapple into whipped cream. Pour into Pavlova just before eating.

Dave's note: We made this in a springform pan and used ice cream instead of whipped cream. Tasted marvelous!

EILEEN HACKETT DEVEAU
MANSFIELD, MASSACHUSETTS

Best-Ever Blueberry Cake

This recipe has been in our family for around seventy-five years. Each summer we would set aside one day to go blueberry picking in the Dresden area of Maine. A more than ample lunch was provided by my mother, but in order to ensure enough blueberries for the whole winter, she called all the youngsters around her and told us that if we didn't eat too many berries, she would make a new recipe for supper that evening. She always called it her Bribery cake.

2 eggs separated
1 cup sugar
1/4 teaspoon salt
1/2 cup shortening
1 teaspoon vanilla
1 1/2 cups flour, sifted
1 teaspoon baking powder
1/3 cups milk
1 1/2 cups blueberries

Beat egg whites until stiff, adding 1/4 cup sugar to keep them stiff. Cream shortening, and add salt, vanilla, and remaining sugar gradually. Combine with unbeaten yolks, beating until light and creamy. Sift dry ingredients and add alternately with milk. Fold in beaten whites and last, the blueberries, lightly floured. Bake in an 8 x 8 x 2-inch pan at 350° for 50 to 60 minutes.

Dave's note: This would be great as a breakfast bread. Not spectacular-looking; it tastes like a blueberry muffin, but huge—and there's nothing wrong with that.

KEN SLATTERY
SCARBOROUGH, MAINE

Old West Virginia Nut Cake

This recipe I got from a friend. We like it very much. When I bake it, I put an icing on it and sprinkle a few ground nuts on it. Either black walnuts, or hickory nuts are good. This makes a delicious cake.

2/3 cup butter or shortening
1 2/3 cups sugar
3 eggs
2 1/3 cups flour, sifted
2 teaspoons baking powder
1 teaspoon salt
1 cup milk
1 teaspoon vanilla
1 1/2 cups nuts, chopped

Cream butter and sugar. Add eggs, one at a time, beating after each additional egg is added. Sift dry ingredients. Add alternately with milk to creamed mixture. Add vanilla and fold in nuts. Pour into 2 layer pans. Bake at 350° for 25 to 30 minutes.

Dave's note: Nice basic recipe. If I were making it, I'd fiddle around with it a lot.

MRS. GRACE REED
STONEWOOD, WEST VIRGINIA

Blarney Stone Whiskey Cake

This recipe was brought here with my husband's grandmother from Ireland. They serve it at wakes and weddings.

2 teaspoons nutmeg
1/4 cup whiskey
1 cup pecans or walnuts, coarsely chopped
1 pound raisins
1 1/2 cups flour
1 cup margarine, softened
1 1/2 cups sugar
5 eggs
1 teaspoon cream of tartar
1/4 teaspoon baking soda
1/8 teaspoon salt

Soak nutmeg in whiskey for 10 minutes. Mix pecans or walnuts together with raisins and ¼ cup flour. Set aside. In a large bowl cream margarine and sugar until fluffy. Add eggs, one at a time, beating well after each egg. Fold in remaining 1¼ cups flour, cream of tartar, baking soda, salt, soaked nutmeg and whiskey, and raisin-nut mixture. Spoon into a greased and floured 10-inch tube pan. Bake at 325° for 1 hour and 15 minutes, or until cake pulls away from sides of pan. Let cool in pan 30 minutes. Remove cake and cool completely on rack.

Dave's note: Many years ago, when I first started cooking, a prominent chef told me I'd never go wrong if I threw booze in the pot first. I guess it works for everybody.

REGINA BELL
DRACUT, MASSACHUSETTS

Daffodil Cake

Yellow layer:
- 6 egg yolks
- 1/2 cup sugar
- 1/4 teaspoon salt
- 2 tablespoons water
- 1/2 cups flour
- 1 teaspoon baking powder

White layer:
- 1/2 cup flour
- 1 teaspoon cream of tartar
- 6 egg whites
- 1/2 cup sugar
- 1/4 teaspoon salt
- 1/2 teaspoon vanilla or lemon flavoring

For yellow layer, combine egg yolks, sugar, salt, water, and flour that has been sifted with baking powder 3 times. Mix well and set aside.

For white layer, sift flour with cream of tartar. Beat egg whites until stiff. Fold in sugar, salt, and flour mixture. Pour white batter into a greased 10-inch tube pan. Pour yellow batter on top. Bake at 325° for about 1 hour.

Dave's note: This is such a pretty cake. I was happy to learn it tasted good, too.

ALICE I. DUNCANSON
CLINTON, MASSACHUSETTS

Old-Fashioned Pound Cake

My Scottish great-grandmother had this recipe when she came to Barnet, Vermont. The pound cake is so named because of the fact that in the 1700s and early 1800s all recipes were measured by the pound and one-half pound for ingredients. As most ladies did not read then, when they went to the grocer they told him what they needed to bake. He would write it down and get the groceries and give the ladies back the list of ingredients as a recipe. Thus recipe became receipt, as some still call them.

- 1 pound butter
- 1 pound sugar
- 10 eggs, separated
- 1 pound flour

Cream butter and sugar, then add egg yolks and then flour. The rule is to beat for 1 hour, but sometimes you get tired before the hour is up. Then fold in egg whites, beaten to a stiff froth. Bake slowly in a loaf pan for 1½ hours at about 300°.

Dave's note: You'll have to beat that butter for at least half an hour so it won't coagulate.

SCOTTY VAUGHN
BOW, NEW HAMPSHIRE

Milky Way Cake

8 large Milky Way bars
2 sticks margarine
2 cups sugar
4 eggs
2 1/2 cups flour
1 cup buttermilk
1/2 teaspoon baking soda
1 teaspoon vanilla
1 cup walnuts, chopped

Melt Milky Way bars with 1 stick margarine. Set aside and keep warm. In a mixing bowl, blend 1 stick margarine with sugar and eggs, beating after each egg is added. Combine with flour, buttermilk, baking soda, and vanilla. Add Milky Way mixture and walnuts. Bake in a greased and floured bundt pan for 1 hour at 350°. Remove cake from pan and frost while still warm.

Frosting for Milky Way Cake:

3 large Milky Way bars, melted
3 tablespoons milk
1 cup confectioners' sugar

Mix all ingredients and pour over warm cake.

Dave's note: Have somebody watch you bake this one: your reputation will soar.

D.J. TOMLINSON
DETROIT, MICHIGAN

Mississippi Mud Cake

1/4 cup cocoa
2 sticks margarine
1 small can coconut
1/2 cup pecans
1 jar marshmallow cream
4 eggs
2 cups sugar
1/2 cup flour
1 teaspoon vanilla

Mix together all ingredients except marshmallow cream and pour into oblong cake pan. Bake for 30 minutes at 350°. While hot, spoon on marshmallow cream on top of cake. When cool, frost with icing.

Icing:
1/2 cup margarine
1/3 cup cocoa
1/2 cup evaporated milk
1 box confectioners' sugar
1 teaspoon vanilla

Mix together all ingredients and spread icing over the cooled marshmallow.

Dave's note: Treat this as you would a Brown-Betty. You'll scoop out servings. It's very sweet.

MRS. G.S. CLACKUM
RICHMOND, INDIANA

Chocolate Cake—Normandie

This recipe was given to me many, many years ago. It allegedly came from a chef on the French liner **Normandie** and was served at tea-time.

      4 tablespoons butter
      3 eggs, separated
 2 1/2 cups sugar
 2 1/2 cups cake flour
 1 1/2 cups milk
      4 squares chocolate, melted
      2 teaspoons vanilla
      2 teaspoons baking powder

Cream butter and add egg yolks. Cream again. Add 1¼ cups sugar, then add, alternately, flour and milk. Stir in chocolate and vanilla. Beat egg whites and add remaining sugar to egg whites, then fold into mixture. Sprinkle baking powder into mixture. Bake at 350° until cake springs back in three 8-inch layer pans or one loaf pan.

Dave's note: Very nice flavor. We had much more success with the layer pans than with the loaf pan.

JANET M. BUECHNER
KALAMAZOO, MICHIGAN

Poppy Seed Cake

This was received many years ago from a friend in California. Since poppy seeds were not available in the Midwest, she also sent four cans of them with the recipe. I make it with black walnuts. She rarely can get them, so I send black walnuts to her. The cake can be frozen, but keeps several weeks in the refrigerator. It is best sliced very thin. Everyone loves it.

 1 1/2 cups cooking oil
      2 cups sugar
      4 eggs
      1 teaspoon vanilla
      3 cups flour, sifted
 2 1/2 teaspoons baking soda
  1/2 teaspoon salt
      1 13-ounce can condensed milk
      1 can poppy seed filling
      1 cup black walnuts, finely
        chopped

Combine oil, sugar, eggs, and vanilla and beat well. Sift together dry ingredients, add to first mixture alternately with milk and poppy seed filling. Then stir in nuts. Bake in an ungreased 10-inch tube pan at 350° for 1 hour and 10 minutes. Let cool as angel food cake. Best if you wrap it well in aluminum foil and refrigerate for a day or two. Slice thin.

Dave's note: You can buy poppy seed filling in some supermarkets—or you can take a shot at making your own. If you're in the mood for something not-too-sweet, this is it

MARY I. PEASE
BURLINGTON, IOWA

Rice Cake

1 8-ounce package cream cheese
1 cup sugar
12 eggs
2 cups rice, cooked
pinch of salt
1 teaspoon vanilla
1 quart milk

Cream cheese and sugar, beating until fluffy. Beat eggs separately until foamy, then add to cream cheese mixture. Combine with cooked rice, salt, vanilla, and milk, and beat. Place in a greased pan. Bake in small roasting pan at 350° for about 1 hour. Refrigerate if desired.

Dave's note: This is more like rice pudding. We added a little more vanilla and some nutmeg. You could use cinnamon as well. Next time I make it, I'll add raisins.

MARGARET ROSS
CONNEAUT, OHIO

Della Robbia Cake

I found this recipe many years ago in a magazine section of a newspaper. And up until today, I know of no one else who has even seen it or even tasted it until I served it. I really feel that I have something special here.

1 cup filberts, chopped
1 teaspoon mace
1/4 teaspoon salt
1 cup butter or margarine
1 1/2 teaspoons vanilla
1 3/4 cups sugar
5 large eggs
2 cups flour, sifted

Toast filberts at 325° for 10 to 15 minutes. Combine mace, salt, butter or margarine, and vanilla in a large mixing bowl. Beat to consistency of mayonnaise. Beat in sugar gradually, then add 4 eggs, one at a time, beating well after each addition. Stir in flour and mix well. Beat in remaining egg. Fold in toasted filberts. Spoon into greased and floured 3-quart ring mold. Bake at 325° for 1 hour. Allow to cool for 20 minutes in pan, then turn cake out on cake rack to finish cooling. Store in a tightly closed cake box. The flavor of the cake will improve with age. Before serving, drizzle with an icing made from confectioners' sugar.

Dave's note: Tastes very good. And I like the fact that it improves with age. Well, within reason.

NANCY GULLO
JAMESTOWN, NEW YORK

$100 Mayonnaise Cake

We've always called this the $100 Mayonnaise Cake because a friend of ours, while eating in a New York restaurant in the 1940s (when so many things were hard to get), had this cake and thought it was moist and delicious. So she asked the chef if she could have the recipe. Gladly he took her name and address. On arriving home a few days later, my friend found that the recipe and a bill for $100 had arrived in the mail. I've used this lots and have given it to many others— with no charge!

> 2 cups flour
> 1 cup sugar
> 4 tablespoons cocoa
> 1 1/2 teaspoons baking soda
> 3/4 cup mayonnaise
> 1 cup cold water
> 1 teaspoon vanilla

Sift together all dry ingredients. Then add mayonnaise, water, and vanilla, and mix well. Put in an 8 x 8 x 2-inch greased pan and bake at 350° for about 40 minutes.

Dave's note: This one will rise a little higher in the center. Put your favorite frosting on it.

MRS. RAYMOND CAREY
WEST BOYLSTON, MASSACHUSETTS

Esther's Cheesecake

If anyone thinks that they don't care for cheesecake, they will quickly change their tune after sampling a slice of Esther's light and rich concoction. Her trademark at family gatherings and holidays was that it was rare when someone did not attempt to get this recipe from her. I don't know how successful they were, but it took me about a year to get Esther to fork it over.

graham cracker crumbs
1 24-ounce package cream cheese
4 egg whites
1 cup sugar
1 teaspoon vanilla

Grease a springform pan that is 3 inches deep and dust with graham cracker crumbs. Put cream cheese in a large bowl and set aside to soften. In a deep bowl, beat egg whites until stiff. Combine with softened cheese. Mix well and add vanilla. Blend well. Pour into pan and bake at 350° for 30 mintues. Meanwhile prepare topping.

Topping:
1 pint sour cream
2 tablespoons sugar
1 can crushed pineapple
(or other fruit of your choice)

Mix all ingredients and spread over baked cheese cake. Increase oven temperature to 475° and bake for 10 minutes longer. Cool for 15 minutes. Chill cake for 2 hours, then eat and enjoy.

Dave's note: I'll have to apologize to the other 200 people who sent in a cheesecake recipe. Maybe we'll do a special cookbook, and you'll all fight it out.

JUDY BARTLETT
NORTH SMITHFIELD, RHODE ISLAND

Rose Petal Cake

This is a special cake indeed! The recipe was given to me by my mother (who also made jam from rose petals). Wild rose petals that are fragrant are especially good to use. The secret to this recipe is to be sure and use fragrant rose petals—their delicate aroma will flavor the cake.

1/2 cup butter
1 cup sugar
3 eggs, beaten
2 teaspoons baking powder
1/2 teaspoon salt
3 cups flour, sifted
1 cup milk
1 lemon
1 cup fragrant fresh rose petals

Cream butter and sugar until fluffy and add eggs. Sift together baking powder, salt, and flour. Then add alternately with milk to creamed mixture, starting with flour and ending with flour. Add a little grated lemon rind, 1 tablespoon lemon juice, and rose petals. Mix well and pour into muffin pans. Bake at 350° for 12 to 15 minutes. Makes 36 muffins.

Dave's note: This ordinarily would have gone into the muffin section of this book. But we don't have a muffin section. You might add a little rosewater for extra flavor.

MRS. EUGENIA F. SWAJIAN
NORTH ANDOVER, MASSACHUSETTS

Pennsylvania Dutch Fennel Cakes

This recipe has been in the family for many years, and has been handed down from one generation to another. The actual spelling should be "funnel" cakes, as the batter is poured through a funnel. However, someone in the family spelled it "Fennel cakes" when handing down the recipe, and that is what my generation now uses as the spelling.

These cakes are made very frequently throughout our area at family gatherings, summer festivals, art festivals, sidewalk summer sales, etc. At such gatherings, they are made in an electric skillet. They resemble a huge, delicate pretzel, but have an entirely different texture and taste.

2 eggs, beaten
1 1/2 cups milk
2 cups flour
1 teaspoon baking powder
1/2 teaspoon salt
2 cups cooking oil
confectioners' sugar

Heat oil to 360°. Combine eggs and milk. Sift flour, baking powder, and salt. Add to egg mixture and beat until smooth. Pour batter into the top of a funnel, but first cover opening of funnel with finger. Release batter by removing finger from funnel opening and dripping batter into hot oil in a spiral shape. Fry until light brown. Remove, drain, and sprinkle with confectioners' sugar.

(Continued)

Dave's note: Delicious—fun for kids to watch. Shaping may take some practice, but all shapes are tasty. "A #1" served hot for breakfast.

MRS. VICKIE E. SHARP
JOHNSTOWN, PENNSYLVANIA

Katarina's Streudel

This is actually a recipe for apple povatietsa, which is what they call streudel in Yugoslavia

    1 egg
    3 cups flour
    1 teaspoon salt
    1 cup lukewarm water
3/4 cup butter or margarine, melted
4 to 5 apples, pared and thinly sliced
    1 cup raisins
1/2 cup sugar
    1 teaspoon cinnamon

Mix egg with flour and salt in a bowl. Add water and ¼ cup melted butter or margarine gradually. Knead until smooth, keeping dough as soft as possible. Grease dough ball and place in a covered bowl for 20 minutes or more. Then place dough ball on a large surface—such as a table—that is covered with a cloth. Roll dough out as thin as possible with a rolling pin. Then gently pull dough from all sides, stretching it until dough is tissue-thin. Patience and gentle pulling does it. If dough tears, keep going and mend it by joining dough ends.

Spread entire dough with ½ cup butter or margarine, then with sliced apples, raisins, sugar, and cinnamon. Roll into a jelly roll shape, then form roll into a circle or coil. Bake in a greased pan at 350° for 1 hour, or until golden brown. Long roll can also be cut in two parts, placed side by side, and baked if preferred.

Dave's note: I suggest you use Granny Smith apples and you can save a lot of time by using store-bought phylo dough.

MRS. DAVID (KATHERINE) LANCTOT
L'ANSE, MICHIGAN

When I first started cooking, every meal was a quickie. In college, I cooked for a mob and my philosophy was "Fill 'em and don't kill 'em."

Cooking is for me not only a way to eat food the way I like it; it's really a form of therapy. In spring, summer and fall, there's always something for Dad to do around the house, but what happens in winter? God forbid I should sit on my rump and watch TV or fix anything. One sure way to guarantee a new appliance in my house is to ask me to fix the old one. "I know a guy so dumb and un-handy that when he fixes a toaster, the bread slides out from under it." That's me. So instead I cook.

Quickies are meant for those who either don't have the time or are not very confident at the stove. The recipes are easy and fairly foolproof. The end result should bring praise around the table.

I agree with Julia Child: Don't begin with lessons. Buy some food and try a few easy recipes. It's cheaper, it's more fun, and the mistakes don't taste that bad. —Dave

Quickies

Angels on Horses

To the best of my knowledge, this has been in our family for many years—too many to remember.

bacon
fresh oysters or clams
lemon juice
black pepper

Wrap half a slice of partially cooked bacon around each fresh oyster or clam that has first been seasoned with lemon juice and black pepper. Secure bacon with toothpicks. Bake at 350° until bacon is crisp. Serve hot.

Dave's note: Scallops instead of oysters are super.

LOUIS L. PROTENA
PROVIDENCE, RHODE ISLAND

Minted New Peas

2 cups new peas
1 tablespoon butter
1 teaspoon creme de menthe
1 bunch fresh mint leaves, blanched

Cook peas (or steam them) in lightly salted boiling water with mint leaves added. When peas are tender, add butter and creme de menthe. Garnish with mint leaves. Serves 3 to 4.

Dave's note: For a change of pea pace.

RACHEL DIBENEDETTO
HYANNIS, MASSACHUSETTS

Bacon Roll Ups

2 pounds bacon
2 cups bread crumbs
2/3 cup boiling water
1/4 cup butter
1 egg, beaten
1 teaspoon parsley flakes

Combine all ingredients, except bacon. Take strips of bacon, cut in half, and spoon some of the stuffing-like mixture on each end. Roll up and secure with a toothpick. Bake at 425° for 8 to 10 minutes on each side. Yields 35 to 50.

Dave's note: Don't forget to drain on paper towels.

MRS. KATHLEEN LATULIPPE
HAVERHILL, MASSACHUSETTS

Crabbies

The ultimate in a tasty hors d'oeuvre, these Crabbies are the thing to serve. They're simple to make and not much "trouble." Make plenty and serve them hot and bubbly!

6 English muffins
1 stick butter
1 jar sharp cheese spread
1 1/2 teaspoons mayonnaise
1/2 teaspoon garlic salt
1/2 teaspoon salt
1 7-ounce can crabmeat

Split muffins and set aside. Blend together all other ingredients and spread on muffin halves. Freeze on a cookie sheet. When frozen, store in a plastic bag in the freezer.

To serve, cut each muffin half into 8 wedges. Broil for 5 to 7 minutes until hot and bubbly. Fantastic! Yields 48.

Dave's note: Don't use a mild cheese. Take Crabbies out of the freezer at least ½ hour before serving. If you have no time—forget it. Broil them frozen.

GAINOR M. VENTRESCO
DEER ISLE, MAINE

Mock Lobster

This is a very quick and easy dish that I have served for years. No one could guess it wasn't lobster.

1 pound fresh haddock
1/4 stick butter or margarine, melted
4 ounces salted crackers, crushed

Cut haddock into bite-sized pieces and add butter and crackers. Mix well. Put in a casserole dish, cover, and bake at 325° for 20 minutes. Serves 4 to 6.

Dave's note: Make this right away before haddock prices go up and match lobster prices.

CLARA CATALDO
REVERE, MASSACHUSETTS

Vegetable Dip (Ab-Duq Khiar)

3 cups yogurt
2 cucumbers, chopped
3 mild onions, chopped
2 sprigs basil, chopped
2 sprigs summer savory, chopped, or parsley, chopped
1/4 cup walnuts, chopped
1/2 cup raisins
1/2 teaspoon salt

Beat yogurt until smooth. Stir in the remaining ingredients and chill. Makes 4½ cups of dip (½ cup is 95 calories).

Serve as a summer salad, as a dip with sesame crackers or vegetables, or diluted with milk and served as a cold soup.

Dave's note: Low-fat yogurt would be a smart choice.

MRS. N. BILTCLIFFE
FALL RIVER, MASSACHUSETTS

Delicious Carrots

10 carrots, sliced
Russian dressing (enough to coat
vegetables)
1 large onion, sliced

Cut carrots in thick, round slices. Boil, but do not overcook. Drain off water, leaving a little water in the bottom of the pan. Pour on dressing. Cut onions in round slices and place on top of carrots in pan. Cook for another few minutes. Serve hot or cold.
Serves 4 to 6.

Dave's note: Nice idea and so easy. Why didn't I think of it?

HELEN E. JONES
PLYMOUTH, MICHIGAN

Gladys's Oyster Pie

This recipe is good hot, warm, or cold. It can be spooned out or cut like a pie. People who dislike oysters, like this. I have had this recipe for over fifty-five years. It was given to me by a friend by the name of Gladys, who has been dead many years.

1 pint oysters
2 eggs
1 1/2 cups milk
12 crackers, crumbled
1/2 cup butter, melted
salt and pepper to taste

Mix all ingredients together in a baking dish. Bake at 350° for 1½ hours. If desired, add a little poultry seasoning. Serves 2 to 4.

Dave's note: I tried it on an oyster-hating kid! It worked!

MRS. ARTHUR B. PARKER
LOWELL, MASSACHUSETTS

Crab Soup

We had this soup on our way to Florida one year. The restaurant people would not give out the recipe for four years, though. We made a point of stopping there every time we went down and every time we came back. After pestering them for four years, I finally wheedled it out of the chef.

1 chicken bouillon cube
3/4 cup boiling water
1 can green pea soup
1 can tomato soup
1 cup light cream
1 7-ounce can crabmeat
1/4 cup sherry (optional)

Mix all ingredients except sherry together. Heat but do not boil. Add sherry, if desired, and serve.

Dave's note: Glad you finally melted the chef. I usually bribe them with champagne.

VIVIENNE RIDDELL
FREEDOM, NEW HAMPSHIRE

Pea Soup

This particular recipe was given to my mother by an elderly French lady from Greenville, New Hampshire. When my brother and I were young (over fifty years ago), we spent our summers just over the New Hampshire border in Greenville, a small mill town. About once a week, my brother used to ask if he could stay at his best friend's house for lunch. We later learned that his best friend's grandmother had made this pea soup every time my brother would ask to stay for lunch. Since he obviously liked it so much, my mother asked for and got the recipe so she could make it for him during the winter months.

      1 pound whole dried peas
      2 quarts of water
      1 pound salt pork or salt spare ribs
  1/2 cup onions, sliced
      1 bay leaf
  allspice to taste

Cook peas for 1 hour. Add pork or spare ribs, onion, bay leaf, and allspice. Cook until peas are done.

Dave's note: Peas are done when you have pea soup and not hot water with peas floating in it. Brilliant, aren't I?

MRS. EDWARD REGAN
SOUTH HAMILTON, MASSACHUSETTS

Lazy Clam Digger's Soup

      1 can condensed tomato soup
      1 cup clam juice
  1/4 cup water
      8 ounces clams (canned or fresh)
        salt, pepper, herbs, spices to taste

Combine all ingredients. Heat and serve. Serves 2 to 3.

Dave's note: Use your herb imagination. Basil, maybe. Oh well, you experiment!

STANLEY DROST
BOSTON, MASSACHUSETTS

Index